I0560674

THE LIFE OF
ST. ALPHONSUS MARIA DE
LIGUORI

THE LIFE
OF
S. ALPHONSUS MARIA DE LIGUORI

BISHOP OF ST. AGATHA OF THE GOTHS
AND,
FOUNDER OF THE CONGREGATION OF THE MOST HOLY
REDEEMER

"Gaude Maria Virgo, cunctas haereses sola interemisti in universo mundo."
—*Antiph. Ecclesiae.*

by
ANTONIO MARIA TONNOJA

Translated by the Congregation of the Oratory
With a Preface by Fr. Frederick William Faber

VOL. III.
The Companions of St. Alphonsus

MEDIATRIX PRESS

ISBN: 978-1-957066-60-8

©Mediatrix Press, 2024.

The Life of St. Alphonsus Liguori vol. 3 was originally published as *The Lives of the Companions of St. Alphonso Liguori* by Richardson and Son, London, 1849, and is in the public domain. Typesetting, additions and editing of this edition are the exclusive copyright of Mediatrix Press, all rights reserved. No part of this edition may be reproduced or transmitted in any form or by any means, electronic or mechanical, including photocopying, recording, or by any information storage and retrieval system without permission in writing from the publisher. *No part of this work may be placed on Archive.org.*

Cover art:
©Ryan Grant, 2024.

Mediatrix Press
607 E 6th Ave.
Post Falls, ID 83854
www.mediatrixpress.com

CONTENTS

We hereby approve of this Series of
Lives of the Canonized Saints and Servants
of God, and recommend it to the faithful of
our District, as likely to promote the glory
of God, the increase of devotion, and the
spread of our holy Religion.

Given at Birmingham, this 29th day
of October, 1847.

Thomas
Bishop of Cambysopolis

Nicholas
Bishop of Melipotamus.

PREFACE

THE LIVES of these fathers and brothers, who were the contemporaries of St. Alphonsus, form an excellent sequel to his Memoirs. The relation in which they stood to their saintly founder causes the recital of their actions to be intimately connected with the history of his life, and throws great light on several epochs in that of his congregation. They comprise many most interesting incidents, as well as several remarkable sayings of the saint, which are not to be met with elsewhere. The holiness of these his first disciples was attended by different characteristics and matter for edification in each one of them, and serves to put the finishing touches to the portrait given of that of their saintly master. "Oh!" exclaims St. Maximus, "how great is the glory of that father who is followed by several children who are full of wisdom and virtue!" They may therefore be looked upon in this work as the secondary form in a picture, which causes the principal personage therein depicted to stand out in bold relief. Their mode of thought and of action throws light on the spirit of the order by which they became sanctified, and they serve as so many precious models to their successors.

Fr. Frederick William Faber
The Oratory, London,
Vigil of St. Laurence, 1849.

INTRODUCTION

The extract which follows has been translated from the "Maximes Spirituelles pour la conduite des âmes par le R. P, F. Guilloré de la Compagnie de Jésus."

It has been prefixed to this volume, in the hope that this short account of the philosophy of God's operations in holy souls, will remove difficulties which English readers of the Lives of the Saints have felt, by serving as a key to phenomena which, unless seen from their true point of view, may naturally enough prove a perplexity or stumbling-block to the beholder.

MAXIM VII

The Spirit of God Enters only into a Recollected Soul, Abides only in a Humble Soul, and Converses only with a Simple Soul.

As all the mysteries of our religion were consummated, as it were, by the descent of the Holy Spirit on the apostles, we may say also, that the consummation of the ways of the interior consists in receiving into ourselves the Spirit of God, in preserving the possession of Him after having received Him, and in experiencing the sweet enjoyment of Him in His possession. For the end of the interior life is to form within us a new being by means of a new spirit, as we see that the body forms with the soul a new being. But as to effect this the body must be fitted with organs to receive the soul, the soul must abide therein by the union which it contracts, and, in fine, must perform therein all its functions; in like manner it is necessary to know what it is which is capable of effecting in us the entrance of this Divine Spirit, of establishing His abode within us, and of procuring us the possession and the enjoyment of Him.

This it is, O Theoneus, which is the aim of all our labors and all our prayers, the destruction of our own spirit, that we may be filled with the Spirit of God. But, alas! generally speaking, what bad measures we take for introducing Him into the soul, how short a time He stays after He has been received, and if He does not depart, yet how little we know how to enjoy His presence and to converse with Him! This it is which I would here try to teach you, in order that you may not be deprived of the presence and of the sweetness of the highest of all goods; and to this end I must tell you that it is the recollection of a soul that gives Him entrance, its humility that secures His abiding therein, and its simplicity that attracts His familiarity and His caresses.

O Spirit of God, Spirit of love, vouchsafe to impart to my heart a little of Thy heat, to the end that I may inspire something thereof into the heart of those who shall read this work, and that they may learn so to abandon themselves thereto, that they may be its victims, at once consumed and animated by it. All the world desires Thee and invokes Thee, O Holy Spirit, all the world aspires to taste Thy sweetnesses; and Thou art so good that Thou refusest Thyself to no one, if he do but know how to prepare Thee an abode. O Spirit, who art all love, Thou rejoicest exceedingly when Thou hast succeeded in the conquest of a soul; but, alas! either Thou art unable to approach, prevented by our dissipation of spirit, or Thou abidest but a little while, banished by our pride; or Thou takest not Thy pleasure therein, restrained by our worldly and carnal wisdom.

CHAPTER I

The Spirit of God Enters only into a Recollected Soul.

I have shown you, Theoneus, in the first volume of these Maxims, book 2, how essential recollection is, by reasons drawn from prayer, mortification, and self-knowledge. If then it has appeared to you to be so for such important considerations, its necessity must seem to you infinitely more urgent in the matter which I am now laying before you, where it is a question of opening the doors of your heart and of your soul to the Spirit of God, and of not keeping Him so long waiting when He knocks thereat. Alas! Theoneus, unfaithful that we are, how we weary Him, closing all entrance to Him alone, while we open indifferently to creatures!

Be assured then, that the Spirit of God will never enter into you to assume the sovereignty of you, unless you prepare Him an entrance by habitual recollection. For this Divine Spirit never enters where there is noise and confusion, seeing that nothing drives Him away from us so much as this disposition; and why? because He is Himself a calm and peaceable spirit, who always brings silence and peace into the soul. He brings silence; for more commonly His language consists only in embraces, in consolations, and in the sweet impressions which He produces in our innermost being; and if sometimes he speaks therein, it is but in plaints, or in some simple word which He lets fall into the recesses of the mind, but which carries more meaning with it and has more effect than the most eloquent discourses.

He also brings peace into the soul; for He pours himself into her, as Isaias[1] saith, like a peaceful river, in which she is happily all immersed; and He produces in her this peaceful disposition, either by applying Himself to all her powers, or by diffusing a certain sweet tempering influence over all her passions. He effects this, says Origen,[2] after the manner of a skillful player on the lute, who insinuates an indescribable sweetness and peace into the senses by the sweetness of his instrument; so this Divine Spirit by the sweetness of His grace, calms the passions and brings them into a most harmonious accord.

This is why, before entering into the soul, He would find her in silence, because His voice is so modest, so soft, and so delicate, that the least sound would prevent its being heard; since, according to St. Gregory,[3] it is seen rather than heard, because it insinuates itself without any noise of words, and banishing darkness carries light into the understanding.

Again, in order to make His entrance, He would find her also in peace; for darkness is not less compatible with light, than is the perturbation of a soul with this Divine Spirit, since, according to the Scriptures,[4] it is in peace that He delights to dwell. So also the peaceful disposition of a soul is the attraction which draws the Holy Spirit towards her, and which opens to Him all her doors, that He may make His entrance therein in person, like a peaceful Solomon.

Let us acknowledge, Theoneus, that theirs is a great

---

[1] C. 66.

[2] On Canticles

[3] *On Job.*

[4] Psalm 75.

mistake who think to attract this dear and Divine Guest into themselves by the noise of their sighs and of their acts, and by a disquieting eagerness to behold themselves filled with Him. Oh! I entreat them with all my heart to learn well to be silent, and to divest themselves of all eagerness, and to make it their principal care to adapt themselves to the delicacy of His voice, and the peaceful nature of His operations.

It is certain, then, that silence and peace of soul form the natural preparation for His entrance. Now I wish you much to understand that it is recollection alone which puts the soul in this state of peace and silence. For is it not recollection which withdraws her from all external noise, and which also frees her from the multiplicity of internal operations, that it may lead her even into a spiritual solitude? Is it not recollection which instantly quells whatever disturbing emotion is inclined to arise in the mind; for it has no greater employment all the day long than that of regulating and moderating its movements. Is it not recollection, then, without which the Spirit of God cannot enter into a soul?

Section I.

Further, it is also absolutely necessary, because this Divine Spirit flows into the soul so softly and so insensibly, that without recollection she cannot perceive His entrance. He does not come ordinarily like an impetuous wind, though He did so heretofore upon the apostles in the cænaculum, when being as yet earthly, they had need of some visible sign to give more confirmation and display to this miraculous communication; but He insinuates Himself into the soul, to avail myself of the idea and the language of the third book of Kings, like the "whistling of a gentle air." Or rather this imperceptible entrance of the Holy

Spirit seems to me still better described by one of the prophets.[5] He says that He makes His entrance into the soul, like as the dawning light rises little by little on the horizon, and descends like the soft rain which falls insensibly and penetrates the bosom of the earth.

Now if it be true that His entrance into the soul is made in so secret a manner, observe that it is recollection alone which can favor it; for it is recollection whose close attention discovers the most imperceptible operations which take place in the soul. And does it not suitably follow, that through this discovery, perceiving the inflowings of this Divine Spirit, it should lead the soul to prepare herself to receive Him by that profound respect wherewith it inspires her? Otherwise, surprised by the secret manner with which He insinuates Himself, so far from treating Him with the veneration which is due unto Him, she might perhaps receive Him with irreverence.

Section II.

But be well assured, Theoneus, that without recollection the Divine Spirit will never enter into your soul; because His object is to find her always alone, and He cannot bear to approach her any more than He can endure to abide, or to converse with her, when He finds her already occupied with company. It is for this reason that He would have her either separated exteriorly from all society, or disengaged interiorly, as though for her no creature existed; or all alone within herself, through some secret occupation, which so withdraws her into her own interior, that she loses, as it were, all communication with objects of sense.

O Spirit of love! who will not willingly consent to a

---

[5] Osee, 6.

total separation from everything to find Thee alone? Is there anything whose company ought to delay my soul an instant, when Thou art awaiting her in solitude? O precious moment! when she shall be able to rejoice as Thy spouse, in having found alone Him whom her love desires, so that nothing can withdraw her from such sweet converse, any more than from her place of retreat!

It is most just, Theoneus, that this sacred Spirit should find our soul alone before entering therein; for how could one wish to make another partner with Him, with whom nothing can be compared? How could one wish to divide so small a possession, seeing that all souls and all hearts are nothing but a point in His regard? Know we not that His eyes are sensitive, and that they cannot brook a rival? Know we not also that the purity of His love has secrets, and familiarities, which the soul is incapable of receiving except when she is alone in His company? But what can a third do but interrupt this divine intercourse? And again, would not the soul be unworthy of receiving the visit of this Spirit of love, unless she divested herself absolutely of everything?

If what I have just said be true, O! how precious and how necessary is recollection, seeing that it is it alone which can put us into this happy solitude! All the senses want to be ever diffusing themselves without, but it is recollection. that closes them to all objects, and which restrains them in the very midst of things, without their scarcely communicating with them or attending to them. Inclination leads us to talk and gaze, but its employment is to render a man's mind no more a prison to him than his chamber is. The heart even in the profoundest solitude has its continual sallies, whereby it runs. and flies about everywhere through its disorderly movements; "But it finds in recollection," says St. Augustine, "as it were, a barrier which arrests its flight, and constrains it to stay alone within itself, that it may taste therein the sweetness of its God."

O then, dear and amiable recollection, who by making the soul capable of this divine solitude, disposest her for the approaches of this Holy Spirit! O golden door! through which He enters in triumph into the soul, without other company than Himself! O rich and precious ground of recollection! whence the treasure of this adorable Spirit springs!

Section III.

In fine, you will understand the absolute necessity of recollection for giving entrance to the Spirit of God, from this most certain truth, viz., that He enters into a soul only when all the avenues thereof are closed. In this, His way is altogether opposed to that of created objects; for the senses must be opened for objects to be able to enter; the eyes must be open to give entrance to all that is visible; the ears must be open to receive sounds and words; and the rest of the senses must likewise be open to allow a passage to their several objects.

But this Holy Spirit would have precisely the reverse; for the senses must be closed to favor His entrance. We have a beautiful figure of His manner of operation in the Acts of the Apostles, where it is said that our Lord entered, the doors being shut, into the place where they were waiting for the coming of the Holy Spirit. This it is that this same Spirit desires, in order to facilitate His entrance into the hearts of men, viz., that all outlets should be shut. His intention in so doing is to preclude the entrance of the images of created things into the soul before Him, and to provide for the better purifying of His abode, by admitting nothing impure therein. He desires by this means to show His power, in that He has no need, like creatures, to have the doors opened for Him to enter; in fine, His design is thus to show the soul, that it is Himself indeed, since He enters not by favor of sensible species or of any exterior objects.

Now I ask you what it is that thus closes all the gates of the senses, if it be not recollection? For is it not this that causes the soul, all folded within herself and withdrawn into the depth of her own interior, to await there the coming and the infusion of this Spirit of love? And that she may not be interrupted by the entrance of created objects, she closes herself wholly to creatures, either by shunning their society, or by a continual mortification of the senses; thus contributing by her occupation and by her diligence to give a free, full, and victorious entrance to the Spirit of God.

Who then will not now desire this spirit of recollection, and who will be willing to dispense with it? Say rather, "O that I may be eternally buried and imprisoned within my own interior, that I may prepare the way for this adorable Spirit! Most precious, most fruitful recollection, who openest to Him a way of entrance into His domain! O that I may lose myself in thy bosom, where I may await with confidence the coming of this Divine Good, and my expectation not be disappointed, for thou art His particular attraction, and thou so well removest all hindrances from His path. Seeing that thou procurest me the infusion of the Spirit of a God, alas! how miserable should I be not to rejoice in finding myself in holy captivity to thee, for thou orderest so well thy preparations, that He comes to visit me even in the solitude of my heart, there to be my faithful companion."

Let us abide there, my dear Theoneus, O let us then abide there, for woe to the soul who, to gratify her natural impulses, prefers casting away the slight restraint of recollection, and losing the communication of the Spirit of

God, rather than sacrifice that of creatures.

CHAPTER II
The Spirit of God Dwells only in a Humble Soul.

There are many into whom this Divine Spirit enters, invited thither by their recollection; but, alas how few of them are those in whom He makes a long abode! He does but pass through without tarrying, says the prophet, because the place is not in a state for Him to lodge in. Are you not, Theoneus, of the number of those who, possessing recollection enough to invite His coming, lack the disposition fitted to retain His presence; for that deep humility is necessary, and perchance you have it not. A humble soul is the only abode in which He rests; and as He commonly finds in you only pride and high-mindedness, He glides away forthwith like the rain from the tops of the mountains. O my God! let us then humble ourselves to the very depths, that we may be capable of retaining this Holy Spirit, and being always His perpetual abode, so as ever to possess His fullness!

I pass by all the advantages of humility; it is sufficient for my purpose to point out to you how a soul which is grounded in this virtue, is the true dwelling-place of the Spirit of God.

Our Lord Himself tells us that He will send Him to work all things in us, which He can do only by abiding in us. St. Paul informs us and assures us that He inhabits the very ground of our being, like another self; and some very famous theologians teach us that He so dwells in us, that being in the state of grace, we are essentially sanctified by Him. But you will ask me, Theoneus, how a humble soul is that wherein this Divine Spirit rests; this is the question.

SECTION I.

I say then that the Spirit of God is Himself all humble; have you ever reflected on this? 1. In that He humbles; 2. In that He disposes others to humble themselves; 3. In that He also humbles Himself.

1. Did He not begin by the Word, whom He humbled even to our flesh, causing Him to annihilate Himself in a little clay? For it was by His operation that was effected that prodigious annihilation to which we may say He caused Him to descend, and to which the Word descended only through the obedience He paid Him. Does He not also every day humble the majesty of God when He abases Himself in the hearts of men to the extent of forgetting after a manner His greatness in His familiar intercourse with them?

2. No less does He dispose the saints to humble themselves. Indeed their humiliation is one of His chief employments; for He causes them continually to run after opprobrium and humiliations, such movement being an effect of the impressions which He makes upon their souls.

3. But does He not humble Himself by a self-annihilation? It was He who abased Himself to seek Mary; it was He who formed with His own hands a body for the Word; it is He who abases Himself even to prevent the sinner every hour with His inspirations.

Judge then whether this Divine Spirit, being perfectly humble in His nature, can have a more natural or a more pleasing abode than humble souls. He reposes therein as in His center, finding there the term of His inclinations; He rejoices therein, as in a place, the low and deep capacity of which can comprehend all His fullness; He takes His delight therein. as with an equal, because the more humble

He is in His communications, the more are these souls annihilated thereby. Oh to what a degree, then, ought we not to humble ourselves, that we may become the ground of the dwelling and of the sweetness of this Holy Spirit! How deep an abyss of humility ought we not to possess that we may be the center of His repose! And can we help annihilating ourselves, when we behold Him humbling Himself in his continual pursuit of our souls, with more eagerness than that of the most passionate lover!

SECTION II.

I say, besides, that a soul in humiliation is the most powerful attraction to oblige the Spirit of God to take up His abode therein, because through a property peculiar to His Person, which is to be communicative, He is there only to communicate His gifts; and who, I ask, are more capable of receiving them than the humble? For have you never observed how God seems diligently to seek out someone upon whom His Spirit may rest? Upon whom, He says, shall My spirit rest? you would say that having sought on all sides dispositions worthy of receiving Him, and not having found such, He is grieved thereat; and now what is the conclusion, do you suppose, to which He comes? He says not that He will rest upon a soul zealous for His glory, nor upon an amiable soul, which might form an agreeable abode, nor on a soul all on fire with His love, which would seem to possess more noble and natural qualifications for this end; but as if He had found all which He had failed of meeting with elsewhere, He concludes by saying, that it shall be upon the humble soul, signifying by this that she is much more fitted than the others for the communication of His gifts, and that she can far better receive and sustain all the excess of His love.

If you desire to know the reason, I must tell you that

the living waters of His grace ever seek some deep spot which may hold them and preserve them; and is there anything more deep and lowly than a humble soul? for her inward abasements are sometimes so great, that she seems to cast herself down below nothingness, whether it be that she is confounded at the sight of her own contemptibleness, or at beholding the greatness of God. Here then it is that this Holy Spirit finding in this soul a depth proportioned to the excess of His treasures, stays to impart them to it in all profusion.

And further, He abides there willingly, because He can pour into her bosom the most signal favors, without her being elevated thereby. On the contrary, you will observe that a humble soul never receives any divine gift save with confusion, and you would do well narrowly to examine the spirit of those who receive such familiar favors; for in general the exalted communications of this Divine Spirit humble and confound the soul which is favored with them. Alas! she says, I almost imagine that these favors have mistaken their proper course, so ill are they suited to me, only serving to make me see more clearly my own unworthiness! Ah, where do I find myself, O my God, amidst so many caresses of Thy grace? And where too art Thou, immersed in my impurity? This humble soul thus draws her confusion from her glory, and so to say, buries herself within herself; thither she flies, and there she hides herself as far as she can from the caresses of this Spirit of Love, who only communicates Himself the more to her, and loves the more to abide in her. She imitates Jonas in her flight, but in a manner much more praiseworthy; the prophet fled from the face of the Lord, to avoid the embarrassment of his mission; but she to conceal herself in the depths of her own being, from the confusion which she feels at the favors with which she is loaded.

She even conceives a fear lest these divine visits should

be her sole reward, deriving thus matter for alarm from that which might rather appear to furnish ground for confidence. O Holy Spirit, she says, this is not the place for Thy bounty, and if Thou bestowest it on me here, have I not cause to dread that Thou wilt not reserve it for me hereafter? There is no attitude of humility which such a soul does not assume in the midst of these gifts; and this it is which constrains this Divine Spirit to take up His abode in her, because He can fully satisfy Himself in His communications, without any danger of their being ill-received.

SECTION III.

In fine, the humble ground of this soul arrests the Spirit of God; for this Spirit is purity no less than He is love, and He is purity only because He is love, Whose sacred fire has this property of not being able to endure anything which is impure; this is why He abides with so much pleasure in a humble soul, for there is nothing that produces purity like humility.

What generally soils the most virtuous souls, is that they contemplate themselves as inwardly enriched; they commit a multitude of faults which they regard as trifling, and they neglect to sanctify many common actions. Now it is from the self-same source that the humble soul derives her purity; for, 1st, how far is she from attributing to herself anything of the favors she receives! since, as we have seen, she draws only confusion from them; 2nd, she thinks lightly of no fault, from the knowledge which she has of the greatness of God, to whom the nothingness of the creature is an offense; 3rd, as she beholds herself so little and so limited, there arises within her not the slightest movement of which she would not immediately make a sacrifice to the greatness of God.

Nothing then being so purified as a humble soul, do you marvel that the Spirit of God should repose therein as in His nuptial couch, where he takes all the chaste pleasure of His love?

Add to this, that God being primal and essential truth, His Holy Spirit is pleased to dwell only in humble souls; and the reason of this is, that every man being a liar, it is the humble man only who is true, because he acknowledges the truth of what he is. And what is this truth? that he is nothing but vileness and sin; and as he always remains in this contemplation, he remains also always in the truth, and the Spirit of God in him; because this Spirit loves only those things which do not by falsehood leave their natural place.

I beg you now to reflect that all which I have just advanced enlightens you with respect to two things; 1st, that ordinary favors are the effects of the entrance of the Divine Spirit into the soul; 2nd, that in general their cessation also is the result of the departure of this Divine Spirit who dwells there no longer. You give Him then entrance into your heart by recollection and sighs, and you drive Him away by a proud temper and high thoughts of self.

Ah! humble yourself, Theoneus, that you may not thus basely banish this Spirit of Love; remember that the greatness of His fullness is measured by the depth of your abasement, and forget not that having thus after a manner struck deep root, His abode is the longer and the more confirmed. Bury yourself so deeply in your nothingness, that you may constrain Him to go and seek you even there, and if you feel yourself possessed by Him, fly still further by your own self-abasement, that you may fix Him more steadfastly in the pursuit of you, since humility of soul is, so to say, the chain which keeps Him.

Chapter III
The Spirit of God Converses only with a Simple Soul.

This Holy Spirit may abide in a soul; He may communicate to her His gifts, but He does not always converse with her in the freedom of familiarity. For this another disposition is wanted, and that is simplicity; for it is certain that He holds no familiar conversation except with the simple. O God! how great are His favors to such souls! would it be credible, did not experience supply a sensible proof?

You must know, then, that with such souls He becomes altogether a simple one Himself; and as their life becomes a sort of holy childhood, so He makes Himself a child with them in His manner of conversing. He adopts different ways of dealing with souls according to their dispositions. You will observe, in the course of direction, certain states of longing and sighing in such as are penetrated with His love, so that, if I may use the expression, they have no other language than that of flames; in such as are touched with sentiments of penance, He speaks only as from a throne and in His majesty; in such as are possessed with the repose of recollection, He speaks only by silence; but in simple souls He seems to feel Himself at perfect liberty, almost like one who, treating the world with ceremony, appears afterward to take His ease with a friend, no longer caring what He does and what He says, in all the self-abandonment of intimacy.

SECTION I.

Would you see to what extent the amiable familiarities

of the Spirit of Love proceed? He is wont, says Origen, to seek on all sides for simple souls, to whom He may discover the greatness of His love and the excesses of His tenderness; and when He has found them He lavishes unspeakable caresses upon them and treats them with a familiarity which cannot be expressed.

He takes as tender, and, if I may so say, as eager a care of them, as the most zealous master ever took in forming his disciple.

1. He instructs them by His illuminations, and teaches them more by one single ray of His light than all the books in the world could do. This is why we see persons of no capacity, who have never received any education, speaking wonderfully of Divine things. It is, says Richard of Saint Victor, because this Spirit of Love does not put them under the tutorage of man, but reserves them for His personal instruction in His own school, where, without the noise of words, He makes them understand everything by simple and sudden views. Oh! what a Teacher of sanctity! and what goodness to occupy Himself with the instruction of persons whose natural intellect is often extremely dull!

2. He takes an especial pleasure in touching such simple souls with the fire of His love. They feel themselves burning with a pure flame, and know not how it has been kindled; their will is all on fire, their heart is a furnace. This it is that makes them speak like seraphim; this is why we see issuing from the mouth of these simple ones, who in other matters have nothing to say, words that burn, when they have occasion to speak of the interior life and of God, and why they inspire the same Divine fire in those who have them. And this because it is this Spirit of Love Himself that kindles the fire, the only care of such souls being to let themselves be sweetly consumed thereby. O holy souls, how profitable to you is your simplicity; it makes you speak only the language of love, glowing

wholly with its heats!

3. But, finally, what does He not say to a soul, to conduct her to the perfection to which He destines her? O! how marvelous is the care He takes of her! Know then, O Theoneus, that He sometimes so attaches Himself to a soul that He, in a manner, importunes her by His incessant movements; whether He never ceases speaking to her, for he does so at all times and in all places, as well in the midst of noise as in retirement, as well by night as by day; or reproaches her with her infidelities, for he does not let a single one pass unnoticed; or urges her to purify herself from the least thing, for He cannot endure the slightest spot; or calls her within herself, for He seems to be happy only in her company; or makes her see that she will never have peace until He is her Sovereign and her only Life, for His holy jealousy will not endure that any other should live in her and reign in her but Himself.

SECTION II.

But He not only speaks to her; this Spirit, all love and all goodness, putting no limits to His operations, fills her wholly with His unction, whether he mollifies her wounds or consoles her in her miseries.

1. The greatest wound of such a soul is her interior compunction, with which she is often stricken at sight of her sins and those of others. And do you know, that His unction so sweetens the bitterness of the pain, that it is infinitely more pleasing to her to be wounded than not to be so. "For," as St. Gregory says, "she passes from compunction for sin to the compunction of love;" and, according to St. Ambrose, "The deeper and the sorer the wound, the fuller it is of sweetness."

2. Again, it often happens that the unction of this Divine Spirit penetrates the whole soul, and sometimes

even the body also, with the sweetness which He causes to flow therein. He infuses a sweetness into the will by the way of love; into the understanding by thoughts of peace; into the whole substance of the soul by a complete silence; into the heart by a sweet flame which consumes it; into the bosom by the pleasant sighs and sobs which issue from it; He diffuses a sweetness upon the lips by those accents of love which they utter; into the eyes by those showers of tears which flow therefrom; and often through the whole body itself, so that it is seized with a holy faintness unable to support such excess of sweetness. "This ineffable sweetness it is," says Richard of St. Victor, "which, destroying the impatience of a multitude of desires with which the mind is commonly agitated, fixes and stays it in the enjoyment with which this divine unction has steeped it."

3. In fine, this Spirit of Love takes care also to comfort the soul in all her miseries by His unction. See now, I pray, the amiable ways with which He does this. 1st, He consoles her by His embraces; for do you not feel at times certain sweet and pleasant compressions of the heart, and an inexpressible something which draws you wholly into yourself? It is the embraces of this Divine Spirit, who compassionates our miseries, and treats us like a mother who folds her infant to her breast. 2nd, He comforts the soul by the thoughts of resignation with which He inspires her, that crosses pass away, glory awaits us, and heaven is worth infinitely more than the pain we suffer. 3rd, He consoles her even amidst His reproaches, for this Spirit, so tender, cannot launch the dart with one hand but He must extract it with the other, and instantly pour oil into the wound.

SECTION III

Ah! my God, Theoneus, what sweet and enrapturing things! And what an admirable ground does simplicity form for receiving operations still more wonderful! If this Spirit of Love is pleased to do so much in the simple soul, she on her part is excited to deal likewise with Him. She speaks to Him with an incredible familiarity, as if she were but talking with her own heart; she discloses to Him like a child all her little secrets; she responds to His sacred movements without much considering what she has to say to Him. When He hides Himself from her, she makes Him return by her cries; sometimes she complains, O astonishing boldness! of Himself to Himself, and He is pleased to listen to her loving reproaches; often she moans together with Him, and makes, as it were, an echo of transports and sighs. She tells Him incoherently and unreflectingly everything that occurs to her, and this it is which is most pleasing to Him, as friend converses with friend, telling Him indifferently everything that comes into her mind; she even calls Him to account for His coldness, when she is treated by Him with indifference. Is not this a marvelous state, on whichever side we consider it, to which simplicity gives rise.

Say then, who will not love thee, O dear and precious simplicity, despised and slighted virtue! O that I may generously take thee for my only portion! O that I may become a little child! Take from me that reasoning and proud faculty, that earthly prudence, that human wisdom, and let me be no less simple and docile than a child. Come, O virtue of my heart, come and make me as simple as heretofore I have been self-sufficient in my conduct. Come, O virtue dear to Jesus, to whom He gave the first rank, and chose to be the characteristic of His own mind. Wretched poison of human policy, and of that spirit wise according to the flesh, in what horror I hold thee, since thou causest me to be held in horror by this Divine Spirit! Yes, my God, I consent to pass as a bye-word among men, and as a person void of discretion, I care not what it costs me, so that I may possess simplicity, and with it the unspeakable confidence of thy Holy Spirit.

SECTION IV

But you will ask me, whence is it that the Spirit of God deals so familiarly with simple souls? This is a point upon which I will satisfy you, Theoneus, and with which I will conclude this Maxim.

1. The simple soul makes no retrospections upon the familiarities and favors of this Divine Spirit; all takes place in such innocent unconsciousness, that she does not even understand what is going on, whether this be the result of her being so much occupied therewith, or whether it proceed of grace which has thus formed her, or from her nature which grace has perfected, or whether it be that she is not aware of possessing anything so remarkable.

Now there is nothing which makes the Spirit of God communicate Himself with more freedom than when the soul makes no retrospections upon His favors; for then they are not soiled by her repeated contemplations, which commonly arrest their course, and no after reflection being made upon these divine familiarities, they remain in their purity, even as they spring from an innocent simplicity.

2. The simple soul is also capable of this divine intercourse, because she offers no resistance to the movements of the Divine Spirit, and because her peculiar characteristic is docility. She knows not what it is to dispute; she is ready for everything, she is willing for

everything, she does everything, she says everything, according as she is desired; for the simple soul honestly believes that all is good, in this differing with a politic mind, which judges everything and mistrusts everything.

This is the reason why the Spirit of God familiarizes Himself with simple souls, because being by His nature sensitive and imperious, He finds in them a disposition to receive all the impressions He wishes to make; and they, on their part, without examining the object, or the causes, or the measure, or the nature of these impressions, yield to His breath like a vessel, they take all forms like soft wax, they are wrought into shape like a well-carved stone. Thus it is that they form a subject of triumph to this Holy Spirit, who in their docility finds all the submission He desires.

3. Finally, in the simple soul I observe a particular disposition for entering into this holy familiarity with the Spirit of God, inasmuch as she does not believe that in this respect she possesses more than others.

I do not say that there are not souls who understand the privilege of the favors they enjoy, and receive them with much purity; you will, however, remark in directing them, that they receive them with I know not what of respect, seriousness, and attention, in order that they may not make a bad use of them; and as they thus deal with God, you will also find that He communicates with them in a manner more grave and more reserved.

But the simple soul, because she does not think that this Spirit of Love treats her in a more privileged manner than others, and because she sincerely believes that all are conscious of the same, behaves towards her Divine Spouse with more familiarity and freedom, and He on His side, as He adapts Himself to all our dispositions, acts in the same manner and is not behind-hand in His holy confidences, returning all those caresses which pure and simple love is capable of suggesting.

I leave you, Theoneus, to reflect seriously on all this discourse; that is, how you should labor after recollection, give yourself constantly to humility and love simplicity, if you desire to have your soul always open to the Spirit of God, if you wish to fix His stay within you, and in some measure long to taste how sweet are His divine familiarities.

The Life of
FATHER D. ALEXANDER DE MEO
Of the Congregation of the Most Holy
Redeemer

The life of
FATHER D. ALEXANDER DE MEO
Of the Congregation of the Most Holy Redeemer

By Rev. Father Tannoja.

ULTURARA, which is a small and agreeable domain in the principality of Ultra, situated in the diocese of Montemarano, was the birthplace of Father D. Alexander de Meo, so celebrated as a missionary, and as a man of letters. Although this territory has not been greatly favored by the gifts of nature, as it is situated in the middle of the tortuous windings of the ice-clad Appenines, it has nevertheless become remarkable through the great prodigies of learning and talent to which it has given birth. The most distinguished of all was Anthony Pennetti, the maternal uncle of our Father de Meo. He was not only an excellent medical man, and well acquainted with physics, but was also thoroughly skilled in poetry, history, and mathematics, and what is still more surprising, in civil law and dogmatic theology. Such vast learning caused him not only to be celebrated in the province, but also throughout the neighborhood.

Father D. Alexander was born on the 3rd of November, 1726. His father's name was Mark de Meo; his mother was called Jane Pennetti; she was of an old family of that country, and had been brought up in the fear of God. Nicholas Pennetti, the arch-priest of the place and the brother of Anthony Pennetti, of whom we have already spoken, was a very well-informed as well as a literary man, and it was by his hands that Alexander was regenerated in the baptismal font.

From his very infancy his face betokened the vivacity of his nature, and evinced a certain degree of majesty which even then foretold the sway he would one day exercise over the hearts of men. When he was between seven and eight years of age, his parents sent him to school; after he had been there a year, he committed some act of levity, (I know not what,) for which his master first struck him severely, and then bound him with cords and locked him up in a room alone. Alexander succeeded in freeing himself from his bonds, and then, as he could not go out by the door, he threw himself out of the window. He was providentially preserved from all injury, but this fall made such an impression on his mind, that he would never see this inhuman master again, and it was with difficulty he could be got to submit to another. It was in this interrupted manner that his grammatical studies were completed.

D. Alexander's mind was formed for science by nature, and although the ardor of youth was a source of constant dissipation to him, yet he profited as much by one hour's study as another would by that of a month. His application was inconstant. If a book chanced to fall into his hands, he always devoured it, whatever might be its contents, to the neglect of his other studies. On one occasion amongst others, when he was certainly not more than fifteen, his uncle Anthony Pennetti found him reading a treatise on theology, and said to him with a smile, "Do you fancy that you understand what you read?" And he then gently reproved him for wasting his time by employing it on subjects which he was as yet unable to comprehend. Alexander however remained unmoved, and said, half in jest and half in earnest, "Uncle, do you take me for a fool?" "Tell me then what you have been reading about?" said the uncle; and he replied by giving him such an accurate account of ten or twelve pages which he had read in a cursory manner, that it seemed as if he were quite versed in such matters.

Anthony Pennetti saw that a jewel of exceeding beauty was in danger of remaining hidden under a bushel. He therefore urged him to take the ecclesiastical habit, awakened his taste for science, and undertook to educate him himself. We must not here omit to mention that Anthony was a partisan of Descartes and not at all a peripatetic, and it was under this master that Alexander became acquainted with the belles-lettres, logic, and a portion of metaphysics. About this time, Mgr. Innocent San Severino, (who was afterwards bishop of Piedmont, and grand-vicar of Naples,) sent for him and some other clerics to Montemarano, of which was his See at the time. He there exercised them in various questions of morals, and from that period Alexander began to devote himself to this study. Although he studied but little, he had always the advantage over his young rivals. One day when he went to Fontanurosa, he entered into a controversy with the other clerics, and vanquished them all on various questions of morals and philosophy; their professor, who was present, began himself to take part in the dispute, on seeing his pupils thus defeated to his own great dishonor, but notwithstanding the inequality of this combat, Alexander also discomfited him, which so astonished those who witnessed his victory, that they instantly carried tidings of it to D. Paul Pandolfetti, who was then the vicar of Montemarano.

Alexander was between sixteen and seventeen years of age at this time, and manifested anything but virtuous dispositions, and still less inclination for the ecclesiastical state. His temper was so fiery that it led him into a thousand extravagances, and I may almost say that there was scarcely a single day in which he did not get into some quarrel with his companions. Mgr. San Severino strove to place some check on his excessive vivacity, and neglected no methods which either gentleness or mildness could suggest in order to attain his end; but all his efforts proved unavailing. On seeing no hope of amendment he was several times on the point of sending him away, and if his vicar, Canon Pandolfetti, had not held him back, he would certainly have done so. In truth, Pandolfetti was extremely fond of Alexander, and admired his talents greatly. "If we send him away," said he, "he will assuredly fall into a thousand irregularities, and we shall lose a man whose talents are not fully known." He therefore put up with Alexander's irregularities, in consideration of his youth and the ardor of his nature, and still more through the expectation of the good he would one day effect.

Alexander was scarcely nineteen when he was called into our Congregation of the Most Holy Redeemer through the mercy and grace of God. Our Father Alphonsus was one day passing through Vulturara, when he met Mgr. San Severino. After the usual salutations, he insisted on holding his stirrup, in presence of all the seminarists, to assist him in remounting his horse, notwithstanding Father Alphonsus's repugnance to his so doing. At this sight the priests who were present both admired the conduct of their bishop, and were filled with respect and veneration for Father D. Alphonsus, and grace acted in a special manner on Alexander at this sight, and he was filled with surprise and admiration. "What!" he said to himself, "can holiness draw down even the respect of bishops to such a degree as this!" and immediately and without hesitation he resolved to follow Father D. Alphonsus, and to become a member of his congregation.

He was so engrossed by this holy desire that he repaired in secret to our house at Ciorani, without the knowledge of his parents. When he reached it, he with many tears earnestly entreated to be admitted. When he was examined for this purpose, he answered with perfect frankness, and as he manifested great talent, Father D. Alphonsus did not hesitate to receive him, although he had no testimonials in his favor. His good dispositions were soon admired by all, though his real value was not at first at all adequately appreciated. But one day it so happened that divers systems of philosophy were spoken of at recreation, when D. Alexander, who had read that of Edmund Purchotius, began to recite the whole of the preface to that work, and to speak on the most difficult subjects with the greatest facility. Everyone was astonished, and our saintly father conceived the greatest expectations regarding his future career from this time. Providence undoubtedly arranged all matters so as to bring about his reception; for had the testimony of his bishop been required, or even that of the parish priest, they could not have been obtained, as his irregularities were too well known by them.

No sooner was he clothed in the habit of our Congregation, than Alexander became quite an altered character; his passions were subdued and even extirpated by the first impressions of divine grace on his heart, and gave place to the profoundest humility, and the most entire submission. He was devoted to meditation and inward recollection, and consecrated all the time at his disposal, either to prayer, or to weeping over the irregularities of his youth at the foot of the cross. He had scarcely become a novice ere he began to practice extreme mortification of the senses, and strove to crucify himself by the severest penances. He daily afflicted his flesh by iron chains, fastings, watchings, and bloody disciplines; in a word, he became gentle as a lamb, and his whole conduct was so entirely changed that no one could have suspected what he had formerly been.

As the devil foresaw what defeats he would have to sustain at his hands, he did not fail to torment young Alexander. When his novitiate had nearly ended, a dark cloud of sorrow overspread his mind and troubled his heart; he was so much assailed by feelings of weariness and sadness, that all in which he had formerly delighted now became objects of horror to him. During these days of discouragement one of his former companions arrived at Ciorani, and as he was not received through his lack of capacity, he endeavored to unsettle him, and to get him to take flight with him. Alexander was persuaded, and yielded, and they both conceived the desperate resolution of becoming soldiers. But Blessed Mary never abandons her children, and from the time he entered the Congregation, Alexander always entertained the most tender and special devotion towards her. While he was passing through the corridor of the novitiate, with his mind in this state of disquietude, Alexander cast his eyes on a beautiful image of the Blessed Virgin, which he was in the habit of saluting in passing, when he heard a voice which said to him, (I know not whether it was in an interior or in a sensible manner,) "My son, whither goest thou? If thou abandonest the Congregation, thou wilt assuredly be damned." Alarmed, and yet at the same time enlightened, the cloud vanished, and his heart became dilated. "My Mother," he exclaimed, "behold here I am. I will serve you throughout my life, and love you through all eternity." His companion set out and became a soldier, but Alexander resumed his first fervor, and gave such edification during the rest of his novitiate, that he was permitted by common consent to pronounce the vows of our Institute at the end of a year.

When he became a student, Father D. Alexander did not fail to make use of the talents which God had entrusted to him. He assisted at the lessons in philosophy, in which he always far surpassed his companions; and besides attending to the scientific studies which the lecturer taught, he pursued various other branches of learning in private and with equal success. On seeing the remarkable talents with which he was endowed, our Blessed Father Alphonsus caused him to go to Naples that he might study Hebrew under the direction of D. Ignatius of Calce, who was teaching it publicly at that time; and to the admiration of this learned professor, Alexander soon became well acquainted with this language.

His fervor sustained no diminution, but remained as great as it had been during his novitiate, nay, it even increased, and required to be controlled within just bounds. His continued application to study did not cause him to neglect spiritual things. Prayer and study were his inseparable companions. He augmented his days of abstinence, and fasted every Saturday on bread and water in honor of the Blessed Virgin, whom he venerated as his mother, and to whom he had recourse in all his necessities. He took the discipline daily, and often to blood. When he had a few leisure moments he went to the church, where he prostrated himself before the Blessed Sacrament or before an image of Blessed Mary, and there exposed the wants of his soul. He loved the rule, and was quite indignant when it was in any degree infringed by any of the community.

It was about this time that the Father Abbé, for whom our young clerks felt great deference, for his spiritual and scientific knowledge, began to disturb the peace of the Congregation; he had already succeeded in perverting most of our students, and it is well known that he even tried to set them against the Congregation, and the observance of our rules. Alexander was one of the most zealous of those who took part against this innovator; he strenuously opposed the extravagances of this ill-advised lecturer, and did not rest till he was dismissed from the Congregation. He thus greatly contributed to reestablish the regular observance of rule amongst our students, as well as to those pious practices which are now practiced by us.

After the Father Abbé's departure, a lecturer to teach our young men theology was required; and although D. Alexander was not a priest but only a student at the time, he then began to teach theology to his companions. His being chosen to fill this post, did not arise from his being the only one qualified to discharge it, for Father Caffaro, and Father John Ricci, were with us at the time, and were both distinguished theologians, not to speak of several others of no less talent: the personal merits of young Alexander therefore alone caused this employment to be given to him, and he fulfillled its duties to the great satisfaction of the inhabitants of Nocera and even to that of his companions themselves.

He obtained a dispensation whereby he was ordained priest underage, and he continued to fill the office of lecturer and to go through the different courses of philosophy and theology for several years. He won the admiration of all men of learning in all the houses where he was sent to teach, on account of his attainments and the powers of his mind. A few moments' conversation with him sufficed to show the vast extent of his erudition. About this time there was a bishop who had a very low opinion of us, and spoke of us accordingly, who changed his opinion after he had heard Father Alexander. This father went to Gargano one day with the students, when he also visited this prelate. His Lordship was astonished to see a lecturer who was younger than his pupils, and his prejudices against us made him anxious to put him to silence; he therefore brought forward different points of controversy for this purpose. Amongst others he alluded to the diversity of opinions which render the question of a universal deluge so difficult. His Lordship imagined that we knew nothing about such matters, and that the little father would therefore have to take the part of a learner on the occasion. Father Alexander replied to all he said, but with the greatest moderation; and as to the deluge, he quietly remarked, that he had read all about these different opinions in Augustin Calmet. "Oh!" replied his Lordship, "I read Calmet before you were born." There could be no doubt that he was much disappointed, but as he did not wish to let this be seen, he invited him to come back to Gargano and take coffee with him, fully determining to enjoy the pleasure of then defeating him.

Father Alexander returned to his Lordship's house in the evening, without the least suspicion or mistrust. He there met a Dominican, who directly began to speak of Divine grace with the assurance of one who was giving instructions. Perceiving that this conversation had not been introduced without design, and seeing that the Dominican meant to attack him, Alexander said, "If we are to speak on this subject, my father, let us first set aside St. Augustine; you know that the Dominicans allege that he is on their side, the Augustinians believe that they understand the true meaning of his opinions, and Jansenius, you know, boasts that he has found the real clue to their interpretation, and that he has published a work called Augustinus. All this proves that they are not of the same mind, although they each glory in being the only true followers of the saintly doctor. It is not befitting us to speak confidently when such great men have differed so widely in opinion." This sally alarmed the master; he replied indeed, but without knowing what he said; and although he had begun the dispute with much parade, he ended it in entire confusion at being compelled to keep silence. As his Lordship was also not very well versed in this question, he had a great share in the shame of his discomfiture, and they were both forced to acknowledge and to praise the superiority of the young Father Alexander.

His office of lecturer did not prevent his exercising his talents in preaching; and he succeeded so well that he gained the admiration of all. His style was lofty and flowery at first; he liked to display his learning, and did not know how to adopt a simple and popular style. After he was told of his fault, he tried to correct it; but he soon fell back again into his former habit, as it were in spite of himself. Humiliation however, that all-powerful mistress, who knows so well how to abase the spirit of the proud, taught him how to preach Jesus Christ with fruit and for the salvation of souls.

One Saturday when he was at Nocera, and when D. Alphonsus could not preach on account of a sudden attack of fever, the father rector commanded Father D. Alexander, though he was quite unprepared to do so, to preach on the Blessed Virgin in his stead. He obeyed, but the whole sermon was filled with nothing but learned matters of erudition; he endeavored to prove that the Blessed Virgin had been honored for several ages before her birth; he said that the Druids, who were the priests of the ancient Gauls, had erected a statue in her honor with the Divine Son in her arms, that the Egyptians were in the habit of adoring a virgin seated on a bed beside an infant lying in a crib; that the Argonauts had dedicated a temple in her honor from the time of the Judges, and that all the sibyls had echoed the prophets in foretelling the glories of the Holy Virgin Mary. Although suffering greatly from fever, Father D. Alphonsus was still present in the choir, and when he saw that the sermon was worthless as regarded the instruction of the people, he could not contain himself. He at first thought that what was said was merely by way of a preparatory digression; but when the discourse went on in the same manner, he called a brother and told him to tell Father Alexander to leave the pulpit immediately, and his confusion can easily be conceived. The matter did not rest here: besides giving him a sharp reprimand, Father D. Alphonsus enjoined him to keep silence for three days, and prevented his even celebrating Mass. Father Alexander saw his fault, and that he might be the better able to make himself understood by the people, he drew out a list of the most common words, and of those which are most frequently used; he rewrote all his sermons, and began to preach with that apostolical vigor for which he was ever afterwards distinguished.

Although he had adopted a simple and popular style, the expressions which fell from his lips were so full of grace that they charmed everyone. In spite of this change, however, he was still often obliged to endure corrections on this point. A singular occurrence once happened to him on this subject, which I will here relate. After he had composed a sermon which he had to deliver in a monastery, he carried it to Father Mazzini who read and corrected it. Before he began to preach, Father Alexander gave his sermon to the clerk who accompanied him, and enjoined him to watch to see if he delivered it accurately. The audience were delighted with his discourse, but no sooner had he returned home than Father Alphonsus was informed of the flowery and sublime tone of his discourse. Our blessed father did not fail to speak to him about the abuse he had been guilty of in regard to his ministry: "If harm has been done," replied Father Alexander, "it is the work of Father Mazzini, who revised and corrected my sermon," and as he appealed to the testimony of the clerk as to his faithfulness in delivering it word for word, he proved that what he said was the case. The examination therefore redounded to his glory, and no cause could be found wherewith to reproach him. However, he in consequence became still more careful to preach in a simple and popular manner for the time to come. Although he was still young and charged with the difficult office of lecturer, his zeal did not remain inactive. He devoted himself entirely to the care of souls on all feast days, and he almost always preached on Saturdays and Sundays, and he was also at the head of a society of artisans. As soon as it was entrusted to his management it increased so much that there were more than three hundred associates. Persons came to join it from the neighboring villages which were about two or three miles off, as well as from Nocera itself. It was a consoling sight to see these pious people frequenting the sacraments every week, and it afforded edification to all the inhabitants of Nocera. Father Alexander had so much to do that he had scarcely time to say Mass on Sunday mornings; and in the afternoon he had again to instruct these worthy men after having previously preached to the townspeople.

Whilst he was still lecturer, Father Alexander had to contend with a doctor who entertained an unduly high estimate of his own powers. He was sent on a mission as a relaxation to him after his constant application, and entrusted with the office of giving the spiritual exercises to the priests. They were offended at receiving instruction from so young a father. However, one evening he insisted much on the necessity of knowledge; a climax was put to their vexation, as their ignorance caused them to feel very sensitive on this point. As they were too ill-informed to be able to revenge themselves, they persuaded a divine, who prided himself on being exceedingly well-versed in all sacred and profane knowledge, to do it for them, and they promised to give him an entertainment if he succeeded in confounding the little father. The doctor was full of presumption, and went to see Father Alexander accompanied by the priests, pretending to do so by way of paying his respects to the preacher. When he arrived, he turned the conversation on scientific questions, and inquired what had been the nature of his studies, and what was his employment in the Congregation. Father Alexander humbly replied that he had studied alone, and named the treatise of theology which he was by obedience enjoined to teach. "I am not so much surprised at what your Reverence does," replied the doctor in an elevated tone of voice, "as at a man of the age and experience of Father Alphonsus giving you such a charge as that of lecturer." At these words Father Alexander answered with vehemence, "I would readily admit all you have said regarding myself; but since you have attacked my Father Alphonsus, I will tell you, Sir, that you may select whatever questions you please, and were it even one of civil law, I shall be equal to reply to you." "I speak of theology alone," responded the doctor. "Well," replied Father Alexander, "I can name a hundred heresies in theology;" and he instantly did so. After this Father Alexander said, "Sir, if you wish to know even the very alphabet of theology, you must begin by returning to the schools, for at least three years, and I much doubt whether you would then be able to profit much by these matters." As the doctor did not know how to reply, he bent down his head, and so did the priests who accompanied him, and they all retired covered with confusion and in silence.

After having taught several courses of theology and philosophy with distinction, Father Alexander began to be sent on missions; and in them his talents were specially displayed, and he excited general astonishment wherever he went. His words were as a two-edged sword which struck home, and penetrated into the very inmost depths of the heart. Sin met with no toleration at his hands, and he pursued it into its most hidden entrenchments. No one could hear him without becoming contrite and humbled. In order the better to destroy vice, he dived into recesses of the heart, and sought therein for the very roots of sin, in order to be able to tear them up and plant the love of goodness and virtue in their stead; and grace everywhere attended his efforts. How many scandals and abuses did he not put a stop to! How many undertakings for the glory of God and for the salvation of souls, did he not carry out in all the places which he visited! His zeal exercised itself on every object, and that grace which always preceded him, accompanied and assisted him in all he did.

He was the soul of missions, and nothing could be wanting where Father Alexander was to be found. He was the first to repair to the church, and the last to quit it; and there was no employment which he did not willingly undertake; and he embraced all kinds of fatigue, and supplied every want, however numerous might be his other occupations. His love for the very poorest people and for the most abject and wearisome offices, won the hearts of his superiors, and gained the esteem of all his companions. He had nothing but the salvation of souls in view, and sought himself in nothing; he had the honor of the Congregation at heart, but the honor of God and the glory of Jesus Christ were still dearer to him.

What did not the stirrings of such a holy zeal lead him to undertake? and to what dangers did he not expose himself whenever sin had to be destroyed, and whenever the honor of God had to be defended? A war was once enkindled between two parties in the territory of Angri; they proceeded to the greatest extremities; everyone was under arms, and they threatened to spread the ravages of fire and sword on all sides. Father D. Lorenzo d' Antonio, who was on the spot at the time, was unable to restore peace among these exasperated men, of whom his own nephews were at the head, so he came to our house at Pagani to request that Father Alexander might be sent to him. When he heard the tidings, he lost no time in flying to the spot, as he well knew how fatal the consequences of such a difference might be, and how much God might thereby be offended. He forced his way amid bayonets and drawn swords, with the crucifix in his hand, and without a thought regarding his own safety; and succeeded in making the contending parties lay down their arms. He obtained the cooperation of the other ecclesiastics, and with an authoritative voice represented to them the outrage they were committing against the honor of God. He menaced them with the punishment of hell, and showed it to them open beneath their feet ready to receive them. He thus succeeded in quieting their minds, and reestablished peace in a lasting manner.

On the last Sunday of one carnival, when he was at Nocera, he went out with the brothers of the society to preach in the square, when he met a vehicle full of soldiers in masquerade. Two of those who were near the door were outraging all decency by their gestures and language. When Alexander perceived this, he approached the car in an animated manner, and loudly and vehemently reprimanded this band of libertines. On seeing that they remained obstinate, he took hold of the horses, and commanded the soldiers to retire. One of them drew his saber and raised his arm to strike him, being indignant at this humiliation. Father Alexander was not the least disconcerted at this. He took his crucifix in his hand, and ordered him to cease to give scandal, but the irritated soldier only redoubled his menaces. Father Alexander then knelt down: "Strike," he said to him, "but strike on the crucifix." These words were so successful that the soldiers turned their horses' heads and retired into their quarters in great confusion.

Although Father Alexander's success was so wonderful in the ministry of the word, yet his special excellence consisted in his manner of giving the spiritual exercises. There was something so persuasive and penetrating in his way of speaking, and he spoke in such a forcible and easy manner, that everyone was filled with admiration and astonishment at his great talents and eloquence. He won all hearts, and caused them to amend, as it were, in spite of themselves, and to abandon themselves into his hands. There was not, I believe, a single diocese, town, or population where he was not earnestly sought for, and the superiors received such pressing solicitations on the subject, that they knew not to which to give the preference. During a great number of his missions, if not all, although his office consisted in preaching to the priests and not to seculars, these latter would not be contented without his giving them at least one sermon; and when he preached to men of the world, the ecclesiastics were not satisfied unless they obtained a triduo or at least one whole day for themselves.

It is difficult to say whether Father Alexander did more good among seculars or amongst the clergy: he was almost adored by all classes wherever he went; indeed, the high opinion which was universally entertained in his regard is almost incredible. The most learned advocates and distinguished scholars rendered homage to his talents in the pulpit. He was everywhere regarded in the light of an apostle. The most wicked criminals became as lambs in his presence, and he could mold them as he pleased. Torrents of tears were shed on every occasion when he preached, and he never did so without inspiring the most lively compunction. The most distinguished persons, those of the most unbelieving and proud dispositions, and who entertained the greatest contempt for the maxims of the Gospel, became quite disconcerted after hearing his sermons; three amongst others were so affected by them as almost to lose their senses in consequence. One gentleman who was present at one of his sermons was so struck by Divine grace, that although he was surrounded by a number of priests and seculars, he was not ashamed publicly to confess his greatest and most secret sins; after he had done so he prostrated himself at the foot of the altar, and struck his forehead with such force against the pavement, that he died in consequence some days afterwards full of contrition.

On another occasion Father Alexander set forth the rigors of God's judgments in such a forcible manner when preaching at our house at Caposele, that all his auditors, both ecclesiastics and seculars, cast themselves with their faces to the earth, loudly invoking the aid of St. Michael the archangel, as if they were really witnessing what he described.

Wherever he preached, scandals were repaired and abuses corrected, restitutions of property were made, and reputations which had been grievously injured received ample reparation. Results such as these were of common occurrence; indeed, he seemed to pluck up and to plant according to his own pleasure. Without speaking of his numerous missions in the Campagna, Salerno, Nole, and Averso can prove the success which he obtained by the force of his eloquence; the whole of the territory of la Pouille can testify its wonderful effects, and the provinces of Bari, of the Basilicate, and of Contado, can also bear witness to the prodigies which were effected by grace through his ministry. D. Philip Mazzochi, who is now the lieutenant of the royal council, once caused him to give the spiritual exercises in the large hall of the custom house at Foggia, where he was then in office. Although the exercises were intended for seculars only, all the clerics and regulars who were in this capital of la Pouille, (and they were most numerous,) hastened thither, and in such crowds, that they quite filled the whole place. The results were so wonderful that Mazzochi sent an account of them to the king, but the whole of the good which was then effected will not be known till the last day. With good reason therefore was he called the conqueror of priests; for all the sermons he preached to them brought forth most abundant fruit. Mgr. Moia, the bishop of Muro, who had often heard him preach, used to say, that were a devil to assist at his sermons he would be converted. One year when he gave the exercises to the ecclesiastics of that town, when his Lordship was suffering from an attack of gout, he caused the seminarists and priests to assemble in his own room, that he might not be deprived of the pleasure of hearing him. One evening he spoke on the obligations of the priesthood, after which three Roman collars were found on the altar; they belonged to three young men who were going to have been ordained subdeacons, but who renounced this state rather than enter upon it without a true vocation. He was sought after in all parts of the kingdom. Mgr. Cavalcanti, who was a very zealous and eloquent archbishop, never rested until he had obtained his services for the clergy of Trani and of Barletta. Mgr. Orlando and Mgr. Gianelli did the same with regard to the ecclesiastics of Molfetta and Bisceglia, and after they had heard him preach they felt as if he were a second St. Paul. What success did he not meet with in Corato during the many missions he gave to the gentlemen and clerics of that town! D. Blaise Rainone, who was distinguished for his learning, was so struck by a sermon which Father Alexander preached in the seminary of Nole with regard to the obligations of priests, and on the small number of those who comply with them, that he gave up his project of being a candidate for that office during the vacation. When the time came for the examination of the competitors, he declared that he would only take part in it by way of exercise, and after he was approved of and appointed to the church at Ottajano and to that of Palma, his native place, his only answer was, "I wish to be saved."

There is one thing which it is well to mention: Father Alexander was not a man of attractive appearance, he was rather below the middle size; his complexion was so dark as to be almost black, and his features were so far from being pleasing, that they were rather repulsive. Mgr. Mastromartino, the bishop of Vicoquenza, felt such an aversion to him on first seeing him enter the sacristy to preach to his clerics, that he would gladly have retired had he been able to do so; but he changed his opinion after hearing him preach, and became so affected by the exercises, that he wished to renounce his bishopric, and would have carried his project into effect had he not been dissuaded from so doing by persons for whom he felt the greatest deference. From this time his Lordship became quite enchanted with Father Alexander, and always designated him as the apostle of Jesus Christ. Mgr. Pirelli, who was then bishop of Sarno, and who is now removed to Ariano his native town, had been misinformed as to our style of preaching, and therefore felt some scruple in allowing his clerics to make the exercises under Father Alexander as they wished; he determined to be present himself, and when the father entered the church before preaching, he said to those around him, "We must make up our minds to hear nothing but nonsense." It was not so however; his Lordship was speedily undeceived, and completely changed his opinion of our Congregation; he even invited our fathers to dinner when they were giving the mission at Sarno, and told Father de Meo, who was one of the company, that he had deprived him of sleep for three nights.

Father Alexander was also peculiarly successful in his method of dealing with the young seminarists, and the bishops and professors preferred his discourses to them to those of anyone else. He was constantly sought after by the celebrated seminaries of Nole and Averso, as well as by those of Avellino, Salerno, Conza, and Muro, but they were specially eager to have him at the seminary of Nole; and once when he gave the exercises there for more than twenty days, Canon Crisci, the president, felt as if he had fully performed all his duties towards the seminarists when he had got Father Alexander to preach to them. Mgr. Lopez, the bishop of Nole, Mgr. Tafuri, the bishop of Cava, and Mgr. Sanfelice, the bishop of Nocera, came in person to conduct him to their seminaries, and it would be impossible fully to describe the great good he effected in these as well as in many other such establishments. His zeal enabled him to win over thousands of young men to God; he reconducted them to the paths of virtue, and they became excellent priests and fervent laborers in the vineyard of the Lord under his direction.

But Father Alexander's labors were not confined to this; his fame as a distinguished missionary was soon spread abroad, and he was eagerly sought after in all the principal towns of the kingdom as well as at Naples itself, where he was even better known than anywhere else. The chief nobles entreated him to preach during Lent in their private houses, to a number of gentlemen and men of letters, whom they wished to assemble together, but there were so many applications that it was impossible to gratify all. Prince Dentice tried to secure his services through the intercession of Counselor Celano, and as he could not obtain the consent of Father Villani, who was then vicar-general, he had recourse to the authority of Mgr. de Liguori. Father Alexander also gave the exercises in the house of D. Balthazar Cito, who is now president of the royal chamber; Chevalier Cavallari assisted at them, together with a number of noblemen, knights, and men of letters. When he was asked what he thought of the preacher, he replied, "He is a true minister of the Gospel; he has the true way of preaching the word of God; his style is both simple and sublime; every word deserves attention, and one is never wearied of hearing him." Amongst the numerous churches in Naples, where it was felt an honor to have Father Alexander, I must not omit to mention that of la Pieta: although that edifice is so very spacious, it was not large enough to contain the crowd of people who hastened thither from all parts to hear him; the audience was composed of ecclesiastics, lawyers, chevaliers, and gentlemen, and they were all at a loss how to admire sufficiently the knowledge of the orator, and the manner in which he exercised it. Even in the tribunals nothing was talked of but the Congregation of Mgr. Liguori, and the prodigious eloquence of Father D. Alexander. His high renown caused us to be so much thought of in that place, that the inhabitants in consequence wished to have one of our houses there. The rector of Pieta said that such a concourse of people had never before been seen in this church, except when Father Pepe of the Society of Jesus preached in it. As the papal benediction was to be given on the last evening of this mission, there was singing and a double orchestra; but the musicians themselves shared so much in the general compunction, that instead of singing they burst forth into groans and sobs, which only served to add to the devotion of this touching ceremony.

The king himself wished to take advantage of the zeal of Father D. Alexander. Being informed of his eloquence and ardor for virtue by Marshal D. Francis Pignatelli, he therefore desired that after he had concluded the exercises

in the church of la Pieta, he should go and preach to the
battalion of the brigade and to the numerous young men
who were being educated at the cadets' college. The great
reputation of the preacher caused them to be attended
from their commencement by as many persons as if they
had been given in the cathedral. "The concourse of people
was very great," said Father Capuano in a letter to Father
Villani, "and it comprised persons of all classes. Numbers
of officers, nobles, equerries, lords and ladies, religious of
divers orders, Theatines and Pious Workmen, etc., were to
be seen there. General compunction was excited; it has
caused many cadets to wish to change their condition and
become religious, and several of them are anxious to join
us. Chevalier Acton, the king's minister, was so satisfied
with these results, and gave such a favorable account of
them to his majesty, that he wished him to go through the
same exercises there every year, and Father Alexander
continued to do so until his death. He led these young men
to frequent the sacraments, and caused them to visit the
Blessed Sacrament, and to practice devotion to Blessed
Mary, amongst the other devotional practices which he
established among them. Many of them consecrated
themselves to God with the consent of the sovereign, and
several of them entered our Congregation.

The esteem in which our Father Alexander was held at
court increased the general estimation entertained
regarding him. After he had given the exercises to the
cadets, he was obliged to go to the Brothers of the
Conception without any delay, and thus his labors
continued until Holy Thursday. He had so much to do
every year that he did not know where to commence; but
he was of course obliged to give the preference to the king,
to his majesty's great satisfaction and that of Marshal D.
Francis Pignatelli.

His labors were also productive of great good to his

majesty's troops who were quartered in the different provinces, and especially to those who were in Nole, la Cava, and Nocera; and he often gave them the spiritual exercises at their quarters. Sometimes all the officers would come to our houses at Nocera, or Ciorani, to hear him. It was a great consolation to us to see these warriors become as mild as lambs in his presence, and after humbly confessing their faults to him, and being restored to the grace of God, begin from that time to lead a new life. The fruit which they reaped from the exercises was manifest to all, both by their exemplary conduct, and by their zeal in performing their duties, and the strict watch they kept over the conduct of their subalterns.

Colonel Count d'Aquila came to Ciorani on one occasion accompanied by all his officers, in order to go through the spiritual exercises there. As soon as he had heard Father Alexander preach, he exclaimed, "If what he says be true, and of this there can be no doubt, we shall all be damned, and if we do not believe him we must either be madmen or excommunicated heretics." He became full of contrition for his sins, went to confession to Father Alexander, placed himself under his direction, and frequently went to see him, when his detachment was quartered at Nocera, la Cava, or any other neighboring town.

On another occasion, when he was giving the exercises in the house at Ciorani, there was a violent-tempered Spaniard among the military who were present, who held the rank of sergeant, and who esteemed himself as much as he despised others. After the second sermon he unmasked himself, and confessed that he was a priest; that he had served in the army of the Bourbons for more than forty years, and that he had not only been present at Bitonto and Villetri but at many other battles, even in Lombardy in the reign of Philip V. This miraculous conversion was wrought by the blessing of Divine grace, through the medium of Father de Meo. When king Charles was informed of it, he gave the unhappy man a pension, and our Father D. Alphonsus took compassion on him, and did not hesitate to receive him as a pensioner; he was afterwards restored to the functions of the priesthood by the permission of the Holy See, and continued to lead a penitent and most exemplary life.

Father Alexander's indefatigable exertions and untiring resistance to fatigue were truly marvelous. Several other missionaries put together could not have gone through his labors during one day; thus it was impossible to imitate his zeal. When he was away from home, he usually preached two or three long and animated sermons every day: they always lasted for an hour and a half and sometimes even for two hours, and yet those who heard him were never tired of them. "When he came here for the mission," Canon D. Michael Ungaro wrote from Ceretto, "he gave everyone the highest opinion of his knowledge and virtue; the sermons he preached to the clergy and gentlemen, were so affecting and convincing, that although they each lasted for two hours, it seemed as if he had only spoken for a moment. Everyone who came away from his sermons was so affected, that half the day was spent in sighs and groans before the altar of the Blessed Sacrament. "Once when he was preaching in the house of D. Vincent Nola, the advocate of the poor at Salerno, he got so enthusiastic that he prolonged his sermon for three hours. He seldom tried to excite the feelings at the end of his discourses, as he said he wished that the truths of which he had spoken should be meditated on at leisure, and that everyone should form their consequent resolutions in a dispassionate and unexcited manner.

Such were the labors of Father Alexander. But it must be owned that his frame seemed expressly fitted to bear fatigue, and he was so robust that labor was really a relaxation to him. His facility in speaking was quite wonderful; he could treat on every subject, and was never obliged to go over his sermons before he delivered them. When he had done preaching at one place, he would immediately go and begin again elsewhere on some fresh subject, and with more ardor than before. He was never at a loss what to say, even though he might have to preach to the most distinguished congregations, such as literary societies, chevaliers, bishops or other learned ecclesiastics; and the ease with which he did so not only excited the admiration of strangers, but even that of our own fathers also.

Such was Father Alexander, and such were his occupations until he had an apoplectic stroke. Yet one of his greatest pains when he was young, or rather his greatest temptations, was to fancy himself unfit for preaching, and that he was a useless member of the Congregation. To the above description of him we may add, that he was the very scourge of the unbelieving. He had a peculiar method of attacking in his missions those who had departed from the right road, or who had adopted maxims which were contrary to those of holy Church; he forcibly defended the truths of religion, especially in large towns where men of letters and would-be scholars are wont to assemble together; when he was in such places he never failed to speak expressly on such topics, and he never did so without advantage to the cause of religion and profit to the souls of those who heard him. On such occasions these poor blinded beings were undeceived and convinced. They came and cast themselves in all humility at his feet, confessing their folly and their ignorance, abjuring their errors, and purposing to lead a truly Christian and Catholic life for the time to come. If he had preserved all the evil books they gave up to him, he would soon have obtained a costly library; but by casting them in the flames, Father Alexander offered them up in sacrifice to Jesus Christ, and raised up a kind of trophy to the cause of our holy religion. On one occasion amongst others, when he was preaching in one of the principal churches in Naples, his discourses all related to the necessities of true faith; some days afterwards he was visited by a dozen persons who were much attached to the doctrines of Martin Luther, and who took great pains to disseminate his errors as far as they could. Father Alexander was delighted at the prospect of aiding in their conversion; they began however by telling him that they wanted to enter into controversy with him. The father listened to them with the utmost patience for several days; after which they became convinced of their errors, made their abjuration before him, and gave up to him more than forty volumes, which defended this impious sect *ex professo.*

It would be an endless labor to try to mention the innumerable conversions he effected with the assistance of Divine Grace: every one acknowledged that he succeeded in converting the most obstinate sinners, for none of them could resist the virtue of his words. But although he was so energetic and animated in the pulpit, he was as mild and charitable as possible in the confessional. When a sinner once came under his guidance, he never left him without his being penetrated with repentance and filled with love and gratitude towards himself. He was most skillful in setting forth the deformity of vice and the affront which sin is to God; but while he thus led men to hate evil, he also well knew how to excite great confidence in the Divine Goodness, and in the efficacy of the blood of Jesus Christ.

God had also endowed him with a special talent for the direction of souls; bishops, grand-vicars, priests, chevaliers, lawyers, officers, and other distinguished men felt proud of calling him their director. But although he rendered them every assistance in his power, he did not therefore refuse his aid to the very poorest and meanest individual. He directed everyone according to the duties of his station, and led all his penitents to frequent the sacraments, as being the only method whereby they could obtain or preserve the grace of God. He was not partial to extraordinary things, as they often proceed rather from the dictates of a heated imagination than from true devotion; but D. Alexander strenuously urged upon all his penitents the mastery over their passions, self-abnegation, love of meditation, of Jesus Christ in the Blessed Sacrament, and of our Blessed Lady, as well as the exact performance of the duties of their stations. He not only set on foot a number of confraternities to which he gave rules of the most solid piety according to the spirit of each, but he reestablished a great many which had been heretofore neglected, abandoned, or ill-attended; he also established congregations of zealous ecclesiastics in divers places, who led the most exemplary lives under his direction, and devoted their whole time to promoting the salvation of others and to the greater glory of God.

Although he was such an indefatigable laborer in the vineyard of the Lord, Father Alexander was no less diligent in the acquisition of knowledge. When he was at the monastery he used to study from morning till night, and as he said, his only recreation consisted in this intercourse with the dead. Father de Matteis, the ex-provincial of the Jesuits, allowed him to make use of the celebrated library of the monastery of Jesus, and he used to stay there all day, scarcely taking even a cup of chocolate during the whole time, yet he quitted it after having been there nearly twenty-four hours, as fresh as when he entered it. The librarian of St. Angelo of the Nile never ceased to admire the way in which he used to begin to study as soon the room was opened, and go on until the hour when it was closed, and at the motionless manner in which he sat there without ever raising his eyes from his books. As he was one of his friends, he often left him there after the door was locked, and Father Alexander would go on studying all day without taking any rest. He was also remarkable for the rapidity with which he understood and retained all that he read, so that he could relate all about it several years afterwards with the utmost clearness and promptitude.

His knowledge was vast and universal; he had fathomed the depths of every subject, and understood them each as thoroughly as he did theology and philosophy. He excelled in all literary pursuits; and numismatics, lithology, paleography, were familiar to him; he had a great knowledge of diplomacy, and understood Greek and Hebrew; he was also versed in civil and canon law. In fact, Father Alexander was deficient in no one branch of learning, and the most wonderful part of it all was, that the greater portion of his knowledge was self-taught.

While Father D. Alphonsus was bishop of St. Agatha, he was attacked in a most improper and offensive manner with regard to his opinion on frequent communion. Father D. Alexander courageously undertook his defense, and discomfitted his adversary with his usual energy. In his work on this subject, he reviews the opinion of all the Greek and Latin fathers, age by age, from the commencement of the Church; he fortifies all by the corroborating testimony of the most celebrated theologians of ancient and modern times; he examines the various changes wrought by time, and defends the doctrine of Father D. Alphonsus with the most profound erudition. Mgr. Theodore Basta, the bishop of Melfi, who was a very learned and pious man, considered this work as a complete masterpiece, and thought it was so complete that nothing could be added to it or taken away from it; it met with general approbation, indeed it was sufficient to cause it to do so, to know that it was written by Father Alexander. His opponent replied to it, but in an obscure and unintelligible manner. But as Father Alexander wished to put an end to the controversy, he then began to write a more voluminous work, not only with reference to his antagonist and to Anthony Arnauld, his teacher, but in order that the subject might be fully entered into, and all its bearings investigated for the benefit of the public and of the Church. The appearance of the work was impatiently looked for, when a person of high rank begged our Father D. Alphonsus not to allow it to be printed, as he wished to spare the reputation of the adversary, who was his friend.

Amongst all the branches of knowledge to which Father Alexander applied, he specially excelled in that of sacred and profane history; he had devoted himself to this study from his tenderest years, and had made immense researches on the subject. He was really profoundly learned on this subject, and his acquirements of this sort formed one of his greatest ornaments. He undertook the difficult task of throwing light on the most obscure portions of the history of the middle ages, especially of that of this kingdom. For this purpose, he searched through all the documents to be found in the provinces, in order to find out of those unpublished manuscripts information on points of which even the best informed authors, such as Mabillon, Muratori, Pagi, and others, were not fully enlightened. He chiefly studied among the archives of the Benedictine Fathers of la Cava. By the consent of these religious, he had access to them at all times, indeed he had unlimited power there. There was not a single library in Naples from which he had not extracted all that was most valuable. He had liberty to go to those of the Nile, and of Tarsia, as well as of those of the Fathers of the Oratory and of the Company of Jesus. He took incredible trouble in these researches, and the journeys which he was obliged to take on account of his numerous missions, procured him a sight of the most ancient documents of the various churches and monasteries he frequented, which afforded him great assistance in clearing up and resolving many historical difficulties.

The learned are greatly indebted to Father Alexander for his many discoveries: indeed the most erudite men used to apply to him as to a first-rate archeologist. A great number of orators and advocates from Naples, as well as the most learned lawyers, often consulted him. Even foreigners came from afar to propose their doubts to him. The profound erudition of Father Joseph Maria Romano, who was a graduated doctor at Rome, and a member of the Congregation of the Servants of Mary, is well known in Rome as well as in Naples, yet once when this extraordinary man had to come to Naples, he considered it a great boon to have been able to converse with Father Alexander, and he went away so enlightened on all the points they had talked over together, that he everywhere proclaimed that he was a prodigy of learning. He consulted him again at Rome, when he was so struck by the wide extent of his knowledge, that he thus expressed himself on the subject in a letter to one of our fathers: "The letter which the learned Father Alexander de Meo has written to me, has caused me to marvel at the depth of his learning and the rectitude of his judgment. When I think of all the researches he has made, I marvel yet more. It would be a great pity were all these discoveries to remain unknown." This learned Servite wished that besides Father de Meo's great work on the middle ages, his different treatises should be published; as he looked upon them as so many precious treasures. "The love I bear towards your congregation," said he in conclusion, "makes me say these things, and I shall be quite delighted if I ever see my wishes fulfillled." This was not because Father Alexander was sparing in making the fruits of his learning available for the use of others; for, on the contrary, whoever had recourse to him was always abundantly satisfied, and he not only communicated his discoveries to us but to strangers also. He never objected to lending his writings to those who asked for them, and allowed the most valuable portions to be copied out of them. How many persons of slender attainments in Naples, in the provinces, and even in Rome, got high renown simply by the use he allowed them to make of his labors. To his friends they were of the greatest service. He gave D. Gaetan Mansi a chronological notice on the Mansoni, and on the dukes of Amalfi, which had taken him several years to compile. He gave another counselor the concordance of the Hegira of Mahomet, with the different epochs of the Greeks; a brother of Father Blasi got a dissertation on the claims of some feudal lords against certain regulars; and one of the king's Counselors received a learned and precious manuscript relating to the village of Balnea, which had formerly been the property of a bishop. It is unknown to whom he also gave away a dissertation on the years of our Lord's birth and death, as well as divers chronological manuscripts on the different sovereigns, pontiffs, and consuls. We have also to regret that an introduction to the general chronology of the world up to our own times has been lost sight of and cannot now be traced. D. Alexander was very intimate with the learned Father D. Salvador Blasi, the Benedictine keeper of the records of the monastery of la Cava. He often went to search through the numerous parchments which are to be found there, and they mutually communicated their discoveries to one another. For some years Father Alexander was engaged on the chronology of the princes of Salerno; when it was finished he showed it to his friend, who had the work printed without his knowledge; he added some notes of his own, and dedicated it to the abbé of St. Justinus at Padua. As Father Blasi had some scruples on the subject, he confessed in one of the notes, although in obscure terms, that Father Alexander was of very great assistance to him in this work: "Diligentissimus Alexander Meo," said he, "presbyter Congregationis Sanctissimi Redemptoris emunctæ naris homo, mihique amicissimus, per quem prima Longobardorum principum chronologia, ut per quos profecerim fatear, fax mihi illuxit (page 6. No. 18. note. 3.) Anyone else would have taken offense at this, but it did not at all annoy Father de Meo, and he only mentioned that he was the author of this chronology in his Introduction to the history at the instigation of his friends.

I pass over in silence a great many other valuable manuscripts which he readily gave up, such for instance, as divers theological treatises which had cost him the labor of years, as well as a compendium of the first volume of Father Petau's work, which he gave to one of his countrymen.

Although he was held in such universal esteem, and all his works met with universal applause, it did not the least interfere with his humility or cause him to think highly of himself. Every sort of distinction alarmed him, and nothing pained him more than to speak in his praise. Once when he was in his native country, in order to attend an uncle who was ill, the archpriest of the place died while he was there, upon which the inhabitants unanimously elected him as his successor. On his refusal they applied to the king, and the auditor of the province came to Volturara with a royal decree to that effect, when a second council was held, and the father was again chosen as archpriest. On seeing that the people were determined on the point, for they watched the house where he was, in order to prevent his escape, he chose an opportunity and fled at once to Naples, where he addressed such earnest entreaties to the Marquis of Marco that he extricated him out of this difficulty.

Several learned men of Naples and other persons of distinction urged him to print his documents on history and to dedicate them to the king, assuring him that he would obtain a bishopric in consequence. Nothing more was needed to cause him to delay their publication.

Marshal D. Francis Pignatelli had an extreme attachment for Father de Meo, and his admiration for his science made him resolve to name him to the king as rector of the College of the Cadets. He promised that he should have thirty ducats a month, and that all his household expenses should be paid; but such a proposition only filled Father D. Alexander with horror. The marshal spoke to our Father D. Alphonsus, who was then bishop of St. Agatha, on the subject, and that with great urgency. In order to get out of the difficulty his Lordship answered that he could not oblige him to accept it, but that he left him at liberty to do so. In answer to all the proffered inducements of the marshal Father Alexander resolutely replied, that he preferred remaining in his poor cell and living as a subject in the Congregation, to enjoying liberty and every other advantage at Naples. On seeing his firmness, the marshal insisted on his at least accepting the honorable title of theologian to the king, and taking the charge of the royal library. On finding himself thus beset, the father took flight from Naples, and did not continue to visit him as he had been in the habit of doing. On another occasion however, when they were seated together on the grass in the garden, he told him that the king and queen wished to have him as their theologian, and as the director of the Calabria, adding that he really ought to think seriously about it. The only reply Alexander made was that he suddenly arose and fled out of Naples, and he did not reappear there again. When he printed his Historical Tables, he sent a copy to all his friends except the marshal, as he preferred, he said, to appear wanting in politeness than to expose himself to fresh solicitations from him.

Father D. Alexander's humility served as a counterpoise to his science; nay, it entirely hid it from his sight. In his own eyes he appeared to be wholly insignificant in the world, and amongst us he always looked on himself as the lowest of all the fathers, and he had a good opinion of every one but himself. When he was at the monastery he remained buried in his room all day long; he never displayed anything he knew, and still less did he seek to enter into scientific controversies. If any prelate or person of distinction came to the house, he immediately concealed himself, and if he were sent for and obliged to appear, he remained silent. If he had no duty assigned to him when on missions, he remained so quiet that his very existence might almost have been forgotten. When occupied in the duties of the confessional he always chose the lowest place, and rejoiced at being surrounded by the poorest of the poor. If anyone happened to say, "That is Father de Meo," he turned aside, and if charity did not compel him to remain in the church, he would immediately leave it. He was also delighted when surrounded by little children; he was glad to instruct them, and gave them rules within the level of their comprehension, whereby they might avoid sin and preserve the grace of God. He was indifferent as to what post was assigned to him, indeed he used even to offer to teach catechism, and considered it a favor to be selected for that purpose. During the first mission he gave in his own country, he was not ashamed to follow the example of St. Augustine, by confessing the irregularities of his youth from the pulpit, and asking pardon for all the scandal he said he had given.

If he presented himself before a bishop to receive his blessing, it was not done as a mere form, but he performed the action with such sincere and unfeigned humility that his very countenance betokened what he felt. There were some persons who thought it well to tell him that he carried his feelings on the subject to excess. "It is our duty," replied Father Alexander, "to humble ourselves thus, and it is by this means that God will bless our labors." When he prayed before the Blessed Sacrament, he did so with such outward humility, and with such a deep sense of his misery and sinfulness, that he resembled the publican mentioned in the Gospels, lying prostrate on the floor, and in the attitude of a suppliant not daring to raise even his eyes to heaven to implore the Divine mercy. To obtain an idea of his profound humility, it was sufficient to have heard him accuse himself of his faults in confession, if it were but once. He condemned himself so severely, and gave such signs of repentance, that he caused his confessor to be at a loss what to say, and when he received absolution he prostrated himself with his face to the ground to second the humility of his soul as far as possible.

Such was Father Alexander in private, but he was quite different when in the pulpit or when engaged in any of the other works of the ministry. He used then to seem to forget, as it were, the lowly estimate he had of himself, and to speak with the greatest authority; even if his audience were composed of bishops, chevaliers, and lawyers, he used to declaim against sin with the animation and freedom of an apostle, while setting before each of them the obligations of his station without the smallest human respect. He openly admonished persons of high rank on several occasions, and did not refrain from once reproving a bishop who failed to perform his duty, to the great injury of his flock, although we had a house in his diocese.

He remembered the fear which the apostle expressed, lest after having preached to others he himself might become a castaway, and so he did not think that he had fully performed his duties if he did not himself make progress in virtue while devoting all his time to furthering the salvation of others. This is not the place to dwell on his exact observance of rule, and on his exalted piety. I will, however, say a little on his ardent love for Jesus Christ and for His Holy Mother. When he preached on the Blessed Sacrament, his audience became enraptured. This subject was such an engrossing one to him, that when preaching on it he sometimes prolonged his sermon for several hours, which happened to him at Foggia and at the Tower of the Annunziata; but what is still more wonderful is, that no one ever complained of their length, as they were rendered most interesting by his zeal and talent.

His love for the Blessed Virgin was no less remarkable; he loved her with filial tenderness, and caused her to be honored by others also. He was also most devout to St. Joseph, and had read all that learned men have penned in his glory. He always had a picture of him on the table; he taught his penitents to honor him in a special manner, and wished his name to be given to children at the baptismal font. One year when he gave a novena in his honor, each of his sermons lasted for at least an hour and a half, and so beautifully did he speak about him, that even priests and gentlemen eagerly hastened from Nocera to hear him, so that the church could not contain the crowds who flocked thither. He had also a special devotion for the archangel Michael, and strove to spread it as widely as he could.

At the assembly of our fathers in 1785, when Father Villani was appointed as Mgr. de Liguori's vicar on account of his advanced age, and was chosen as his successor in the office of rector-major, Father Alexander was nominated consultor-general. This election met with unanimous approbation, and we were congratulated on the excellency of our choice even by those who did not belong to the Congregation. As Father Villani cared more about domestic wants than about the good works which might be performed among strangers, he again sent him to the house at Nocera to teach theology to our young men. On reaching it Father Alexander found that the Congregation of Artisans had lost much of its original fervor, and in fact it was almost entirely broken up. The rector of the house thought very highly of the zeal of Father Alexander, and again entrusted it to his direction, and the society was soon restored to a more satisfactory condition. The brothers regained their former spirit when they saw Father Alexander at their head, and eagerly strove to obtain new proselytes; members came to join them from all parts, and the thirty brothers who were left soon multiplied into a hundred and eighty.

Many bishops and the united population of many towns earnestly solicited to have a share in his labors, but the rector-major continued to prefer the good of the Congregation. Mgr. Tafuri, who was then bishop of la Cava, asked that he might be allowed to give the exercises to his clergy, but he received a negative answer; not daunted by this he went to Nocera in person, and managed so that it was impossible to refuse to allow him to take Father Alexander with him in his carriage, and as soon as the exercises at la Cava were ended, Father Alexander had to go to the high town of Nocera to give the retreat to the gentlemen there.

A body so worn out by study and broken down by fatigue necessarily sunk ere long. On the second day of the exercises, while he was in bed, this excellent father had an apoplectic stroke; he came to himself again but without the use of his senses; his head was greatly affected, and his tongue was so contracted that he could scarcely speak intelligibly. After he had obtained medical aid he was taken home, where various remedies were administered to him, after which he got gradually better, indeed, almost quite well. In the month of May Father Villani sent him to visit the houses at Caposele, Iliceto, and Ciorani, for the benefit of his health, and these journeys were of such use to him, and he got so well, that doubts were entertained as to whether Father Alexander had really suffered from an attack of apoplexy at all. When the season became more advanced he went to the Tower of the Annunziata and took the baths at Agnano. All these remedies had the most salutary effects, and his head got into a much better state, but as a precautionary measure, his superiors interdicted all kinds of study, and gave him every relief which was compatible with the spirit of his calling.

In January, 1785, our fathers gave a mission at Pozzuoli, and Father Alexander accompanied them that he might enjoy the air of this salubrious climate. When he was there he gave instructions to the young seminarists, in compliance with the wishes of their bishop and of the rector of the seminary. After Easter our fathers took him with them when they went to give a mission at Ottajano, by way of giving him a little relaxation: he heard some confessions while he was there, and in order to satisfy the people, he gave two short exhortations on the crimes of drunkenness and blasphemy after the evening sermon.

The illness which had endangered the life of Father de Meo caused general sorrow; men of letters especially feared that at least his History of the Middle Ages might thereby be lost. When he recovered therefore, his friends urged him to have it printed. He resisted their entreaties for some time, but in August he consented to send his labors to the press, whether through a presentiment of his death, or in consideration of the distinguished rank of those who solicited it, I know not. And so, on the 12th of

September, 1785, his Historical Essay appeared before the public. D. Francis Conforto, who revised it, assures us that the only reason which caused the Father to get the approbation of the work, was that he felt that he was approaching the end of his course, and that he wished before he died to have the consolation of at least publishing this portion of his works, which he considered as the key to his Annals; he also said, that he literally tormented him with repeated solicitations that no time might be lost, which he justified by constantly repeating in clear and distinct terms that the hour of his death was at hand.

If Father Alexander had always been much applauded for his great learning both at Naples and elsewhere, the publication of his Historical Essay increased his renown tenfold. Mgr. Laëzza, so distinguished for his extensive acquirements, said to one of us when speaking on this subject, "Father de Meo's work has caused the greatest sensation at Naples, and that not only among men of learning, but also among free thinkers and scoffers; all unite in bestowing the most heartfelt praises on such profound erudition." Battilore also said to one of our fathers, "I have made great researches and carefully studied this epoch of history; but Don Conforto has shown me an inestimable treasure by referring me to the Essay by Father de Meo." He entertained such esteem for the author, that he went in person to visit him, to thank him for the great service he had thereby rendered to the cause of science. The Duke of Toritto also went to call on Father Alexander. "What!" he exclaimed with admiration on seeing him, "are you the Father de Meo, who wrote the new Essay? Are you really the author?" And he repeated three times over, "Is it really true?" Then laying his hand on his shoulder, he said, "Father de Meo, allow me to call myself your disciple; speak and I will listen with docility."

Mgr. Gervasio, who was very celebrated for his learning, thus expressed himself to one of our fathers when speaking of this work, "It has made a great noise in Naples, and what increases the sensation is that he has been able to controvert other great authors. Mgr. Gestari, whose numerous labors on the history of this kingdom are well known, exclaimed with surprise on seeing the Essay of Father de Meo, "I despair of continuing my Annals now," said he; "I confess that he has vanquished me, but although he has surpassed me, I must own that his work is truly admirable."

The author of the Encyclopedical Journal of facts concerning this kingdom wrote as follows, in December, 1785: "In this work, that is to say, in the Historical Essay, a number of interesting dates are to be found, and a great many errors are brought to light into which Father Paggi, Mgr. Assemandi, Muratori, Canon Mazzocchi, Pellegrino, Patrillo, and others of our most celebrated writers on the history of those distant ages had unconsciously fallen." When afterwards speaking of the fall of the kingdom of the Lombards into the hands of Charlemagne, he adds, "None of the modern historians of Europe have hitherto been able to give exact information regarding the year of the birth of Charlemagne, but by the most solid reasoning deduced from the most accredited authors and the most authentic manuscripts, he has happily been able to prove that it took place on the 1st of June, 1773." And again, in alluding to the chronological table to be found at the end of the work, he bestows the highest eulogiums on it, saying, that it forms a fitting crown to so precious a labor, and enhances the merit of its author in the highest degree.

In speaking of this chronological table, the abbé Gestari says in the appendix to the tenth volume of the fifteenth epoch of the Annals of this kingdom, "If we do not quote it at length, it is not from want of respect for the talent of this great man, but only through typographical reasons, which prevent our being able to insert such a voluminous work here." He went on to mention the way in which Father de Meo had been opposed by Father Biasi; he said, "It is possible that Father de Meo may have been mistaken on certain points, and that Father Biasi may have some reason for what he has said, but we have such a high opinion of the knowledge and accuracy of the former, that we cannot alter his chronology in any respect."

The fame of this Essay spread even beyond the mountains. A learned Dane came from Naples soon after its publication, on purpose to make Father Alexander's acquaintance, and to consult him on divers subjects. When he heard that the author had just died at Nole whilst preaching there, he became filled with indignation against those whom he believed to have caused it, and said, "The superiors who have killed him deserve to be branded! Are subjects like these to be destroyed by preaching?"

As it was generally believed that Father de Meo was entirely recovered, the bishops as well as the Faithful began to recommence their solicitations for the happiness of hearing him preach again. Amongst others the lords of Gargane, who were great friends of his, entreated him to come to the Tower of the Annunziata to give the spiritual exercises during the Novena of the Conception, and they assured him that this was ardently wished for by the whole of the population. He complied with their request, and by his mission he not only brought forth many fruits of salvation to the souls of his hearers, but caused them to resolve to build a new parish church. He went about the neighborhood collecting money for this great undertaking; and as large sums were given in consequence of this, he had the satisfaction of seeing the work commenced, nay, he even assisted the people in carrying the materials for the building, to their great edification. Cardinal Zuroli was much pleased on hearing of all this; and when Father Alexander went to pay his respects to him, he not only thanked him for all he had done at the Tower, but begged him to return again for the carnival, to preach at the adoration of the forty hours; and the cardinal did so, because he wished him to exhort the people to continue their alms until the church was completed, as it was much wanted there.

When his recovery became known at Nole, and when people heard of what he had done at the Tower, Canon Lucia, who was his intimate friend, sent him a message through D. Michael Ruopoli, the priest, to let him know that they were very anxious for him to come and give a retreat to the brothers of the Congregation during Lent. The good father hesitated for some time, as he did not like to refuse, yet felt almost unable to undertake it. The matter was settled in the following manner: Ruopoli applied to his superior, who sent for Father Alexander about it. He at first said that he must not reckon on him. "Very well! that settles the point," said the rector. "But what shall I say to the canon?" replied Father Alexander; "it pains me to have to refuse him." "If that be the case, let it be arranged that you give the retreat," answered the father-rector. And thus after much hesitation Father de Meo was led to promise to give the wished-for exercises.

At the end of the carnival, Chevalier Acton, the minister at war, was informed of Father de Meo's restoration to health. Being aware of the spiritual necessities of the cadet's college and of the brigade regiment, he ordered the grand-almoner to inform the superior of our Congregation, that he wished Father Alexander and some other father to be sent to give the exercises to the cadets and to the marine guards. When Father Alexander set out for the Tower, Father Villani, the vicar-general, gave him this new mission for Naples, but he did so with regret. Father de Meo had never before refused any amount of fatigues, but on this occasion he felt bound to say that he had not strength to undertake it, and that the hand of death was upon him. "Does not your Reverence know," replied Father Villani, "that a good soldier ought to die with his arms in his hand?" Upon this Father Alexander bent down his head and took leave of the rector. "My father," said he, "recommend me to Jesus Christ; I will go, but I shall return no more." "Go cheerfully," replied the rector, "the air of the Tower is very good, you will recreate yourself while you are there, and yet you will be laboring for God at the same time." "But I assure you," said Father Alexander, "that I set out never more to return."

He began the exposition of the Quarant ore on Quinquagesima Sunday, the 26th of February, 1786, and terminated it on Ash Wednesday; he set out for Naples on the following Thursday, out of obedience to his superiors. They sent a carriage to the Tower to fetch him, accompanied with every mark of esteem. A superior officer went for him attended by D. Dominic Lombardi, the chaplain of the marine guards. On the 5th of March, which was the first Sunday in Lent, he commenced the exercises to the soldiers in the interior of the port. When he went to pay his respects to the grand almoner and to Cardinal Zuroli, they received him with the greatest consideration. His Eminence thanked him for all the good he had effected during the adoration of the Quarante ore. He was anxious to know where the new church was, and was much comforted by what he heard about it. Father Alexander also visited the Marquis d' Espluè, the commander-in-chief, and his Excellency Dominic Pescara, the commander and general of the armies in the kingdom.

The regiment profited greatly by his sermons; everyone talked of the apostolical zeal of Father Alexander, of the simplicity and clearness with which he set forth the word of God, but especially of the powerful way in which he attacked vice and preached Jesus crucified. There was not a single officer or soldier who did not assist at his discourses; and this not because they were obliged to do so by their commander, but because their high esteem for him made them go and hear his sermons, and sometimes it was as if in spite of themselves. Although overwhelmed with business, Commandant Espluè and General Pescara assisted at them several times. Chevalier Acton expressed unfeigned regret at being prevented from doing so by his numerous occupations. A great many persons of high rank joined the military in attending them. The exercises succeeded perfectly, to the great good of souls, and to the glory of Father Alexander and that of the whole congregation.

Notwithstanding the general satisfaction, the officers regretted that the soldiers who were quartered elsewhere, of whom there were many, could not share in such a great benefit. They therefore begged Father de Meo to give a triduo to these soldiers after he had taken a little rest. He could not refuse this; so it was fixed that after resting on the Monday, Wednesday, and Thursday, he should open the triduo on the Thursday evening.

This rest was but nominal however, for during these three days Father Alexander did nothing but hear the confessions of the officers, who came to speak to him and to consult him all day long.

So much exertion, day after day, could not fail to terminate in a deplorable and tragical manner, in the case of one whose frame was already broken down by infirmities. Whilst he was saying Mass on the Wednesday at the church of St. Louis of the Palace, our poor father felt a sudden giddiness in his head which quite took away his sight. He did not become quite insensible, but his senses were so affected that he did not know where he was. He was at length restored to consciousness by the use of strong scents, and finished the Mass, but with great difficulty. The malady did not attack him again for some little time, and though the seeds of death were in him he would not yet give way. By a great effort he commenced the triduo on Thursday as before agreed on, and continued it during the following Friday and Saturday. On Sunday morning he set out for Nole in a carriage with Father Rastelli, to give the promised exercises to the Associates of the Conception. An officer and three chaplains of different regiments accompanied him to Nole.

Father Alexander's residence at Nole was a fatal epoch as regards himself as well as the Congregation, or rather it was a glorious epoch for him, but it was one of heart-rending sadness for us. In what I am now going to relate, I shall faithfully follow the account which I received from the priest D. Ignatius Vecchione, who was an eyewitness of all that he related, and a great friend of Father Alexander's. Father de Meo arrived at Nole on the 19th of March, and with him Father Rastelli, who was to give the grand sermons. After he had made his meditation he went to say Mass in the church of the religious, called the Nuns of the College, and after having heard another on his knees, he retired into the house of D. Croce Mastrolilli, where he was lodging. When invited to dinner he said, "I hope you will excuse me, for I do not feel well." "At least I hope you will take something or other," replied D. Croce. "I would rather not," answered Father Alexander; "how can I eat, when I have to go to the church?" He at last yielded to Father Rastelli's entreaties however, and took a mouthful or two; after which he conversed with the people of the house for about half an hour, but he only spoke of death and eternity; he then retired to his room, took some coffee, shaved, recited Matins for the next day, and then walked about saying his rosary. After that, D. Croce tried to persuade him to go out for a little relaxation, but he excused himself, and begged to be left alone until it was time to go to the church.

Before the instruction, (for he had reserved this part for himself,) Father Alexander knelt down before the altar of the Blessed Virgin for about half an hour. When the members of the confraternity and the other Faithful had finished reciting the rosary, he ascended the pulpit, and commenced preaching in the following manner: "My brethren, may the grace of our Lord Jesus Christ, which has assembled us together in this place, cause you also to derive benefit from these holy exercises. I will own to you that I do not mean to give an instruction this evening, for I wish that we should unite together in making an act of faith. I do not, however, intend by this merely to cause you to recite the ordinary formula, but to join with you in meditating on whether we really believe what we profess to believe.

"It is an inexplicable thing for a Christian to believe that he will merit eternal punishment by one mortal sin, and yet to have the temerity to commit it. Such a sight has been a marvel to good men in all ages, and fills the saints in heaven with astonishment. If you ask anyone whatsoever if he would venture to traverse a forest, wherein he knows there are assassins, he will tell you, no. Yet it might happen that these malefactors would allow him to pass through in safety, nay, they might even escort him on his journey and show him the way he should take. 'That may be,' he would reply, 'but can I risk my life on a chance? It would be madness to do so.' Ask another to go into a country where the air is full of pestilence, and tell him that it is possible he may not be infected, and he will make you the same answer. In like manner, if you tell a person to throw himself out of the window, trusting that he very possibly may not be killed by it, you will infallibly again receive the same answer. How then comes it to pass that a Christian, whose faith tells him that he will have to dwell in eternal flames for one mortal sin, that his brain will become as a burning fire within his head, that his blood will be congealed within his veins, and the marrow in his bones, can have the courage and the daring to commit sin? Verily, I feel pity and commiseration for those who profess to be men of sense and learning, when I see them fall into folly such as this. No, my brethren, we have not faith, we have not faith. We do *not* believe in the eternal torments of hell, where there will be fire in the intestines, fire in the breast, fire, fi–." He here ceased to speak; he supported himself against the pulpit, and bent his head and fell as if he had been going to kneel down. The auditors were filled with horror at such a spectacle; the cleric who was behind him caught him in his arms; the spiritual father of the brothers hastened to him, and so did Canon D. Salvadore de Lucia, who gave him absolution on the spot. He was taken out of the pulpit, and placed at the right-hand of the statue of the Blessed Virgin which was placed near the pulpit. He was immediately bled; and from the high opinion the people entertained of his sanctity, they preserved the blood in several phials. Groans soon issued from all parts of the church, and he was surrounded by gentlemen, priests, and canons, amongst whom were the dean and chanter of the cathedral. All were eager to render him some assistance; some supported his head, others wiped away the perspiration in which he was bathed, and strove to restore him to consciousness by strong scents; there were some who loosened his cassock and other garments, while others prostrated themselves before the altar of Mary reciting the litanies for him; all were in tears, and earnestly prayed to God and the Blessed Virgin to preserve the life of their dear Father D.

Alexander. Meanwhile, several persons went about the town in all haste seeking the aid of the most celebrated physicians and surgeons.

Whilst every exertion was being made for his relief, the sick man only grew worse and worse. As the doctors found that his pulse only beat at intervals, they ordered Extreme Unction to be administered to him with all haste; they continued however to make use of every remedy which could be available in such a case: they applied cupping-glasses to the nape of the neck, and bathed his extremities with hot water; blisters were placed on the legs, and mustard poultices on the soles of the feet; but all was of no avail, and failed in affording him any relief. The tidings of this calamity soon became known throughout the town, and persons of all ranks hastened to the church. As night was far advanced, people were to be seen running from all parts with lighted torches in their hands, for everyone felt eager to see the holy missionary once more before he expired. The crowd was so great that the soldiers were obliged to be sent for to guard the door to prevent the confusion and tumult likely to arise from such an assemblage of people.

As soon as Mgr. Lopez, the bishop of Nole, was informed of what had happened, he went in person to see the holy father, accompanied by his own physician. This latter coincided with the others in thinking it unsafe to move him elsewhere, for fear of his dying on the way. His Lordship therefore had a bed placed beside the statue of the Blessed Virgin, in which the dying man was placed. "Father Alexander," to quote the words of a priest of the name of Vecchione, "looked like one in a peaceful slumber; I could have fancied he was only preparing for his sermon, as I had so often seen him do before, with his eyes half closed, and his head erect, as if absorbed in God." His Lordship showed signs of the most lively sorrow, for he had loved him with tenderness and entertained the greatest esteem for him. After he had remained for two whole hours by his bedside, he saw that all further assistance was unavailing, and as he could no longer endure to witness such a sad spectacle he retired to his palace at about nine o'clock. The pious father continued to be attended by a multitude of people, of priests, of men of distinction, and among them we must specify D. Felix Zamparelli the chanter, D. Xavier Pesce the rector of the hospital, and the two treasurers of the cathedral, who never left him. The malady grew worse however, and the agonies of death came on. At half-past twelve, that is to say on the 21st of March, 1786, Father Alexander gave up his pure spirit to his Creator, amidst the tears and prayers of many pious souls who were animated with the sincerest attachment towards him. The inhabitants of Nole felt this calamity so deeply, and it was such a shock to them, that more than six hundred people required to be bled the next morning, and although at first this seemed only to proceed from natural causes, by comparing notes it was discovered that it had often been foretold by Father Alexander. It was also found that on the different occasions on which he had previously visited Nole, he had several times predicted that his mortal career would terminate in that town.

This martyr of obedience had scarcely breathed forth his last sigh, ere a prodigy happened which increased the amount of veneration which was already felt in his regard. One of those who were assisting the painter to take the cast of the deceased's face, managed by some accident to plunge an iron instrument, of which he was making use, into his hand. It pierced it through and through; but the artist immediately recommended himself with faith to Father Alexander, immersed his hand in the water which had been used for his foot-bath, and drew it out entirely healed, with the exception of a scar, which remained as a sort of testimony of the miracle. This unexpected prodigy caused everyone to desire to possess some relic of him; some took one thing and some another, all esteeming themselves most fortunate if they could obtain a morsel of anything he had worn. The inhabitants of Nole gave the most ample marks of gratitude on this occasion towards him who had sacrificed himself for their salvation.

The brothers of the Congregation resolved to celebrate his obsequies with all possible solemnity, as they were anxious to perpetuate his memory. The body of the deceased was clad in sacerdotal vestments, and placed between four torches which were lighted beside the statue of the Blessed Virgin, where he had expired; a magnificent catafalque was then hastily erected, which was commenced on that fatal evening when his death might be so surely predicted. This funeral decoration was of a square form, and above thirty feet in height. It was not adorned with gloomy decorations, but with rich brocades, trimmed with plates of gold, and it was lit up by more than two hundred candles. The body, which had remained flexible, and bore an air of indescribable sanctity, was placed on the top of the platform in a coffin covered with leaves of gold and of silver; and the mortuary trophy was embellished by several beautiful epitaphs, which were composed by Canon D. Salvadore de Lucia, who was a great friend of the deceased.

The people were summoned to the church on the morning of the 21st, by the mournful sound of the bells; but the sight there presented was so far from one of woe, that the decorations on the contrary inspired feelings of the greatest gladness. On the preceding evening everyone had been plunged in sorrow; but this morning joy was shed through the hearts of all. The preparations resembled the festive decorations of some great solemnity, rather than those for the obsequies of a corpse. The church looked still more beautiful than on days of a plenary indulgence, and a kind of fair was set up in front of the sacred edifice. The following inscription, which was also composed by Canon D. Salvadore de Lucia, was placed at the door:

"Quisquis ades
erectam feigners pompam
contemplaturus
admirandum Congregationis S. S. Redemptoris
lumen
Alexandrum de Meo
fato cunctis acerbissimo extinctum
ne lacrymare
quem
pro re christianorum publica
immortalia gesta
nunquam interiturum æternabunt."

If the brothers of the Congregation manifested such ardor in adding splendor to the obsequies of Father Alexander, the God of the elect contributed to it far more by the most signal graces and prodigies. After the miraculous cure of the painter became known, there was not a single invalid who did not have recourse to the intercession of the deceased, and who did not obtain some of the water which had been sanctified by contact with his body on the preceding evening. The right foot of Samuel Troccola, the son of a man of the name of Nicole, had been so crippled from the time of his birth that he could not make use of it without the most acute pain; he was carried to the church, and it was bathed in this healing water, after which it was entirely cured. Christiana de la Montagne had a tumor on her knee, which had given her great suffering for a long time, but after she had bathed it in this water, she too obtained a perfect cure. A man whose throat was much swollen, and who bathed it in the same water, was also instantaneously cured. A lady, who was a convert, having been a Lutheran, and who had lived at Nole for some years, had such a diseased arm that she could not dress herself without the aid of her maid; on hearing of the miracle which had been wrought in behalf of the painter, she instantly hurried to the church, plunged her arm into the hallowed waters, and was perfectly cured. Another lady, whose arm had been completely paralyzed for several years, was healed in like manner. A young man, who was reduced to extremity by an internal complaint, and who was so ill as to have been just anointed by his priest, applied this water to his stomach, and was immediately cured. Prodigies such as these rendered the obsequies extremely striking, and everyone spoke of him through whom they were effected under the title of blessed or saint.

At this same time the authorities of the town caused the holy sacrifice to be celebrated for this blessed spirit by all the clergy both secular and regular, so that masses were going on at every altar from morning until noon. But a great number of priests were only anxious to honor the memory of Father Alexander, and refused the rich retribution which was offered to them. The clergy of the cathedral repaired in procession to the church at seven o'clock in the morning, by the desire of the bishop; the Office for the Dead and Mass were then sung with the utmost solemnity. All the inhabitants of the town of Nole assisted at the function, and the Faithful of the neighborhood repaired to the church in such crowds that guards were obliged to be stationed at the church for the preservation of order.

As Mgr. Lopez also wished to honor the memory of Father D. Alexander in his own person, he had his pontifical throne conveyed to the church in the afternoon of the same day, and at half-past nine o'clock the next morning, he repaired thither in person, assisted by his chapter and by all the seminarists, to sing high Mass with all the ceremonies usually employed on such occasions. All the staff who were stationed at Nole assisted at this ceremonial, together with the colonels of the different regiments. There was not a chevalier or a lady of high degree who was not present at these obsequies, not to mention a multitude of people who flocked thither from all the surrounding country. The funeral sermon in honor of the deceased was delivered by Canon D. Salvadore de Lucia, who is unrivalled in this kind of eloquence.

The fame of the numerous graces which had been obtained from God through the medium of the relics of Father Alexander soon spread throughout the adjacent villages, and the people in consequence came in such crowds to visit them, that it was not only necessary to cause the doors of the church to be guarded by the soldiers, but even the chapel where the body was laid, for well-grounded fears were entertained that their devotion might overstep due bounds, and thus lead to some confusion. But it was not only the poor who crowded to the church, persons of the highest rank were to be seen there, including nobles, priests, religious, ladies, chevaliers, and the military. They were all anxious to kiss his feet, but as the height of the catafalque prevented this, they were obliged to be satisfied with devoutly kissing the bottom of it. This day was also rendered memorable by fresh miracles; the saintly body was exposed for forty-five entire hours, yet so far from becoming the least offensive, it remained flexible to the last moment. His cassock was divided among the people into small pieces, and all his hair was taken away, so great was the opinion entertained of his sanctity, and the eagerness which was felt to possess some of his relics.

Obsequies in his memory were also celebrated in other

parts of the diocese and even beyond it. The archdeacon of the cathedral of Nole, D. Anthony Acierno, who was a great friend of the deceased, happened to be at Ottajano at this time, where he was preaching the Lent, and he had a solemn Mass sung for the repose of his soul as soon as he was informed of his death. All the priests of Ottajano followed his example from a sense of gratitude for his kindness in often giving them the spiritual exercises, and they each offered up the holy sacrifice for him. No sooner did the sad tidings reach Somma, than the canons and the clergy celebrated his obsequies with great solemnity. The Congregation of Constantinople at Cerreto did the same thing, and all the priests of the town also said Mass for the deceased.

As the members of the Congregation at Nole did not possess any right of sepulture in the church either for themselves or others, they entreated the bishop and the chapter to allow them to inter the father, and to erect a splendid monument to him on the very spot where he had expired. Their wishes were readily granted, although his Lordship and the canons regretted not being able to preserve these precious remains in their cathedral. The corpse was laid within two wooden coffins; and his Lordship insured its safety by having the inner one secured by a double lock, of which he himself kept the key. The grave was walled in with brickwork, and the first coffin was covered over with pitch, after which the interment took place on the 22nd at nine o'clock in the evening, in presence of the rector of the hospital, of the spiritual father and of all the members of the Congregation. After that, the best sculptors were sent for from Naples, who were ordered to carve a magnificent monumental stone, resembling that which is to be seen in the cathedral upon the tomb of Mgr. Sanchez de Lune, the former bishop of Nole. A portrait of the deceased was hung up in the sacristy of the Congregation, in which he was represented in the act of preaching with the utmost zeal, and with a crucifix in his hands. The stone was not finished until the 29th of the following May. The epitaph was composed by Canon D. Salvadore de Lucia, and ran as follows:

> Quieti æternæ
> Alexandri de Meo
> Congregationis Sanctissimi Redemptoris
> presbyteri
> qui Evangelii præconio
> singulari doctrina ac pietate
> omnibus regni ordinibus carus
> heic
> herculeo morbo correptus
> concionabundus obiit
> an. æt. suæ LX.P.M.
> civibus advenis convenis
> illacrymantibus
> sodalitii hujus magistri
> locum ubi ante hac nemini
> dedere
> an Rep. S. MDCCLXXXVI."

It would be too tedious to relate here all the favors which continued to be obtained through the invocation of Father Alexander; I will confine myself to mentioning some which were granted immediately after his death and even during his life.

He was yet alive when Don Francis Avella, one of the gentlemen who was with him during his last moments, asked and obtained a singular favor from him. From the time he was attacked by apoplexy, he constantly supported his head, and kept wiping away the perspiration in which he was bathed until he drew his last breath. Whilst he was in this extremity, Don Francis Avella, for that was his name, prayed him to beseech God to grant that he might die the same death at the close of the exercises. The notary was only forty-five years of age, and he was in robust health at this time. When he went home, he related all about the holy death of Father Alexander to his five sisters, and he also told them of the favor he had solicited from him. "Well," they replied, "but Father de Meo could not die with a wish to injure anyone; now you know that you are our only support, and that all our hopes are centered on you." However, Father Alexander was too grateful to his benefactor, to neglect to obtain from God the favor he had desired. The exercises were recommenced by another father on the 23rd of March; D. Francis assisted at them, made a general confession, with sentiments of the deepest contrition, and communicated several times during this holy period. He was attacked by a cold three days afterwards, which the doctors however pronounced to be far from serious; and in a few days more he was able to take his meals as usual. But on the 13th of April, and at the very hour when Father Alexander expired, that is to say, between twelve and one at night, the notary was like him attacked by apoplexy, and in ten minutes afterwards he was dead.

There was a priest in the territory of Lioni, who had a wound on his head which endangered his life, and which was supposed to be already mortified; but after he had applied a relic of the clothes of Father Alexander to it, his state suddenly changed, a profuse perspiration came on, after which his malady was completely cured.

There was a lady in the same place who was suffering from a tertian fever, who was instantaneously cured after she had taken some water in which some threads of the shirt of the deceased were placed. A priest of St. Vitaliano, in the territory of Nole, was suffering much from gout which had got to his chest; he recommended himself to Father Alexander, and after he had applied some linen which had been steeped in his blood, he instantly got out of bed and began to eat. Emmanuel Sirignano was so ill in consequence of a vomiting of blood, that he was unable to receive the holy viaticum; but he too took a mouthful of the water of which we have spoken, when the vomiting ceased and he was entirely cured.

Don Vito Nola was attacked by a bleeding in our house at Ciorani, which lasted from seven in the morning until eight in the evening. Two monks did all they could to relieve him but in vain. The life of the sick man began to be despaired of at eleven o'clock, when he remembered that he had a relic of Father Alexander, He placed it on his neck and recommended himself to him; and he was immediately cured, as several strangers as well as such of our fathers as were present, can testify.

I will conclude by giving one more instance of the glory which he, whom we number among our patrons, now enjoys in heaven. The president of the Congregation of Nole had a bottle of Father Alexander's blood in his house. One night his son perceived that the room in which it was kept was quite resplendent with light. He uttered a loud cry, and called all the household together. They all witnessed the miracle, and hurried to the spot, which appeared as if it were on fire, but when they reached it, the light disappeared.

Wonders such as these occurred in divers places, and even now whilst I am writing this account (20th of June, 1786,) these miracles have not ceased; for D. Ignatius Vecchione the priest, and D. John Baptist Santoro the physician, testify that people are continually repairing to his tomb, even from distant countries; that they confidently invoke his aid in all kinds of suffering, and always go away relieved.

Thus gloriously did the mortal career of Father D. Alexander terminate, whose memory will never die. He was an honor to science, rendered essential service to souls, and was an illustrious member of our Congregation. He was a prodigy of nature as well as of grace, and he won the esteem and love of every heart; the bishops looked upon him as a new apostle; the missionaries of Naples were wont to say that he had a breast of iron, and he was compared by all the learned men to a flowing river, in consequence of his persuasive eloquence, while they looked upon him as a prodigy of erudition. Mgr. Moia, the bishop of Muro, called him a walking library, and one of the king's Counselors designated him as an incomparable man. After his friend, the learned Benedictine Father D. Salvadore Maria Blasi, had heard of his sudden and premature death, he thus expressed himself regarding it, in his eighteenth Letter, (page 103,) "I cannot tell you what I felt when I heard of this unexpected calamity, it was a sword of sorrow which pierced my very heart; I know not whether the loss of this apostle, who led so many wandering sheep into the right way, should be more keenly felt by the religious world or by the republic of letters, which in him loses an indefatigable laborer, whose knowledge was as vast as it was profound." We cannot conclude these eulogiums better than by quoting that which was bestowed on him by our blessed Father Alphonsus Maria de Liguori. After hearing Father Alexander preach, Mgr. Borgia, the Bishop of Aversa, said to him, "He is indeed a perfect wonder; he never has had or can have an equal." To which Mgr. de Liguori added, "His excellence is such, it conveys some notion to us of the wisdom of God." We can add nothing to this eulogium. Saints are not lavish in their commendations, and their words are weighed in the balance of the sanctuary.

The Life of the
REV. FATHER D. PAUL CAFARO
Of the Congregation of the Most Holy
Redeemer

The life of
REV. FATHER D. PAUL CAFARO,
Of the Congregation of the Most Holy Redeemer

By St. Alphonsus de Liguori

 ATHER D. PAUL CAFARO was born on the 5th of July, 1707, in the diocese of la Cava, and in a place called after the Cafari. His father was called John Nicholas Cafaro, and his mother Cecily also bore the name of Cafaro. Cecily was a woman of great piety, and her husband led a most exemplary life although only a secular. He belonged to a congregation the obligations of which he never neglected. He was much given to mental prayer, and he also taught his family how to practice it; his children daily received instruction in the Christian doctrine from him; and he was scrupulously obedient to his spiritual father; in fact, when he died his director did not hesitate to say to his wife, "You have now a saint in Paradise." These virtuous parents had six children, four girls and two boys, of whom Paul was the second. His temper was so sweet and gentle even in his very cradle that his mother used to be obliged to awaken him when she wanted to suckle him. His childhood was quite different to that of other children, and quite free from those acts of levity which usually accompany it. He had a very serious illness when he was ten years of age, which he bore without a murmur, and with such patience that the doctor who attended him was quite delighted with him, and made his virtues generally known. When he began to

study, he was always modest and attentive to his duties, he never deserved any reproof or punishment from his masters; but, on the contrary, he excited their admiration and that of his companions, as well as that of all who conversed with him.

As soon as he was old enough to do so, he began to frequent the sacraments and to meditate chiefly before the Blessed Sacrament; and he did so with such devotion that it afforded matter of edification to all who beheld him. On account of his great piety and regularity his mother entrusted the care of his sisters to him; he watched over them most sedulously, and was very careful in seeing that they did not leave the house while she was out. If either of them happened to transgress on this point, he punished her by shutting her up in a room, in which he obliged her to remain for some time, which varied according to the length of her stay and the distance to which she had gone.

He became a cleric at the age of thirteen, and led such an edifying life in the seminary which he entered, that the president, D. Dante della Monica, used to say, "The sight of this child leads me to God and makes me recollected." He therefore made him zealator over all the seminarists, and as he never failed to accuse those who transgressed the rules through the dictates of human respect, they revenged themselves on him by ill-treating him one day when they found him by himself. Paul, however, did not therefore in the least slacken in his zealous vigilance, and thus corresponded to the confidence reposed in him by his superior, who had entrusted the superintendence of the whole seminary to him, notwithstanding his extreme youth. When the seminarists asked leave to go to any fête, or place of amusement, the president used to reply, "I will consent if Paul will go with you." One day the seminarists were invited to assist at the office in the church of the convent of Preato, and as it was late, the nuns wished them to stay dinner. They sent to ask permission for them to do so from the president D. Simon Sambiasé. He sent the following line in reply: "Let Paul decide; if he will remain with them, I consent." Such was the confidence which all the superiors had in the wisdom and prudence of our D. Paul, although he was still but a mere boy.

At this early period, and although he was scarcely initiated into the office of cleric, he began to manifest his zeal for the spiritual advancement of his neighbor. He went from village to village on all feast days, teaching the Christian doctrine to children and to the most ignorant and abandoned people; he even stirred up the other clerical students who were his companions, to imitate his example, and he was most solicitous in aiding them to become holy and learned priests, and capable of leading souls in the way of salvation. For this purpose, he used to instruct them and teach them how to meditate. He was thus occupied for seven consecutive years, and we know that his labors were crowned with success, for these clerics became good priests and excellent laborers.

Paul was so mortified, and such a lover of the interior life from his earliest youth, that he used often to retire into a secluded chamber, in order to hide his mortifications and abstinences from observation, and take his meals alone there, that he might be able secretly to let them down out of the window to the poor, who were stationed below ready to receive them; he used only to reserve a morsel of bread or some such nourishment for himself, and with that he was in the habit of mingling bitter herbs. He used to fast at least twice a week on bread and water. Sometimes he would confine himself to soup without bread, and throughout his youth he constantly abstained from meat and fruits, which was a great mortification for one so young. Besides this, he used to mortify his body by haircloth and the discipline in the privacy of his cell. When he was only thirteen he wore an iron chain with such sharp points that the very sight of it was enough to appall, and when his mother discovered it she took it from him by force. From that time he used to sleep on the boards, or oftener still on the bare ground, with his head resting on a bench. He then began to reflect that a good priest ought to be well-informed, so he began to study Greek and Latin, under the direction of D. Ignatius della Calce, with the greatest ardor; after that, he studied philosophy, and above all, theology; this science appeared of such importance to him, that he founded an academy at la Cava, which he directed himself for several years, and of which he was both the head and the support; he was lecturer in dogmatic and in scholastic theology in our Congregation, and he treated on the different branches of both in some learned papers which we still preserve with veneration, and we have attached still more value to them since it has become the custom in the Congregation for the young men only to study from books, as experience has taught us that they make much more progress by this method, that a great deal of time is thus saved, and they are thereby freed from the inconveniences of writing, which is very prejudicial to the health.

After he became a priest, which he did in obedience to his director, D. Paul strove to unite himself still more closely to God than before, and to devote himself to the exercises of a holy life. He meditated for four hours daily, according to the rule laid down for him by his spiritual father, two of which he passed before the Blessed Sacrament, and two others were subtracted from his sleep. Besides this, he used often to put in practice the counsel of St. Augustine: "Go, young men, go, ye grey-haired, and visit the sepulchers of your fathers." For he used often to go to the parish cemetery and pass several hours among the bones, occupied in meditation on death; and sometimes he even spent the whole night and slept there. At times he would take the skeleton of his deceased father, who was interred in this place into his hand, and say, "O my father, how light death hath made thee!" At this same period he used also to retire for some days into a very solitary hermitage, where he spent all his time in prayer and macerations of the flesh.

He was appointed confessor and almoner of the ecclesiastical prison soon after his ordination. He had also at this time the consolation of converting by his gentleness and by his instructions, or rather by his prayers and penances, two Calvinists of noble birth who came to la Cava at this time. After he had been in the priesthood for a year, his bishop insisted on his filling the post of parish priest in the church of St. Peter, and he accepted this office out of pure obedience, and after much resistance, in 1755, when he was in the twenty-eighth year of his age.

From the time he became a parish priest he devoted himself entirely to the service of the souls in his parish. I will here cite what was said of him by a priest who had witnessed his good works and his zeal. "Whilst D. Paul was parish priest," said he, "he never shrunk from any fatigue which could procure the spiritual advantage of his parishioners. In order to be always ready to fly to the assistance of the sick, as soon as he was sent for, he used to go to bed quite dressed, so that if he were awakened in the middle of the night he could set out directly. More than once, to the great astonishment of those who came to fetch him, they met him at the door of his house, as if he had foreseen the message, for he would say directly he saw them, 'Here I am. Let us go.' During the month when he was on duty in the parish, (for it was served by several priests,) he spent the night in the church, as he promised that those who wished to apply to him should always find him there, and he remained seated in the confessional even during the short interval he allotted to repose. He was so full of zeal, and so anxious to attend to the parishioners who had recourse to him without delay, that when the sacristan came in the morning to open the church doors, he found that he had been kneeling there since two or three o'clock, and he never once got there before him."

He not only preached in the parish church as often as possible, but he went about from chapel to chapel, giving spiritual assistance to the poor who were unable to repair to the church, by preaching to them, by giving them instructions, or by hearing their confessions. He went through the neighboring villages, with his crucifix in his hand, after twelve o'clock on feast days, and he made a special point of visiting all places of the greatest resort and of a suspicious character, in order to prevent sin being committed against God. He used to return thither again between eight and nine o'clock at night, even in the cold of winter, and give short instructions on the truths of eternity, setting the chastisement of heaven before sinners, and inspiring terror into those who were living at enmity with God. One evening when he was preaching before the house of a gentleman, who was probably in a state of alienation from God, he was accosted by him in the most offensive and insulting manner, he even treated him as if he were mad; to which D. Paul only replied, "No, Sir, they who perform their duty are not madmen, and I am only doing my duty in taking care of the souls entrusted to my care." One amongst the good fruits of his labors was that of withdrawing several women from a life of sin by either placing them out of the reach of temptation, or by supplying their necessities out of his own pocket; and when his purse was empty, he went about begging for them from house to house. He took particular pains for one woman whom he extricated from a criminal connection by causing her to change her abode, and

supporting her there by the alms he collected until she at
length married the accomplice of her guilt. He often went
about begging for bread for the poor, and when he
obtained any, he used to distribute it amongst them
himself. One day his brother found him engaged in this
charitable work, and being ashamed to see him acting the
part of a beggar he loaded him with invectives in the
public street, and reproached him for thus dishonoring his
family and himself. Reproaches such as these however
produced no effect upon him, and did not therefore in the
least slacken his zeal in the exercise of those labors of love,
by which he led a great many women of bad character to
live in the fear and love of God. He had much to suffer
from his activity in putting a stop to scandals. He was
several times even threatened with death in consequence.

He introduced the practice of monthly confession and
general communion for the children in this territory, as
well as to the frequentation of the sacraments by the adults
not only of his parish, but of those of nearly the whole
diocese. He also established the exercise of mental prayer
in common in the church, and of visits to the Blessed
Sacrament. He took infinite pains in preparing everything
for the erection of a community of twelve priests, who
were to be specially entrusted with the care of destitute
souls in the diocese, viz., those of prisoners, sailors,
children, and the poor; for this reason it was to have been
called the Congregation of the Destitute. The rules were
drawn up under his direction, and approved by the bishop,
and several priests offered to join it, but an obstacle was
put to the completion of the undertaking, from the
impossibility of finding a suitable place of residence.
Another happy result of his zeal was that the priests of la
Cava were thereby led to give the spiritual exercises in all
the numerous villages of this country, or at least in those
where they were most required. By his means these

exercises were given every year in the chapel of St. Roch-au-Bourg, as they were much needed by the inhabitants of this locality, who chiefly consist of carters, tavern-keepers, butchers, and persons of the same stamp, who are generally very indifferent to all that regards the concerns of the soul. Whilst these exercises lasted, he went about every evening in all directions, collecting together all the persons he could, after which he used to conduct them to the chapel, and either instruct and preach to them himself, or assist others who were doing so; he spent the rest of the time in the church or in the sacristy, and generally without eating, saying that he did not require anything, owing to the robustness of his constitution. In fact, although but one individual, he took upon himself the care of every soul within his reach, so that Mgr. de Liguori, the bishop of la Cava, called him "the watchful guardian of all the churches." From hence it happened that when D. Paul retired into our Congregation, the inhabitants of la Cava began to blame us, and said to us, "O what have you done? You have deprived us of a saint and an apostle!" Paul was so highly thought of in his own country, which is far from being a common occurrence, that once after a report was spread that he had died in a place where he had been giving a mission, a multitude of people from la Cava and Salerno came out to meet him on his return, to testify their joy at seeing him.

Although D. Paul performed his duties of priest in so holy a manner, he was tormented by scruples, from the fear of not fulfillling his obligations properly; he was therefore continually urging his confessor to allow him to resign his post, but the confessor always refused, being convinced that his fears were quite unfounded, since in reality he did even more than his duty; so whenever he renewed his demand, he told him to banish such an idea from his mind. But D. Paul still continued to be a prey to the deepest sorrow. One day when he was at home, his parents heard him break forth into tears and sobs; they were quite alarmed, and inquired what misfortune could possibly have befallen him. Paul continued to weep, and replied, "For charity's sake, assist me to obtain the favor of resigning my curé; my confessor refuses to give me leave to do so, and I am dying with terror in consequence." Some days afterwards his parents found him shut up in a chapel, in which he was giving vent to his sorrow by continuing in tears. Although they had opposed him at first, they were now touched with pity, and resolved themselves to strive to have his resignation accepted, which was carried into effect in the year 1740, to his own great satisfaction, but to the great regret of his parishioners; however, he labored for the salvation of their souls with as much zeal as he had done before.

It was by a special leading of Providence that he gave up this office, for God called him to another state of life, and wished to withdraw him entirely from the world, for no sooner had he resigned it than He inspired him. with the thought of quitting all earthly things, and of entering into our Congregation, to lead a life of obedience, as He caused him to feel that the most agreeable sacrifice we can make to God is to strip ourselves of our own will. He wrote to me about this inspiration, for I was at that time his director. In order to be sure that this was truly his vocation, I told him to reject the thought as often as it arose in his mind, for I well knew that if it really came from God, He would Himself strengthen it. He endeavored to obey me, but as God wished to draw him wholly to Himself, the more he strove to banish the thought, the more ardent did his desire to retire into our Congregation become. At length, after much reflection and discussion, our D. Paul determined to go through the spiritual exercises alone, (ere taking his final resolution,) in the

Hermitage of the Cross, situated in la Cava, on the summit of a mountain. When he was there, he determined to abandon the world entirely in order to give himself wholly to God; although when in it he had never loved it or been of it. He thus expressed himself on the subject when writing to a nun just before he quitted it: "I do not wish to have anything more to do with earthly things," said he, "I wish to belong wholly to God, and to forget myself, and for this reason I wish to place myself in the hands of others, so that I may have nothing to think of but eternity."

He entered into the Congregation and left home without telling anyone of his resolution, and joined me at la Barra, which is a suburb of Naples, where I was then living with several of my brothers, in a house provided for us by Cardinal Spinelli the Archbishop of Naples, who sent for some of the fathers of our Congregation to give missions in his diocese. It was here then that Father D. Paul came to aid me. Soon afterwards his brother heard of his having resolved to abandon his family, and came to see him; he was transported with indignation, and did not cease to address him by the most offensive epithets for two whole hours, but D. Paul prudently remained silent, not offering a single word in reply. I say he did so through prudence, because the most logical reasoning and the most eloquent language are unable to convince a passionate man; indeed the more forcible and clear they may be, the more they harden and embitter him. When his bishop, Mgr. de Liguori, heard of his retirement from the world, he too was filled with great displeasure, and made loud complaints against him for so doing. He met him one day during his journey to join us, when he stopped his carriage, and tried to persuade him to return to la Cava; but on finding that D. Paul remained unshaken in his resolution, he ended by saying, "Well, since this is your decision, do not let me see you again, and do not re-enter my diocese."

After this, D. Paul commenced his novitiate, during which he gave the greatest edification, especially by his exercise of the virtue of obedience, which is a most painful and difficult thing for one who enters a community after having reached a certain age, and after having been long accustomed to do his own will, even although he may have been always engaged in the most holy actions. Paul increased his penances, and especially his meditations, during this period, which latter he extended to seven or eight hours a day. During his novitiate and throughout all the remainder of his life, including the six last years, when God tried him by excessive desolation of mind, as we shall relate hereafter, he never had the least temptation to abandon his vocation. When it was time for him to make an oblation to God, that is to say, when he had to pronounce the vows of poverty, chastity, obedience, and perseverance, according to the rules of our Institute, he did so with such love and compunction, that tears choked his utterance, and prevented his being able to repeat the words of the formula which is usually pronounced at profession.

At the termination of the novitiate, his superiors at once employed him in the work of the missions. Let us here pause for a little, however, and admire some of the virtues which this excellent priest practiced during his holy life. And first, let us speak of his zeal for the salvation of souls. He was singularly devoted to the work of the missions. Indeed, he had been ardently attached to them from the time he became a priest. When he was a parish priest he used to go on missions with his companions, the missionaries of la Cava, as often as he could do so without neglecting the duties of his curé; and they attest that he was indefatigable in these exercises, that he never spared himself for a single moment, and that he did not even shrink from what might endanger his life. Whilst he was at la Cava, it once happened that he had to go to a part of the country near the territory of Eboli, called Piesti, where the air was dangerously unhealthy at that time. All the rest declined to go there but Paul, who offered to go of his own accord. He cheerfully set out, notwithstanding the danger he was running; he remained alone there for a week, during which he was constantly employed in preaching and in hearing the confessions of the inhabitants, and by God's mercy he left it full of joy and in perfect health. His love for missions was so great, that when he had resigned his curé, and before he had decided to enter the Congregation, he made a plan to go about through the kingdom incognito, begging his bread, and giving missions in those places which were the most destitute of spiritual assistance; he even wrote to this effect to a bishop of Calabria, but as he did not know anything about him, he did not accept his offer. He at the same time wrote to the bishop of Capaccio, offering to exercise his ministry in his extensive diocese; but this proposition was equally unsuccessful.

When he was in our Congregation, he made a private vow never to manifest any repugnance for any mission to which his superiors might send him. He also made a vow to go as a missionary among the unbelievers should such be the will of his superiors. It will be well here to quote the letter which he wrote on this subject to Father Mazzini, his director: "My Father, I know not whether it is through the spirit of God or through that of pride, that I feel impelled to write to your Reverence, to lay before you the desire which I have always had of offering myself to the father-rector for the missions among the heathen. From the time of my novitiate, I have vowed to obey the superior *pro tempore*, by undertaking any office, even that of a foreign missionary; and I made this vow with the strong desire and lively hope of realizing it some day or other. This desire is less fervent than it was, it is true, but I am still perfectly ready and willing to carry it into effect, and what is more, this desire has never left me since my novitiate. I know that I am full of faults, but yet I feel a holy envy for those who are more perfect. If I compare what I was with what I am, I find that I have changed for the worse, and this makes me long still more to go and labor among the heathen, for if I were once embarked in an enterprise like that, I should be, as it were, compelled wholly to renounce myself and my own ease and comfort. My favorite maxim is that of St. Augustine, who says, 'O happy necessity which forces us to amend!' Now as I know that if I were sent on a mission among the heathen I should be almost forced to do good, to suffer, nay, perhaps even to die for Jesus Christ, I feel the greatest desire for it. It is true that I suffer much from seasickness, and that I might perhaps die on the voyage; but I should not therefore hesitate to set out, let the consequences be what they may. My Father, I resign myself to you," etc. He succeeded in obtaining permission from his director to make this request, and he afterwards most earnestly besought me to grant his petition, imploring it as the greatest favor I could possibly grant him.

D. Paul was a truly indefatigable missionary, and spared no pains, especially in the laborious office of hearing confessions. Yet it must not be imagined that this was an easy duty to him; on the contrary, it caused him the greatest anxiety, as he was always afraid of having been guilty of some negligence regarding it. From hence it arose that this employment was a positive martyrdom to him, and the state of excessive weakness into which he sometimes fell during its administration was a plain proof of what he then endured. This however only enhances our admiration for the immense zeal and ardor of Father D. Paul. In the morning he was the first to enter the church, and in the evening he was the last to leave it, as he spent the whole day in hearing confessions, generally those of men, which are usually the most embarrassing and tedious. When he returned home in the evening after the sermon, he entered the confessional again, without allowing himself a single interval of rest, and when he had attended to the penitents around him, he left his room to see if there was anyone else who would like to go to him, although every confession was a source of torture to him. Once when he went on a mission without an alarm, D. Paul used to keep awake for several hours every night in order to be able to awaken his companions at the appointed time; during which he would get up from time to time without shoes or stockings, to go and see what o'clock it was. On another mission he preached and heard confessions, although suffering from an attack of fever; in fact, his labors in the work of the missions during winter and spring were quite incessant. Whilst he was at home, he spent the day in giving the spiritual exercises to the ecclesiastics and seculars who asked for them, in fact he never shrunk from any fatigue or inconvenience which he met with in the service of souls. One day when he was at the house at Nocera, he heard that a man had just been mortally wounded; he immediately flew to his assistance, without waiting to put on his cloak, hat, or shoes; and in order that he might go still quicker, he even took off his slippers, and carried them in his hand till he reached the sick man.

When he was in the pulpit he preached with admirable zeal and energy. Everyone owned that his sermons produced an extraordinary effect, quite different to that which followed those of other preachers. Even in the conferences which he delivered to us in chapter, which takes place once a week among us, his words seemed like burning arrows which pierced our inmost souls, for he uttered them with such penetrating energy, that we felt that they sprung from the depths of his own heart, and above all, when he spoke of eternity he caused all who heard him to tremble.

This burning zeal, as that of D. Paul may be aptly designated, caused him to write those ardent Letters which he sent to divers subjects whose skill in gaining souls for God was well known to him, in which he urged them to redouble their pains and labor in this holy work. One of the fruits of his zeal was manifested in the abundance of prayers which he addressed to God when a bishopric became vacant, and in the active measures which he took in order to cause the election to fall on a good prelate. It was to his zealous efforts alone that the elevation of one worthy prelate to the episcopate must be attributed, who is still alive, and who governs his church with a solicitude which is most advantageous to the souls of his people.

Whilst D. Paul was thus laboring for the good of souls, he devoted as much time as possible to the exercise of mental prayer. The love of meditation indeed was his strongest passion, or rather it was his greatest delight. From his earliest years, and especially after he became a cleric, he set apart several hours a day for this purpose; he always spent two hours in prayer before the Blessed Sacrament in the afternoon; sometimes he was kneeling, sometimes he was seated, but he always preserved an air of such great devotion, that the Faithful used to say to one another, "Let us go and see the saint." He also made frequent visits to the cemetery, where he used to stay for a long time meditating on death and eternity. After he entered our Congregation he used to make two meditations in church before the Blessed Sacrament, besides that of an hour and a half, which is prescribed by the rule, and he also made another one of half an hour in his own room before going to bed. He would have liked to prolong this exercise through the night, but the superiors would not permit him to do so. Besides this we used often to find him kneeling in his room engaged in meditation through the day, and it was also noticed that when he went out to walk in the wood, as he sometimes did, he retreated behind a tree and knelt down in prayer. He spent every spare moment, when he was on missions, before the Blessed Sacrament, or else he used to recollect himself wherever he might be, saying, "God is everywhere."

He made his preparation for his sermons on his knees; thus this time was also to him a time of prayer, and it was for this reason that his sermons made such an impression as they did, for they were the fruit of his own meditations. I also think that the reason why his discourses so often turned on death and eternity, was because they were the ordinary topics on which he himself meditated. I have already mentioned how much he liked to visit the burying-ground. One day when he was speaking on this subject to a nun who admired his firmness in remaining in such a place, he said, "I should like to spend all the days of my life there." When he was a parish priest, every evening after his studies were over he made an hour's meditation on death, in concert with a worthy priest who lived with him, during which they used each to place themselves in a corner of the room in the attitude of corpses. "O death! O eternity!" were words which were continually on the lips of this servant of God, whether he were alone or with others. When he was engaged in conversation he would often say to one of his companions, "Tell me how you would feel, were death at hand?" He often spoke of death and eternity in his letters to his penitents and friends. In one he said, "Earthly things will soon be at an end, and will avail nothing for all eternity." In another, "Let us think of eternity, for time is short." In a third, "We must arm ourselves with the buckler of faith, which is the thought of eternity. Let us reflect that all here below will soon be at an end, but that eternity will never end. Let us remember that it is better for us to be one of God's meanest servants, than to possess the most exalted worldly dignity. Think of what on your deathbed you would wish to have done during life." His most powerful discourses were those in which he spoke of death and eternity, and they were his favorite topics. When he was a priest, he used to conduct the Faithful to the cemetery from time to time; when he would take the bones of the dead in his hand whilst he was preaching, thus striving to impress them with the fear of death, that he might the better instill into them a contempt for the world and the thought of eternity. Indeed, almost every one of his public discourses contained some reflections on death and eternity.

But we must now return to the subject of his meditations. Except while he was very young, when D. Paul experienced nothing but sweetness in prayer, he exercised it without any sensible consolation, although he received great lights in it during his after years, especially with regard to the majesty of God, on which he once composed a sermon which filled all who heard it with astonishment. During meditation he spent nearly all the time in saying prayers which he counted on his rosary, repeating almost always these words, "Lord, deliver me from sin, and make me holy," or else, "My God, come to my assistance, come quickly: 'Deus in adjutorium meum intende,'" etc. He used also to recommend this method of praying to others: "Without prayer and humility," he wrote to one of his penitents, "man cannot preserve either favor or grace. Humility! humility! Prayer, prayer without ceasing! let these be our watchwords. He who prays obtains. We must therefore pray without ceasing. Ask continually for alms at the gate of Divine mercy; let at least an hour a day be consecrated to asking spiritual favors from God." On another occasion, when writing to the same individual, he said, "Meditation is necessary, and without it we shall never be where we desire to be, and where we should be with meditation. I entreat you to pray unceasingly. It is the first, the second, the third, and the last method of vanquishing our enemies."

He often felt such interior desolation, that he felt as if he were so sinful that God had abandoned him, and began to weep; and when he recalled to mind his former transports of love towards God, he would tearfully and sorrowfully exclaim, "Lord, there was once a time when I loved you, but now I love you not!" One of us once asked if he had ever felt joy in contemplation. "I once enjoyed it," he replied, "but I have lost all pleasure in it now." Yet it often happened that when anyone wished to speak to him whilst he was engaged in meditation, it was necessary to shake him several times in order to arouse him enough to make him hear what was said to him. But from the time of his youth, as we have already said, God treated him as a strong soul, and reduced him to a state of entire suffering, so that the whole course of his life from that period was an uninterrupted succession of aridities, temptations, and terrors.

However, he rejoiced in the superior portion of his nature, and desired that God would always deal with him thus, as he well knew that the love of God does not consist in sweetnesses, but in the accomplishment of the Divine will amidst tribulations, as St. Theresa said, and as he himself was constantly repeating to his penitents. To one of them, amongst others, he wrote as follows: "Souls who are enlightened by special grace can alone comprehend the value of a cross which is borne for God; but in the next world all will clearly see that this grace is preferable to the possession of the whole world. Let us then pray God to give us strength to suffer, for otherwise our weak nature will sink by the way; meanwhile let us maintain a lively faith in eternal life." He wrote to the same person on another occasion: Saints are formed by crosses, and not by meditations. We see a great many people who practice meditation without becoming saints, because they have nothing to suffer, whilst others, who are in the midst of tribulations, become so although they can meditate but little. The chief benefit of meditation is, that it gives us strength to suffer, and thus to please God. Patience then is the way to heaven, and we obtain it by meditation." He also said, in writing to a father of our Congregation, "Your letter tells me of your pains as well as of your consolations; both of your trials and of your consolations. I wish your Reverence loved tribulation more than pleasure; crosses are indeed precious treasures, for they were sanctified by the death of Jesus Christ on the cross; we ought therefore to desire that our crosses may be multiplied everyday until we at length die nailed to the cross with our Blessed Redeemer."

Thus highly then did our D. Paul esteem and love the cross; and he wished others to do the same, but he could not be insensible to the thorns with which his path was thickly strewed, nor to the terrors which tormented him without cessation. In his latter years especially he had to endure the most cruel temptations which can be inflicted on the soul who knows and loves God. The secrecy by which I am bound forbids my disclosing its nature; were I able to reveal it, it would fill the hardest heart with tenderness. I have no hesitation in saying that his sufferings during these latter years were as intense as any which were ever endured by any martyr of Jesus Christ. He was in such a state of desolation and terror, that he was afraid that God had abandoned him, and he used to sigh and exclaim in the bitterness of his heart, "Alas! I have lost the right way, and I do not know what will become of me!"

In writing to one of our fathers, who was so ill as to be given over by the physicians, and who had asked him to pray to God to grant him a happy death, he said, "Would that I had as well-grounded a hope as that of your Reverence! the great work of my salvation is in a most hazardous position, and for this reason I entreat you to intercede for me when you are in the presence of God." In writing to another father, he said, "I entreat you to recommend me to Jesus Christ, for I labor in uncertainty (*laboro quasi in incertum*), and none but God can know the state of my conscience." In another letter to the same father, he said, "If your Reverence had to endure my sorrows, it would assuredly banish all joy from your heart, but may you continue to possess happiness, and leave me to groan under my misery. Yet have pity on me, at least you who are my friends, for the hand of God has afflicted me, 'Misremini mei, saltem vos amici mei, manus Domini tetigit me.' Now you will ask in what manner God has struck me, and I will tell you. He has afflicted me by withdrawing His mercy and support from me, as a punishment for my infidelities. You will say, Oh! what humility! but I reply that it is an incontestable truth, therefore, pray to God for me."

His love for meditation also caused him to love silence and solitude, which are its inseparable preservatives and companions. Even whilst he was a priest, and whilst he was really absorbed by the anxiety and pains he endured for the salvation of souls, he used to retire into remote and lonely places from time. to time, to hold converse with God in meditation and in penitential exercises. It was this which caused D. Paul to have such a predilection for our house at Iliceto, which is situated on one of the mountains of la Pouille. He used often to retire into a little grotto below the monastery, called the Grotto of the Blessed Felix, to meditate, or else he would plunge into an adjacent wood, where he felt as if he had met with a solitude like that of the first hermits. He thus expressed himself regarding a letter to a priest who was his great friend: "When I am in our new house of our Lady of Consolation at Iliceto," said he, "I feel as if I were enjoying the solitude possessed by the solitaries of Egypt. We retire here after the missions which we give in winter and spring, and enjoy such great tranquility and solitude, and are so removed from the tumult of the world, that we never hear anything about what takes place in it. We live apart from all converse with men in the midst of a wood, where the air is pure and the view agreeable, so that it may really rival the rocky cave of St. Peter of Alcantara. Blessed be God for having brought me hither! but yet I have to mourn over my ingratitude in working out my sanctification so tardily. But I still hope by God's grace to effect it someday." This love of solitude caused him to take delight in studying the Lives of the Hermit Saints. At an after period, to the one to which I have alluded, he went with us to Nocera of the Pagans, and as we were then only building the monastery our fathers were obliged to lodge in a private house. As it was very small, and a great many people came on business, it was difficult ever to be alone there. To obviate this, after the exercises in common were at an end, he used to retire into a confined loft full of straw, where the heat was insupportable, for it was summer, yet this servant of God went there at noon, although that is the hottest part of the day, to seek for a little solitude amid this burning straw, to be able to converse without interruption with God.

D. Paul was no less attached to the virtue of obedience, both with reference to the rule and also in regard to the orders of the superiors. He gave the most perfect example of implicit obedience even to the most unimportant rules, and during the whole period of his sojourn in the

Congregation, no one ever detected him guilty of the slightest infringement of them. One day when he arrived at the monastery of the Blessed Trinity, in the territory of Ciorani, quite wet through, he was recommended to go and dry himself in the kitchen; he replied, "No, that would be contrary to rule, as it is now silence-time." Our deceased Father D. Cæsar Sportelli, who was also a great observer of rule, said one day when speaking of D. Paul, "I always knew that Father Paul was a most mortified man; but I now perceive that he is also a rigid observer of the rule." He not only loved regularity himself, but he was equally desirous to see it loved by all our brothers. He could not bear to see anyone break the rule in any respect, and so the strict observance of every regulation was always to be found wherever he was the superior.

D. Paul was equally attentive in obeying the least sign from his superiors. He manifested perfect submission to his parents from his very infancy, and his mother asserted that he had never offended or distressed her in any respect. He made a vow of entire obedience to his confessor in his youth, and it was in order to be able to resign his own will to that of others that he entered into our Congregation. He said to a nun, on taking leave of a convent of which he had been the confessor, "God calls me to live under obedience." For this reason he used to say that the holiness practiced in the Congregation was worth more than that in the world. He expressed this sentiment when writing to D. Francis Margotta the priest, who was then thinking of joining us, which he afterwards did: "I write to your Reverence on bended knees, on account of the respect with which your holy resolution of retiring into our Congregation has inspired me. I cannot tell you what pleasure it has afforded me. Blessed forever be Jesus Christ, who has given your Reverence the courage to bid a last adieu to the world to give yourself wholly to God. Until now D. Francis Margotta has appeared to me to be a saint, but he has been so in his own way. At present however I see that he wishes to become a true saint, according to the will of Jesus Christ. We are all expecting you: make haste and come to us."

His esteem and love for obedience were so great, that when he received a letter from the rector-major, he read it on his knees and replied to it in the same manner. He also used to carry about with him the circulars which the superior sent to the houses every year, and which contained several minute regulations for the good government of the Congregation, and he often read these letters over in order that he might punctually observe all that they enjoined. Thus when any question arose amongst his companions as to what should be done in certain cases, he cleared up their difficulties by reminding them of some decision given by the superior under similar circumstances. One year, one of the superiors ordered him not to assist at the meditation which we make in common in the evening, and to employ the time in preparing the theological treatises, which he was to explain to our students. Notwithstanding his love for meditation, D. Paul obeyed without objection or uneasiness. On another occasion the superior ordered him to give all his instruments of penance to one of our lay-brothers; this obedience cost him much, but he instantly obeyed and without a word of complaint.

I will now relate another instance of obedience, and one which was still more painful to him, on account of the wound it inflicted on his humility. When he was at Nocera, we had a large picture painted, which is now to be seen at the entrance of this house, representing our Father Mgr. Falcoia, who was the bishop of Castellamare, and the first director of our Congregation, in the act of giving our fathers the rules he had drawn up. The rector of Nocera wished Father D. Paul to be included amongst the personages therein represented, and ordered the painter skillfully to portray his features whilst he was looking on; he then sent for him, and in order that his humility might not be pained, he merely told him to stand there for some time whilst the painting was being done, that he might be able to suggest any requisite alterations. D. Paul assented; but he probably suspected the real object in view, for he kept changing from one position to another, and turning his head about, first on one side and then on another, so that the painter declared that he could do nothing. Upon this the superior openly said to D. Paul, "Go and sit down and remain motionless, for we wish to have your picture taken, and do so without objecting." As the poor father was thus bound down by obedience he sat perfectly still on his chair, but his heated countenance plainly showed the torture which his modesty had to endure during the process. When the portrait was done, he exclaimed, addressing the superior, "Ah! God has justly punished me! some days ago I gave a sharp rebuke to a priest who had had his likeness taken, and now God has so ordered matters that I have been obliged to have it done myself." He was no less obedient to his spiritual father, and he never did anything without his permission, as we shall see when we begin to speak of his interior mortification. One day whilst he was suffering great interior desolation, he went to his confessor and took a paper out of his pocket on which he had written down his sins preparatory to making a general confession; but no sooner did his confessor tell him to leave it alone, than he tore the memorandum and became tranquil.

We must now speak of the profound humility which D. Paul preserved throughout his life. This virtue was, as it were, the very apple of his eye; it was the ordinary subject of his meditations, and he constantly offered up this prayer to God, "Humilem fieri, igne flagrari, in sanctum cito conversi pati, et contemni pro te."[6] And he used to repeat the words, "pati et contemni pro te," over and over again with all possible fervor. He often conversed with his brethren on humility, and when he spoke on this subject his words were so full of ardor that he seemed to be carried out of himself. See what he said about this virtue when writing to one of his disciples: "You may rest assured that you are in a state of grace. As to the consolations you experience, 'nec laudo, nec vitupero,' (I neither praise nor blame them,) and as to the desire for martyrdom, it may be good if it does not proceed from the devil, who often seeks to make us entertain some secret complacency and vainglory by his suggestions. Your sensitiveness when neglected seems to me to proceed from self-love, which is not entirely dead within you." In a letter to another of his friends, he said, "Without humility, man cannot continue to preserve the grace of God in his soul; I therefore earnestly recommend you to cultivate this virtue. I wish you to picture to yourself your place in hell, if you feel that you have ever done anything to merit it, and the abyss of the misery of your sins, if you have committed any. Let us strive to become saints rather than philosophers; let us determine to conquer or die." He also wrote as follows to one of our fathers: "The meditation of a soul under desolation should consist in patience, resignation, and prayer. If she cannot be recollected in God, let her at least be so in herself, that is to say, in her own misery, which is always an incentive to recollection of mind."

As for himself, he believed that he was the most

---

[6] O Lord, make me humble, give me grace to burn with the fire of Divine love, to become soon a saint, to suffer and to be despised for Thee.

unworthy of all, and after his death a number of self-accusations were found among his spiritual memoranda. He used often to accuse himself of his faults in public when he was superior, and he placed some of the other fathers under obedience to accuse him of all the faults they might see him commit, and to humble him without scruple. Once when he was minister in a house, he begged the zelator publicly to accuse him of his faults in the middle of the refectory, and after he had done so, he thanked him for it with much gratitude. But whilst D. Paul spoke and acted thus, he did not resemble those who loudly proclaim that they deserve the contempt of the whole world, and who yet shrink from the least offensive word, or the slightest instance of neglect. He not only did not complain when he was despised, but he rejoiced interiorly. I will now give a beautiful instance of his humility. We have already said that his discourses were generally sought after, for he spoke with so much zeal that he filled the hardest hearts with compunction. Once, however, when his superior sent him to a place in the territory of la Pouille, his first sermon was so much disliked by the inhabitants that they sent him away again; yet he returned full of peace and even satisfaction at having received such a palpable affront. On another occasion, (upon which I was present,) a religious, who is now dead, was conversing with him upon some theological question. He not only differed with him in opinion, but treated him as one quite ignorant of what he was saying, so that when he came to himself, he went and asked his pardon; but D. Paul did nothing but admire the humility of this father, and said, "What humility! the idea of coming to beg my pardon for a hasty word!"

His favorite book was the Hidden Life, and he said that he did not think it could be surpassed by any spiritual book. During one of his illnesses, although his strength was quite prostrated by fever, he read it over five times.

His love for the hidden life made him say, "If I had ever been unjustly accused of the greatest crimes, and afterwards degraded and publicly punished with ignominy, I might then be able to do something for God." Thus would D. Paul reveal the secret desires of his heart, although he did so unconsciously. Nothing pained him so much as to hear himself praised. One day someone said to him, "My father, you are a saint." But his face became glowing as a burning coal, and he replied with much agitation, "What sort of a saint, what sort of a saint!" He was always seeking to mortify himself at his meals, but when he was discovered, he hastened to conceal his mortification. Once when he was preaching at la Cava before Mgr. de Liguori the bishop, who had been, and indeed still was, an excellent preacher himself, he received high eulogiums from him; but in another sermon which he delivered before the same prelate he spoke incoherently and confusedly, in order to lessen the reputation he had gained by the first; he even went so far as to pretend to be quite perplexed or to have lost his memory, and stopped short in the middle of the sermon, but everyone saw that he had done it on purpose to efface the memory of the praises he had before received. Before his death, that is to say, during his last sickness, which continued for thirteen days, this servant of God spoke so little that his words might have been counted, and we imagine that he acted thus through a humble fear that his last words might be treasured up as it is usual to do in regard to great servants of God.

He was also always most careful to practice interior and exterior mortification. His efforts to overcome all his inclinations were incessant, and formed one of his chief resolutions during the spiritual exercises, as we find by reference to his notes, but as these acts were interior, we know little of their nature or extent. They are fully known to God alone, and we trust that he is now enjoying their reward in heaven. As for exterior mortification, we have already said that he began to practice it in the most rigorous manner from his very childhood; he even made a vow to abstain from meat. In order to mortify himself still further he confined himself to one meal a day, and it was so slender that he sometimes felt his strength quite prostrated in consequence; when he was with us he used to speak of such acts as instances of the indiscretion and folly of a thoughtless young man. When he was a priest his meal often only consisted of a morsel of bread and a glass of water, which he used to take in a corner of the church. His sleep never exceeded four or five hours at this period, and he went to rest in his clothes. When he entered the Congregation, he used indeed to take two meals a day, in order not to offend against obedience and to avoid singularity; but he might be said even then to keep a continual fast, for he only took a few ounces of nourishment in the evening, and eat so little in the middle of the day, that he generally arose from table half famished with hunger; so that his superiors at length ordered him to take more at a time. He used also often to mingle bitter herbs, and sometimes even the peel of decayed oranges, with what he did take. In order to mortify his thirst during dinner, for he never drank anything at other times, he only took small quantities at once.

He always carefully abstained from all amusements while he was in the world, indeed he was never known to enter into the least earthly gratification. He never went to plays, games, public walks, or field sports. In la Cava, his birthplace, his family possessed the shooting ground for ringdoves, and this sport is carried on every year there, and is a great amusement for the children; but D. Paul never took part in it. One year when he was the superior of our house of St. Mary of Consolation at Iliceto, which is an extremely cold place, he took care that all the fathers should be provided with warm clothing in winter, but said nothing about himself, so that the tailor forgot to make any for him, and he went through all this rigorous season with nothing but his cassock and shirt without the least complaint. When he was traveling it often happened that night came on whilst he was at a distance from any of our houses; and as he was always careful to lose no opportunity of mortification, he used to avoid going to our friends on such occasions, for fear of the hospitable reception they would give him; he used therefore to go to inns instead, where he was often obliged to lie down either on straw or even on the bare ground. He made a vow of obedience to his confessor whilst he was in the world, and as he was fond of exterior mortification, D. Paul readily got him to consent to all that his fervor inspired him to ask; and all that his director permitted regarding mortification and meditation, he executed most punctually as a rigorous obligation to which he was bound by vow. Disciplines to blood were common with him, and for this purpose he used sometimes to use bunches of thorns which he had gathered in the fields, but he generally scourged himself with a thick cane filled with lead and covered with large, long iron spikes, which not only pierced the flesh but penetrated far deeper. He also afflicted his body by binding his arms and legs with large chains armed with points, and he used to wear them even whilst he was preaching and hearing confessions; but his superior once perceived them during a mission, and took them away from him, and gave them into the charge of a lay-brother.

It was also noticed that when he went to walk in the woods of Iliceto during recreation, he used to strike his hands on the thorns every now and then in order to mortify himself; in fact, D. Paul never had any amusement or relief whatsoever; his whole life and constant study were spent in crucifying his inclinations, in refusing himself every pleasure, and in afflicting himself by every possible penance. He was often heard to repeat, "We must fight in order to become saints; we must be always fighting, always striving to mortify ourselves in everything, in eating and drinking, in sleep, in our method of sitting, and in short, we must be mortified in all things." This is a beautiful maxim, for it is a saintly one, but how rarely is it put in practice, unless indeed by those who have entirely consecrated themselves to God.

D. Paul was also a great lover of poverty. Even whilst he was in the world he made a vow to his confessor, by which he bound himself never to have more than five carlins in his possession at once, and those he only kept that he might be able to bestow them on the poor, whose wants it was his duty to relieve, as he was a priest at the time. His clothes were so shabby, that once when his brother met him looking as ragged as any beggar, he treated him as a madman and loaded him with reproaches in the public street. After he entered our Congregation, where the vow of poverty is one of those we take, he always observed it most zealously. When he was superior, he was very rigorous on this subject, and never forgave any member of the Congregation who was guilty of the least offense against religious poverty. He even carried its observance to excess, which was contrary to true economy, for he would not allow of any store of provisions, saying, "Poor people never lay in stores;" and he was the first to set an example of this rigorous poverty, by always putting it in practice himself. In his notebook he had written, "I should be much more afraid of being rich than of being poor; I wish to love poverty more than men of the world love riches." And in order to carry this resolution into effect, he never even made use of scissors, needles, thread, ink, paper, or of any other such little necessaries, without the permission of the superiors.

When he was superior on the missions, he always chose the worst horse, the worst bed, and the most inconvenient confessional for himself. It is the custom in our Congregation for even the priests to take it in turn to wash the dishes on certain days in the week, as an exercise of humility. The other fathers used to make use of soap or bran afterwards, in order to clean their hands, but he only employed cinders, saying that it would be contrary to holy poverty to use anything else. Our fathers are allowed to carry some book of piety about with them, such as the New Testament, the Imitation, the Visits to the Blessed Sacrament, and others of the same kind, with the consent of the superior; they also keep some devotional pictures in their breviary or on their table. But D. Paul would have nothing of the kind, and when our fathers told him that there was no offense against poverty in so doing, he replied that his motto was, "Nothing, nothing, nothing." During his last illness, and when he had lost his speech, he perceived that a silver watch was hung up in his room, and as he could not speak, he made a sign to have it taken away, as a thing contrary to poverty, but the father-minister told him that it served to regulate the administration of his remedies, which set his mind at rest.

He was as detached from his relations, as he was from the goods of this world. When he was at our house of the Holy Trinity, in the territory of Ciorani, his mother asked him to obtain permission for her to go and see him, for she had not done so for many years; but he sent her a message by a priest, telling her to let the matter alone, for her wishes only proceeded from earthly affection. The mother renewed her entreaties, protesting that she wished to have the consolation of visiting him before she died, both for the sake of seeing him and also that she might be able to give him her last blessing. D. Paul again replied that it was unnecessary, and that she could give him her blessing where she was, as it would be as valuable at a distance as near at hand. On another occasion, when he heard that his sister was seriously ill and in great suffering, he positively refused to go and see her, and contented himself with replying, "I wish that her pains may become still greater, that she may thus be more conformed to the suffering life of Jesus Christ."

Although D. Paul was so austere with regard to himself and to his relations, he was as charitable and considerate as possible towards all besides. He strove to comfort and relieve those who were oppressed by temptations or other trials; and although his natural disposition was severe, charity rendered him mild and affable to all, especially to those who came to confess their sins to him. He was in the habit of visiting the prisons at la Cava and at Salerno before he entered the Congregation; he began by preaching to the poor prisoners; he then heard their confessions; after which he distributed a basket full of bread amongst them, and gave them each a carlin. There was a nun who experienced great distress of conscience, who applied to D. Paul while he was a priest. He attended to her with the most painstaking diligence for eight days consecutively; this happened during the octave of Corpus Christi, and as the nights are very short at this season, and as the servant of God wished to arrive at his church in time to attend to his parish and people, he went to this religious before daybreak. This fact has become known through the testimony of the religious herself. When he was superior amongst us he was always trying to relieve the wants of others, and specially of those who were ill, and not satisfied with recommending them to the care of the infirmarians he often waited on them himself. One day when he saw that one of those who were sick had rather an uncomfortable bed, he immediately gave him his own. During the hours of rest, he used to walk about the corridors of the monastery on his toes, to avoid disturbing those who were in their rooms.

As for the virtue of purity, he preserved it with the utmost vigilance, and watched over all concerning it with the most scrupulous attention, and as far as we can tell D. Paul never sullied his saintly soul by the foul stain of impurity throughout his whole life. He had a horror of this vice from his earliest youth, and could not even bear to hear it spoken of. Once when he was very young, he was going to school with another child who was related to him; but upon his uttering an indecent expression, Paul blushed, and ran off, leaving him behind. On another occasion when this same companion repeated the same word in his presence, he could not help giving him a blow, and from that time he resolved never to be in company with this relative again, nor with any other boy who might resemble him, and he carefully carried his purpose into effect. With still greater reason was he always most reserved in his intercourse with women. He never looked at them, and he never spoke to the oldest female without casting his eyes down; but as he was afraid that his eyes might someday betray him into evil, he prayed to God to weaken his sight, and God granted his petition. He was so careful on this point even with regard to his mother and sisters, that they complained that he had never even once looked at them.

When this servant of God was on missions, he generally began by hearing the confessions of men, and it was only when he had heard them all, that he made up his mind to listen to those of women, in order not to remain idle. When he was obliged to converse with them on any indispensable business, he rigorously followed the advice of St. Augustine: "Cum feminis sermo brevis et rigidus," and he sent them away as quickly as he could, and with all possible gravity. If he had to give the spiritual exercises in a convent, he remained in the confessional in the morning and afternoon; but he never revisited them when the retreat was over, unless in cases of absolute necessity, however pressingly he might be asked to do so by the religious, for fear of contracting any attachment to them.

To purity of body he united that of soul also. He owned to the priest who succeeded him, that he was not certain of ever having committed a mortal sin during his whole life, adding that he only feared that he might have done so, but fears such as these are the scruples of saints who are afraid even when there is not cause for apprehension. Father Balthasar Alvarez said that mortal sin is such a horrible monster, that it cannot enter a soul which loves God, without making itself clearly known, from whence theologians are unanimous in concluding that when a timorous person is only in doubt, and is not sure of having lost the grace of God, it is certain that he has not done so. As for our D. Paul, although he affirmed that he had doubts on the subject, the priest who heard his last general confession on his deathbed, affirmed without hesitation that the servant of God had passed into another life without having lost baptismal innocence.

D. Paul had also great devotion towards the Passion of Jesus Christ. One day when he was preaching on that subject, his countenance became so inflamed and radiant, that it seemed as if a seraphim were in the pulpit. Another time, in the territory of Oliveto, when he was preaching on the love of Jesus Christ, in presence of the Blessed Sacrament, he remained silent and motionless in an ecstasy for a long time in the sight of all his auditors, which affected them more than the finest discourse could have done.

He was no less devout towards the Blessed Virgin. He had cherished a tender affection for this Divine Mother from his infancy, and this tenderness used to be plainly manifested in all his sermons, and to those who went to confession to him. His great delight when he was dying consisted in fixing his eyes on a picture of Blessed Mary which was placed beside him. His last illness took place during the Novena of the Assumption. While he was ill, D. Paul one day said, "If I do not die before the 15th of August, I shall not die now." He spoke thus because he had a confident hope that if he were to die, our Blessed Lady would grant that his death might happen during this novena, and he was not disappointed of this expectation.

But amongst all the admirable virtues of D. Paul, the most striking was his perseverance in goodness. He used also to strive to inculcate it on all with whom he held any intercourse. "Constancy in good resolutions," said he; constancy was indeed, as it were, his watchword, and the firm and unwearied energy with which he carried out his resolution of always aiming at the greatest perfection, and of doing what was most pleasing to God was truly wonderful. During the whole time this good father lived with us, no one ever perceived the least voluntary fault in him, or the slightest appearance of tepidity. What rendered this most remarkable was, that he preserved this constancy during the severe aridity of mind with which he was tried for the last six years of his life, when no spiritual relief, no ray of consolation was afforded him to soften the pain of this grievous martyrdom. There are some men in the present day who boast of having very strong minds, because they despise the truths and maxims of the faith, which they call the prejudices of the feebleminded. With far greater justice may we say that D. Paul was a man of a strong mind, for he courageously persevered in his good resolutions, and unceasingly did he advance in the love of God; he never slackened in his fervor, for he was always striving to attain the greatest sanctity which it is possible for a man to acquire. One of our fathers, who was a man of great virtue and discernment, said that if he had to depict

D. Paul, he would represent him on a marble pillar with this inscription: "Semper idem." His fervor was always the same, he was always equally solicitous in seeking God and His greater glory; he was ever constant in advancing in the practice of virtue, without ever making a retrograde step; and he was at all times careful to overcome and mortify himself, without ever indulging in the least bodily relaxation whatsoever. For him there were neither theaters, feasts, concerts, sports, games, parties, or any other worldly amusement. In a word, he was always the same, and his actions were always uniform, full of fervor and heroism. For this reason, his countenance was always serene, both in prosperity and adversity, because his only passion was that the good pleasure of God might be done. These words were therefore constantly on his lips, and he wrote on a paper which he kept before him on his table, that it might always be in his sight, "The adorable will of God." This was his favorite and accustomed topic in preaching, and that by which he most inflamed the hearts of his hearers.

He even declared that he did not wish to become more holy than God willed, but he did not therefore cease always to aim at the highest possible degree of holiness. One day when he was conversing with a religious, the latter said to him, that he did not wish to do anything more than was necessary just to secure his salvation; at these words D. Paul stood up, and said with emotion, "O my father, what do you say? We who are religious ought to be saved as saints and men of perfection." He then brought forward a great many proofs in support of what he had advanced, so that at length the religious said, "Well, I admit that is true, my father, and I will try to do better in future." When the servant of God read the Lives of the Saints who gave themselves up wholly to God, he shed tears of joy. Neither could D. Paul restrain his tears when a member of our Congregation made his oblation after the year's novitiate, by pronouncing the accustomed vows of poverty, chastity, and obedience, of renouncement of every dignity or ecclesiastical benefice, and of perseverance in our mode of life. When he met with anyone inclined to lead a pious life, he did all he could to induce him to give himself up wholly to God, and to lead him to entire conformity to the Divine Will. His letters contain admirable passages to this effect. To one of his sisters, who experienced many tribulations, he wrote, "Think of nothing but of offering yourself unreservedly to God; abandon yourself entirely to His Divine will, beg Him to dispose of you as He pleases, and be assured that the best devotion of all consists in doing the will of God." In writing to one of his penitents, he said, "We must suffer much if we would please God. He asks us for courage, not for tenderness." And when he was conversing with us, it seemed as if he could only speak of striving to please God, and of seeking in all things to do what is most agreeable to Him.

Such was the life of Father D. Paul, of which we have here given a slight sketch, and his holy death perfectly corresponded to so virtuous a life. He was superior of the house of St. Mary Mater Domini, in the territory of Caposele at the time it took place, and while he was there he often predicted his death, even before he became ill. He spoke of nothing but of eternity and Paradise for some months before he died; and he often said to his brothers, "Tell me, what do they do in Paradise?" On one occasion he positively said, "I shall die this year." And the event verified these words. On the 5th of August, 1753, when he was still in good health, he spoke still more definitely about his death, and said, "I shall die this month. The fever will come on today." And that very day, after dinner, fever attacked him, and the symptoms were so bad that the doctors despaired of his life on the third day. His illness lasted for eleven days, during which he filled all who approached him with admiration, so great was his calmness, patience, and obedience towards the infirmarian when he administered the prescribed remedies to him. He received all without complaint, and asked for nothing.

We cannot relate anything regarding his sentiments in this last illness; for he said very little throughout the whole time. We have no doubt that he acted thus through humility. He knew that the last words of those who are looked upon as great servants of God are carefully treasured up, he therefore remained in a state of constant and silent recollection, keeping his eyes constantly fixed on the image of Jesus crucified and of the Blessed Virgin. When his brothers begged him to say some words of edification to them, he did not reply, and he even manifested some displeasure at the request, fearing that even the last words he had uttered during life might be treasured up after his death.

One of our fathers begged him to order the community, as their superior, to pray to God to restore his health, for the welfare of the Congregation. He then spoke, and said, "No, it is expedient for me to die." When I heard that he was so dangerously ill, I sent him an obedience by virtue of my authority as his rector-major and superior, to get well, should such be the good pleasure of God. But when he heard of this command, he raised his hand in silence, thus signifying that his recovery was not the will of God. He was somewhat tormented by his habitual fears at the commencement of his illness; but after his director ordered him to have confidence, he became quite calm, and with celestial peace, with eyes fixed on the crucifix, and amidst his weeping brethren, he gave up his pure soul to God at about one o'clock on the 13th of August, 1753, being only forty-seven years of age. We confidently trust that he is now united to his God, whom he strove so much to please, and Whom alone he sought throughout his whole life. When the toll of the bell announced his death, there was general lamentation among his brethren as well as amongst the strangers who were then in the house. One of his veins was opened before he was buried, and immediately the blood gushed forth. Since his death a great number of the Faithful have obtained prodigious favors by means of his relics. These miracles have been carefully registered, and will be published in due time, should it ever please God to cause him to be honored on His altars.

The Life of
FATHER D. JANUARIUS MARIA SARNELLI
Of the Congregation of the Most Holy
Redeemer

The life of
FATHER D. JANUARIUS MARIA SARNELLI
Of the Congregation of the Most Holy
Redeemer

By St. Alphonsus de Liguori

 ATHER D. Januarius Maria Sarnelli was born at Naples, on the 12th of September, 1702. His parents were D. Angelus Sarnelli, baron of Ciorani, and D. Catherine Scoppa. They had eight children, of whom six were boys and two were girls. D. Januarius was their fourth son. D. Andrew, who was the next to him in age, is that secular priest who set on foot at his own expense, a house of missionaries in the territory of Ciorani, who were instituted that they might go about in the diocese of Salerno, and in the neighborhood, laboring for the salvation of the destitute souls in the country.

D. Januarius manifested most pious dispositions from his very infancy; and he was even then remarkable for his angelic modesty, which caused him always to keep his eyes cast down in presence of women, even in that of his sisters and mother. His obedience and submission to his parents were equally exemplary, and when he perceived that he had at all annoyed them, he used instantly to beg for forgiveness, and would kiss their hand or even throw himself at their feet in order to appease them. He evinced the greatest love of mortification from his earliest youth, and even then always abstained from fresh fruit from a spirit of penance. When his parents gave any entertainment, he used instantly to leave the house and go to the Church of St. Francis Xavier, which was just opposite to where they lived. In a word, from all we know regarding his childhood and the whole course of his life, it is easy to infer that he never lost his baptismal innocence.

When he was fourteen, he earnestly begged his father to allow him to leave the world and to enter into the Society of Jesus, but as he was so young he would not permit him to do so. From this time, however, D. Januarius redoubled his fervor in the service of God; he increased the number of his meditations, and led a still more retired life than before. He never conversed with those of his own age, but after he had gone through his studies, his love of solitude caused him to retire into the church, to pray to God before the Blessed Sacrament to enlighten him as to his vocation. After that he would return home, where his conduct towards his parents was a source of great edification to the whole household. At an after period, he embraced the profession of the law in obedience to his father, and he succeeded in it in a wonderful manner. Although he was still very young; the management of the revenues and of the rents of the Duke of Cirifalco were soon entrusted to him. But amid these different occupations, he never omitted to assist at Mass everyday, or to make his visit to the Blessed Sacrament and his daily meditation, and he had such affection for this exercise, that when he was at liberty he used always to go to the Church of St. Francis Xavier, where he would remain in prayer for such a long time, that when anyone came to speak to him and he was not at home, the servants, who knew his custom, used generally to reply, "You will be sure to find him if you go to the Church of St. Francis Xavier." When he went to his father's estate, the only recreation he took was that of shutting himself up in the parish church, where he would spend half the day in meditation. This was asserted by the priest of the place.

He used also to visit the sick in the hospital of the incurables several times a week, and he said that he received such great lights from God when he was there, that these visits gave him constant food for meditation, and he came away full of consolation, and replenished with the spirit of God. It was also in this place that God made known to him that he was called by Him to leave the world. After consulting with his director on the subject, he immediately resolved to do so, quitting the bar and becoming a priest. As soon as he was ordained he gave up all earthly possessions; he distributed all the money he had laid by amongst the poor, as well as the clothes he had worn in the world. He gave himself up unreservedly to God from this time, and spent all his time in prayer, study, and the assistance of his neighbor.

In order to live in still greater solitude, and to give up all connection with the world, he retired into the Congregation of the Holy Family, or, in other words, into the Chinese College, which is established at Naples. During all the time he stayed among these exemplary priests, his constant occupation was either meditation and study, or else going about the neighborhood teaching the Christian doctrine; he also went several times a week to the hospital, where he would spend as many as six hours consecutively, in teaching, consoling, and attending the poor patients.

About this time, he became a member of the Congregation of apostolical Missions, which was set on foot in the Archbishopric of Naples for missionary purposes, in which he labored in a most exemplary and efficacious manner from the moment he entered the priesthood. Some years afterwards he heard that a congregation of missionary priests had been recently formed in the town of Scala, under the direction of Mgr. Falcoia, the bishop of Castellamare, and that they were to devote their time to the service of the destitute country poor, by means of missions and other spiritual exercises; and as he heard that regular observance of rule was strictly attended to among them, and that besides the simple vows of poverty, chastity, and obedience, a fourth vow and oath of perseverance was taken by its members, he felt a great desire to enter it. In order therefore to satisfy his desire to lead a life of greater perfection, and one in which he would be entirely consecrated to God, and animated by the counsels of Father Manulius, of the Society of Jesus, (who died some years ago with a high renown for sanctity,) he resolved to enter the new congregation, and quitted Naples for Scala. He did not, however, lose sight of the Congregation of Apostolical Missions, of which we have already spoken, but continued to support it as far as possible whenever it called upon him for help.[7]

He spent the rest of his days in the rising congregation, in which he edified all his brothers by the constant practice of every virtue, above all, by his mortification, obedience, and charity towards others. It was specially noticed that he was so exact in obeying the sound of the bell, that if he were writing, he arose immediately, and would even leave a letter unfinished. Such was his mode of life while he lived in our house at Scala. His superiors afterwards sent him to Naples, both because the air of Scala did not suit his infirm health, and to enable him to continue the great undertakings he had already commenced in the capital, especially that of delivering it from women of bad character, as we shall relate more at length hereafter, and it was here that his life terminated.

------

[7] As this Congregation was established on a large scale, there was nothing to prevent his still serving it with the consent of his superiors even after he joined us. Thus St. Alphonsus himself never ceased to belong it.

Although he labored with the most indefatigable zeal in the duties of his own institute, he did not neglect to assist the brothers of the Congregation of missions from time to time. Although engaged in the laborious enterprise of expelling all abandoned women out of Naples, he yet found time to devote himself with such ardor to the salvation of souls, that when Cardinal Spinelli, the present archbishop of Naples, (1752), sent for Father D. Alphonsus de Liguori, the rector-major of the said Congregation, to come with his companions, and give missions in the villages of his diocese at his expense, he wished that Father Januarius Maria might be one of the missionaries; and he gave them a permanent abode near the village of St. Sorio, to enable them to go about in the neighborhood more easily. When Father Alphonsus was obliged to leave the city on business connected with the affairs of his congregation, the cardinal left the whole charge of the mission in the hands of Father D. Januarius, who thus continued the good work which had been commenced by that excellent missionary D. Matthew Testa, who is at present a most worthy canon in the capital. Our father continued to labor in these missions with the utmost success until his blessed death, which took place some years afterwards. This loss not only grieved the very zealous pastor of the town of Naples, but also his own faithful flock; indeed D. Januarius was generally regretted, as a great laborer in God's vineyard, and it was everywhere said, and it is still declared, that he alone was worth ten other missionaries.

But before relating his precious death, it will be well to give some brief details regarding his virtues. He was so fond of meditation, that even when he was a secular, he used to steal time from business to go and pray in some church, but from the time he became a priest, he gave himself up unreservedly to this holy exercise. He used daily to repair to the Church of the Cross of the Palace for this purpose, where he would shut himself in a little cell behind the sacristy, and remain in prayer from dinnertime until the evening; this was his daily practice until he entered the Chinese College, except when he went to the hospital. He received so much celestial light, and felt such holy ardor in meditation, and had such a gift of tears, that he himself owned that he had nearly lost his sight in consequence. The Gospel was the book from whence he derived all his light and consolation. "Scarcely had I read a few verses," said he, "ere I was so enlightened by the Divine Goodness, that I melted into tears, and the world then appeared to me as nothing but smoke."

He was several times seen going up and down the cloisters of the Church of the Cross and that of the Holy Ghost, with his arms extended, his eyes raised to heaven, and giving vent to such passionate sighs that several persons who saw him thought he was beside himself. When once told that such actions caused him to be taken for a madman, he replied, "That is very true, for he who does not love God is mad, and I do not love Him." On another occasion, when a priest asked him why he did such things, the color mounted to his cheeks, and he confessed to his friend that he did so unconsciously. From this time he would only speak of, and listen to conversation about, God and the salvation of souls, as I can myself testify; and when he heard people talking on indifferent subjects, it pained him so much that he always strove to turn the conversation on spiritual things, or else tried to steal away if he could do so without giving offense.

Our Father D. Januarius Maria had also a great devotion for the Blessed Trinity, in Whose honor he celebrated Mass as often as he could, and tried to inspire everyone with a devotion to this mystery. He also published a very pious book to propagate this devotion.

He was also specially devout towards the Passion of

Jesus Christ. His room was full of crosses and pictures to remind him of the sufferings of the Incarnate God, and he caused a great many to be made, which he distributed, that they might be placed in the different houses and streets. His devotion was no less great towards the holy sacrifice of the Mass, as we can see by his works, and he never omitted to celebrate it for a single day to the end of his days, although he was several times on the point of fainting at the altar through his infirmities, and once he really did so, yet even then he persisted in finishing it as soon as he recovered, although it cost him a great effort, as he declared that all his hopes were centered in this august mystery. He had such a deep conviction of the love which we owe to our Blessed Savior, that he said that we should be always preaching to souls. in these words, "Love Jesus Christ! love Jesus Christ!" He had also the greatest devotion towards the Blessed Virgin, and especially towards her immaculate conception. In order to spread this devotion, he gave away a great quantity of pictures of her as well as of scapulars and rosaries, and his great delight during the recreation established in our Congregation after dinner and supper, consisted in making rosaries, images, or scapulars. He had also a special love for the holy name of Mary. Once when he was present at a sermon on the Blessed Sacrament, which was delivered by a most zealous preacher, he was quite satisfied with the discourse, yet it grieved him to think that he had not once pronounced the sweet name of Mary. He therefore humbly entreated him never to omit the name of the Blessed Virgin in his sermons for the future, assuring him that it would add greatly to the benefit they already produced. He was really proud of being called by the names Januarius Maria, and could not help mildly showing some dissatisfaction when he was only addressed by the name of Januarius, without the addition of that of Maria. He begged his friends to unite with him in praising the Divine Mother in the month of September, as he said she always granted him all the favors he asked for during this month. Before he went to bed, he was in the habit of winding his rosary round his arm to remind him of his Divine Mother during the night, and he told one of his confidential friends, that in his greatest trials and combats with the powers of darkness, he was always quite fortified when he held his rosary in his hands. He preached on the glories of Mary wherever he went; he recommended devotion to her in all his sermons, and made every exertion to get novenas celebrated in her honor. He even composed a very devotional little book in honor of the Mother of God, entitled, "The Grandeurs of Mary," which is to be found amongst his spiritual treatises. He had but one cause of regret at the hour of death, viz., that he had been unable to finish his large work on the glories of Mary, of which he had already collected all the materials.

We will here mention that after the great consolations with which God favored him for so many years, He ordained that on a certain feast day for which he had prepared with much fervor, his soul should fall into a state of frightful aridity and profound desolation, which lasted throughout the remainder of his life. At his last moments indeed God restored the sense of His grace and presence to his soul, and gave him the favor of dying inflamed with an ardent desire of seeing God; but with the exception of these happy moments his heart always remained dry and cold, both during meditation and also in his labors for the salvation of souls. It seemed to him as if God had abandoned him, and he felt no consolation in any of his spiritual exercises. He also endured the most horrible temptations, especially to infidelity, gluttony, and despair, which caused him to say that he had become quite incapable of occupying himself in the service of God, and that it seemed to him as if these words of the Psalmist were constantly resounding in his ears: "Multi dicunt animæ meæ, non est salus ipsi in Deo ejus." At times he could scarcely breathe, but even then he would sigh and say these two words, "My God! my God!" This took place even during his apostolical labors for the salvation of his neighbor, by which he certainly shortened his life; for notwithstanding his great zeal for the glory of God, all that he did was performed by a great effort, being destitute of consolation and accompanied with extreme repugnance. He was indeed a man of great strength of mind, and full of ardor to spread the glory of God and to do His holy will. The words which were always on his lips, in his heart, and on his pen, were, "The glory of God and the will of God." All that he did was done for God alone, and if he sometimes felt tempted to vainglory on seeing the success of the works which he undertook for the glory of God, he used earnestly to pray, and get others to pray, that he might be delivered from this secret satisfaction.

During this bitter privation of all celestial consolation, he always maintained a firm confidence in God, and placed all his trust in the efficacy of prayer. He said that amid the torture he suffered from temptation and desolation his only strength was in these words of Jesus Christ, "Si quid petieritis patrem in nomine meo, dabit vobis." He declared that if God had given him no other grace than that of prayer, he should be abundantly satisfied, as there are so many great promises attached to that holy exercise. In fact, this confidence in meditation purchased for him all the favors with which God endowed him. By it he triumphed over the many difficulties he had to contend with in his immense labors for the glory of God, for he had recourse to his own prayers and to those of others on all such occasions, and he was wont to say that he had a secret by which he could be certain of obtaining even more from

God than he asked for. To meditation he united mortification of the senses. When he was ordained priest, he fasted three days in the week on bread and water; his failing health afterwards compelled him to give up this practice; but even then, he always abstained from taking fruit except when his superiors made him do so through obedience. His mother related to one of his confessors, that when there was any delicacy at dinner he never touched it even when a mere child, and he limited himself to such sparing quantities that what he took hardly sufficed for the support of nature. Although his health was much impaired he never omitted to take the discipline. Yet he could only have struck on bones, for his penances, sufferings, and labors had reduced him to a mere skeleton. When he could not do anything else, he bore the stings of insects without endeavoring to escape from them, and they often cause greater pain than haircloth and disciplines.

He also had such a great wish to be despised for the love of Jesus Christ, that he made a firm resolution never to justify himself before anyone when he might be accused of a fault. He prayed for the love of humiliation in all his masses; and for this end he said the Collect ad petendam humilitatem, as often as he could. He confided to a brother of the Congregation that God answered this prayer soon after he began to say it, by sending him a great many opportunities of practicing humility, and that he not only granted him grace to bear humiliation with patience, but also with interior gladness. Whenever he received any slight, he thanked God for it, and he confided to the same brother that he was so far from dreading reproach and shame, that he felt an ardent desire to be dragged through the mud in the streets of Naples. In order to look contemptible, he always wore old and ragged clothes, such as are hawked through the streets by Jews, declaring that he wished to have nothing in common with the world; and when his parents reproached him for thus dishonoring his family by his shabby appearance, he told them not to distress themselves about it, for that if anyone asked his name, he would never say that he was the son of the Baron of Sarnelli, but would call himself Father Januarius Maria, as if the former were his Christian name, and the latter his surname. One day when he entered the church of our Lady of Good Help at Naples to say Mass, the cleric on duty on seeing his ragged attire sent him away most unceremoniously, and would not permit him to celebrate. Our father was afterwards revenged on him, but it was only with that revenge which saints are wont to take on those who injure them; for by his assistance the uncourteous cleric was afterwards enabled to become a priest. In a word, he lived and died in such poverty, that the priest who assisted at his death procured new clothes to bury him in, as all his own were worn out and in rags.

Our Father Januarius Maria possessed charity towards his neighbor to a heroic degree. When he was absent from our houses he lived as scantily as he could, ate little, and wore the most wretched clothes, not only to draw down contempt on himself, but also to enable him to have more at his disposal for the poor. He would sometimes even take off his clothes, go without shoes, and deprive himself of the food which was served up to him, that he might bestow them on the indigent. He would often go about Naples collecting the poor together, after which he would conduct them to his own house, where he washed their feet, waited on them, and supplied their wants. To enable him to do this he selected a room midway on the stairs, which was so very dark and out of repair, that one of his friends even saw the mice jumping up and down on his bed. Here, however, he received all the poor who came to him, for had he attempted to do so anywhere else the servants would have sent them away. He did not receive women there, but when any of them wished to speak to him, he went to some church to hear them. After he entered the Congregation, his greatest happiness consisted in obtaining leave from his superior to bestow alms on the poor.

He had an incredible affection for the sick in the hospital, and bore any amount of fatigue to assist them in spiritual or temporal necessities. When he was only a secular he went about begging for provisions from his relatives. He collected together as much as he could, after which he arranged it all in baskets with his own hands, and sent it to the hospital. Whenever he went to visit these poor sufferers after he became a priest, he would carry some little luxury in the shape of fruit or sweets or such like, which he concealed under his cloak, and which he had either procured expressly for them, or which he had deprived himself of in order to bestow it on them. He even went the length of having long earthenware vessels constructed to hold roast meat; and he carried them to the sick by hanging one on each side. He used also to make up and distribute a number of little packets of tobacco among them. He would make their beds for them, and wash their feet; in fact, he never omitted charity which could contribute to their relief. In all works of spiritual mercy and zeal for the salvation of souls, D. Januarius Maria Sarnelli attained to the most heroic degree of perfection. From the time he left the world to devote himself to God in the ecclesiastical state, he was always studying how he could be most usefully engaged for the salvation of souls; and all his thoughts and words were directed to this one point, even during his familiar conversations during recreation. Whilst others were then seeking for relaxation, he looked preoccupied and sad; and if anyone asked him what he was thinking about, he replied, "I am thinking what had better be done to assist the souls whom God died to save." When he spoke of how much the poor require spiritual assistance and priestly instruction, his countenance glowed with zeal, and sometimes even tears of pity would flow from his eyes. He often said that he felt that he had a special call to assist the poor and destitute, and applied these words of the prophet Isaiah to himself, "Evangelizare pauperibus misit me." He added, that he believed he should be damned if he did not devote all his energies to this purpose, and that it seemed to him as if these words of St. Paul were addressed to himself, "Vae mihi si non evangelizavero!"

Whilst he was at Naples, before he entered the Congregation, he determined to join two other priests in giving missions in the provinces of Calabria and Abruzzi, as he thought these places the most destitute of spiritual aid. The patron saint who was most dear to him, was St. John Francis Regis, on account of his love for the poor. It was this same predilection which caused him to enter the Congregation of the Most Holy Redeemer, for he knew that it was chiefly instituted for the assistance of the destitute country poor.

He was unceasingly engaged in preaching and hearing confessions whenever his health permitted it. After he had been nearly worn out by his laboring in church all the morning during missions, he would only take a bit of bread or a few raisins, which he ate in the sacristy, and spent the rest of the day in preaching and in the confessional. Once when he was in the territory of Bracigliano, he bore the fatigues of a mission for two months consecutively without having even a coadjutor to aid him; yet he was in the confessional by day-break. His only refreshment consisted in a cup of chocolate, which he took very late in the day, after which he immediately began to preach and hear confessions, so that he alone heard the confessions of about two thousand people. On another mission, which was given in the village of the Slaves, in the diocese of Cajazzo, where we had then a house, he labored for five weeks, during which he heard confessions until four o'clock in the afternoon, when he took a little refreshment; he then returned to the pulpit, and after he had done preaching he re-entered the confessional, where he remained until ten at night.

His zeal carried him even further than this; it was several times observed that he passed two days without tasting food, when he was particularly occupied about the salvation of certain souls. Yet he was almost always in bad health. When he was advised to try and get well before undergoing such fatigue, he replied, "If I were only to labor when I am well, I should have done little or nothing, for I see that it is God's will that I should always be in suffering;" and when it was replied, that if this were the case his life would not last much longer, "Well," said he, "and can there be anything more glorious than to wear out one's life for God?"

It was therefore by a sort of constant miracle that he was able to labor for the salvation of souls without taking any rest, notwithstanding his infirmities and weakness. When he was composing his admirable works on spiritual subjects, he often wrote until midnight, and only ceased writing when overcome by fatigue. Thus, a lay-brother who waited on him at this time, used to reply to those who asked what he was doing, "If he is not writing he must be ill." He said himself that when he had to go through any special undertaking for the good of souls, he almost always felt more suffering and weakness than usual beforehand; but that his strength increased when the time for action arrived. He often began to preach when he was much fitter for his bed; but he felt much better after the sermon than he had done before.

He preached with so much zeal, and his sermons

produced so much effect, that they often led sinners to give public signs of sorrow, and loudly to ask for a confessor. All who attended his missions said, "Let us go and hear the saint. It is a saint who preaches." When he was at Naples, he often went to the Church of St. Januarius, beyond the city walls, in spite of the great distance, that he might preach to the old men there, and he used afterwards to say to his brothers at Scala, that he was quite distressed to have to abandon this work of charity.

He was also very fond of ministering to the wants of poor children, and used to say that nothing would please him more than to have to teach them the Christian doctrine on all the missions. When he was at Naples he sought out with holy diligence the little children suffering from the ringworm, in order to instruct them, to exhort them to go to confession, and to give them some little treat, and he used to do this with so much charity that they were in the habit of calling him their father. He also went about the public squares of Naples, seeking for the little street porters, who are generally very ignorant of their faith. He would then conduct them to his own house, where he taught them the Christian doctrine, prepared them for the sacrament of penance, and gave them something to eat. In order to spare all trouble to the servants, he himself prepared their food, and after he had dismissed the poor little creatures, he went to the kitchen and washed what they had made use of with his own hands.

We may truly say that our Father Januarius Maria was really fond of the sick in the hospital, for he was almost always there. If he arrived in the morning, he did not leave it until noon; or if he reached it after dinner, he stayed there until it was nearly eight o'clock, and then he only quitted it with regret and a wish to be able to remain longer. I cannot express the charity he exercised towards them, or how tenderly he exhorted them to bear their sufferings with patience, instructed them in the things appertaining to God, and in the proper manner of making a good confession, and before he was himself a priest, he procured good priests to hear their confessions. One day he formed a plan of living in the Hospital of the Incurables, that he might be able to assist these poor creatures with more facility, especially at the hour of death; he even obtained a room for this purpose; but an unexpected difficulty arose which prevented his carrying his project into effect. His zeal once nearly caused him to lose his life in the Hospital of the Galleys, where he used also to administer the succors of religion to the poor criminals.

It is well known what this same zeal caused him to undertake at Naples, in order to rescue prostitute women from sin. He went to preach in the parish church of St. Matthew on all feast days, in order to convert these unfortunate beings, and it was through his suggestions that the Congregation of the archbishopric undertook to give the spiritual exercises in this parish every year for the same purpose. In order to relieve the wants of these poor creatures, he gave them all he received from home, and even did without necessaries himself to have the more to distribute among them; and he gave a great many of them enough for their livelihood in the shape of a monthly allowance, in order to prevent their selling their honor and their soul; and not satisfied with relieving those who asked for his aid, he sought for them throughout the whole town. He placed sixteen of them in asylums, and enabled a great many others to get married. We know that he provided for the subsistence of two of these women for two years, and that he afterwards furnished them with means to enable them to keep house. As his own income was not sufficient for all this, for he spent from five to six hundred ducats a year in such ways, he went about Naples begging alms for these unfortunate people, and that not only in pious establishments, but in private houses, which he nevertheless did with so much repugnance, that he said he sometimes felt as if he would die of shame, for he had not only to bear the great annoyance of having to pay repeated visits, but he had also to endure reproaches and even insults. He confided to a friend that several persons who had formerly esteemed him highly, and welcomed him courteously, changed so completely when he came to them on this errand, that they then quite shunned him, and sent him away with roughness and incivility.

In striving to realize the plan he had formed of compelling all the women of bad character to leave the town, and take up their abode in some remote quarter, he had to endure inexpressible fatigue and persecution. As he saw that these unhappy creatures did immense harm by being scattered about in all parts of the town, he was convinced that the only method of remedying so great an evil would be to compel them to go and live together out of Naples. All the town, and God above all, knows what labors and expense this project occasioned him, for the furtherance of which he composed several books entitled, "The Abuses of Prostitution." This undertaking also drew down on him the opposition and reproaches of his friends, for as they looked upon the thing as impossible, they were always striving to make him abandon it, and ridiculing it with bitterness; but his confidence in God was strong and unshaken, although he was alone and devoid of the help of man, and he managed so well with the first ministers of the king, our protector, that he at length had the satisfaction of seeing his desires fulfillled. For a decree of nine articles was sent to the Duke of Giovenazzo, the president of the first chamber of the ministry, on the 4th of May, 1758, in virtue of which sentence of banishment was pronounced against all prostitutes, who were thenceforward to live without the town, in places which were allotted to them. This royal mandate was executed with such rigor, that justice seized on the effects of those who would not quit their houses, and all their furniture was thrown out of the window. From thirty to forty prostitutes were thus expelled from Naples; some of them married, others retired into asylums, and the rest either went to the places assigned for them, or fled elsewhere. As for our Father Januarius Maria, he several times ran the risk of being assassinated on account of the share he had in their expulsion, and for this reason his parents did all in their power to prevent his going on with this good work, as they were afraid some fatal accident might be the result both to himself and to all his family; but he declared that he was ready to suffer all, and that he should even think it a great privilege to die in an undertaking which was so glorious to God.

It was this same zeal for the salvation of souls which supported him through all the labors which he went through in preparing all his works, in which the choice of subjects and the manner in which he treated them, clearly proves how much he would have liked to sanctify the whole world, had that been in his power. Besides the book of which we have already spoken, on the special abuses which the prostitutes of Naples caused to that town, he published another for all the towns and villages of the kingdom, in which he proves that women of bad character are not tolerated in any one of them or in any of the smaller towns, and he sent a copy of this work to all the bishops in the kingdom. After this he published a book called, "The World Sanctified," (1752.) In some respects we may say that this work really has sanctified the world, for it has been the means of extensive good; it has been in almost everyone's hands, and spread through several kingdoms as well as that of Naples. He also put forth a whole work against blasphemy, as he was eager to extirpate this accursed vice from the kingdom, where it is so deeply rooted; and he published in a work called "The World Reformed," a treatise on the respect due to churches, in which the inhabitants of the kingdom are also most wanting.

I will now give a list of several other works which he published to the great profit of souls: a treatise on the obligation of parents to bring up their children properly; another to serve as a guide to souls in the paths of spirituality, entitled, "Discernment of Spirits;" "The Ecclesiastic Sanctified," which was written for priests; "An easy Method for all the Exercises of Missions," which is most useful for missionaries; "The Enlightened Christian," which cost him the greatest labor, as he himself owned, for he composed it amid all the sufferings of the malady of which he died; "The Desolate Soul," for the comfort of souls in desolation of spirit; and "The Enlightened Soul," which contains some most devotional meditations. He also published several other little works which we will mention elsewhere. Death prevented his finishing several others, which he had already begun to get printed, such as a treatise to excite compassion for the souls in purgatory; another on the methods of appeasing God's anger in public calamities; a selection of pious reflections for every day in the year; a collection of sermons on the Blessed Virgin for every Saturday throughout the year and for all novenas; and a book of instructions on faith and morals. Thus all his works were destined to promote the salvation of souls, whom he desired, as he said, to assist even after his death. When he was on the point of death, he said to Canon Sersale, "Canon, I wish to go on preaching until the judgment day."

We must now give an account of his last illness and of his happy end. Januarius Maria labored for many years, as we have already seen, although he was always ill and oppressed with fever. His last mission was given at Posilipo, during which his sufferings were very great, as he was quite worn out by fatigue and pain. From that he retired to St. Agnello, where his maladies increased so much that he was obliged to give up all his labors, and was no longer able even to say Mass; this was viewed by all as a sign his death was at hand, for he had never before abstained from celebrating it. One day he made the most surprising efforts to say it, but he could not succeed, and fainted in the attempt. As the malady grew worse and worse, he went to his brother's house at Naples, where he was ill for a month. Although his sufferings and weakness continued daily to increase, he never abandoned meditation, and as his interior trials were as great as ever, he tried to obtain consolation by conversing with the servants of God who came to visit him. The doctors advised him to try the air called the saving air, but he was too weak to be moved.

About a fortnight before his death he took to his bed, from whence he never arose again. From this time, however, God freed him from the heavy cross of spiritual desolation, and he began to enjoy the greatest peace, every disquieting thought was banished from his mind, and he felt nothing but an ardent desire to be united to God in the mansions of the blest. Once, when a servant of his father's said that he hoped God would restore his health, he replied, "Oh, if I could exclaim aloud now, my sole cry would be that my only consolation is to think that I am going to die, and you speak to me of recovery!"

He also now showed the extent of his patience and charity, for amid the almost insupportable pains he endured, which caused him to stand in need of constant attendance, he felt the greatest compassion for those who waited on him; and when he required anything he said to the brother whom the superior of the Congregation had sent to assist him, "Brother, have patience with me for the love of Jesus Christ, for I shall not live much longer." At this time he made his last will, and as he wished all he had to be employed in alms and other good works, he disposed of all his possessions in favor of the Congregation of the Redemptorists.

One day he said to his brother, who did a great deal for him during his life and at his death, "Brother, the time is at hand when I hope I shall be able to make you a fitting return for all you have done for me."

At this same period the devil appeared to him under the form of an abbé, and tempted him to vainglory, saying, "Don Januarius, your illness has caused general lamentation throughout Naples, on account of the loss which would be sustained by the death of such a great man." Upon this the dying man instantly pronounced the names of Jesus and Mary, and the evil spirit disappeared and returned no more. One day when Canon Sersale came to visit him, he said that he hoped he might get well. "Dear Canon," he replied, "I was tormented by scruples for a long time, but thanks be to God, I am now free from them. I shall therefore die tranquilly and without any disquiet. All that I have done has been done from a pure intention of pleasing God. The sacrifice is now complete; do not then speak to me anymore of living, for I wish for no other life than the possession of my God."

During his last days he was always repeating devout aspirations; sometimes they were addressed to the Blessed Trinity, when he would say, "Benedicta sit sancta Trinitas et individua unitas; confitebimur ei, quia fecit nobiscum misericordiam suam;" sometimes either to our Blessed Savior or His adorable Mother, and he would kiss and embrace their images from time to time. Just before his death he addressed the following affecting words to God, which were carefully noted down by the lay-brother who attended him: "Father, behold the time has come for me to depart hence and to go to my Creator and my Father. O Lord, I sigh for the moment when I shall see Thee face to face, should such be Thy good pleasure; for I wish neither for death nor for life. I wish only for what Thou willest. Thou knowest that all my actions and all my thoughts have been for Thy greater glory alone." Words such as these in the mouth of a dying man, on the point of appearing before God, are sufficient to manifest what must have been the innocency of his life. On the morning of the day he died, he said to the brother who waited on him, "Brother, go and get out my oldest clothes and bury me in them, for I do not wish anything to be wasted."

The doctor came to see him at about eight o'clock in the morning of the same day; and when he was going away, he said that he would see him again in the course of the day. "I shall gently enter into my agony today," he replied. He told the brother not to forget to make him say the rosary, "For," said he, "I wish to die whilst I am reciting it." And so it was, for when he had reached the third decade that same day, he became very weak, and the damp perspiration of death began to flow. "I feel the chill of death," said he to the brother, upon which he instantly called for a priest, who began to suggest pious affections to him; but the dying man interrupted him, and asked him to allow him to speak himself; and he then began to speak to God in the most tender manner, but it was almost impossible to hear what he said, for his speech was well-nigh gone. Just as he entered into his agony, the two brothers of the Congregation who assisted him at this last hour asked for his blessing; and he gently raised his hand and blessed them. His agony was peaceful, and lasted little more than half an hour; his rosary was around his arm all the time, and he clasped the crucifix in his hands, kissing

it from time to time. The priest gave him absolution during
this interval, after which he calmly expired, at ten o'clock
on Thursday morning, June 30th, 1744, aged forty-two. His
happy death took place the day before the eve of the feast
of the Visitation; thus the wish he had often expressed of
dying during a novena to the Blessed Virgin was gratified.

As soon as he was dead his countenance suddenly
became most pleasing and beautiful, and a smile
overspread his lips; his body exhaled such a sweet odor,
that it scented the room where he died for a long time, and
it was not only perceived by those who assisted at his
death, but also by the strangers who came to see his
corpse. His brother, D. Dominic Sarnelli, said that he could
not bear to leave the room, as he experienced the greatest
spiritual consolation when in it. His body was conveyed to
the church of our Lady of Good Help, accompanied by the
brothers of the Congregation of Apostolical Missions in
the archbishopric of Naples, who all followed him to the
church, being filled with the greatest sorrow for his death.
When the body arrived there, a great number of people
crowded round it weeping and exclaiming, "Alas, for the
saint is dead!" and this cry was repeated throughout all the
neighborhood. They then began to tear up his clothes, and
everyone tried to carry away as much of them as possible;
he would soon have been stripped of everything, had not
some limits been put to this pious eagerness. His body was
exposed for forty-eight hours, after which a great many
priests and other persons testify that it remained quite
flexible, and did not emit the least unpleasant odor, and
that bright blood flowed from incisions which were then
made in his arm and head. His relics were sought for in all
directions, and the renown of his sanctity spread far and
wide. Persons came to visit through devotion, and
exclaimed with many tears, "O the well-beloved saint of
Jesus Christ! he is not prized sufficiently!" In consequence

of this reputation for sanctity, several persons recommended themselves to God through the merits of Father Januarius Maria, and received signal graces thereby, which I must however pass over in silence, that I may not exceed the narrow limits allotted to me. I trust however that the time will come when these interesting facts may be collected by others, and that a more detailed Life of this great servant of God may one day be given to the world.

The Life of
FATHER D. ANGELO LATESSA
Of the Congregation of the Redemptorists

The life of
FATHER D. ANGELO LATESSA
Of the Congregation of the Redemptorists

By the Rev. Father Tannoja

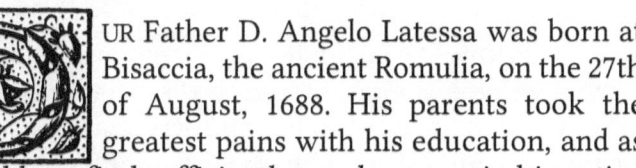 UR Father D. Angelo Latessa was born at Bisaccia, the ancient Romulia, on the 27th of August, 1688. His parents took the greatest pains with his education, and as they could not find sufficiently good masters in his native town, they sent him betimes to Acerno to study literature under the direction of an excellent professor who resided there. As D. Angelo was filled with grace from his very childhood, he never allowed his studies to interfere with his progress in virtue; he selected D. Horace Sansoni, the archdeacon of the cathedral, as his director, who was a man of rare piety, and he made it a rule never to deviate in the least from any of his counsels. D. Angelo remained six years at Acerno, and made still more progress in the science of the saints than in earthly lore and literature. He was devoted to prayer and meditation, he abhorred idleness, and shunned all intercourse with the world. His chamber, study, and the church, comprised the history of his life.

When he returned to Bisaccia, he resolved to embrace the ecclesiastical state, and he therefore devoted himself to theological studies with all possible diligence. He wished to be ordained subdeacon at the age of twenty-one; but as Mgr. Galliani, his bishop, was very scrupulous in admitting young clerics to Holy Orders, he would not then give his consent. D. Angelo bore the delay with resignation, and from this time he led a still more secluded life than before; he abstained from all kind of society and amusements, devoted himself to study and the frequentation of the sacraments. After Mgr. Galliani's death, his successor, Mgr. Mastellone, perceived the indisputable signs of a true vocation in the young Latessa, he therefore conferred Holy Orders on him, and ordained him priest at the age of twenty-six.

At this time D. Gaetan Julian, a famous missionary and a great servant of God, retired to Bisaccia at the end of a life of labor in the work of the ministry; this priest was the worthy disciple of the venerable Father D. Anthony de Torris, of the Congregation of Pious Workmen. D. Angelo immediately chose him for his director, and he grew so attached to him, that he remained under his guidance for thirty years.

As D. Julian wished to give up all thoughts of everything but God and his own soul, he had no sooner returned to Bisaccia, his native country, than he retired into a solitary spot, where he could live apart from all his relations and friends, and as he had not provided anyone to attend to his wants, D. Angelo undertook to do all that he might require, and his affection for D. Julian was so great, that he waited on him more like a servant than a son. If he went to his room, and D. Julian was busy or absorbed in his meditations, which generally lasted for three or four hours, or if he had not heard his knock, D. Angelo would remain quietly at the door until D. Julian happened to open it. He had all the food required prepared at his own house, and carried it to him every morning and evening. As D. Julian did not have a fire in winter, he four times a day carried some hot coals in a foot-warmer to him. There are persons now living in Bisaccia who remember having often seen him waiting with angelic tranquility and admirable patience as if he were a beggar at D. Julian's door until he was ready to open it.

As Mgr. Mastellone had a high opinion of D. Angelo's virtue, he made him canon of the cathedral of Bisaccia in the year 1768. As he was an enemy to everything like pomp and ambition, he would not accept this dignity without the permission of his director, and as he did not think it right to grant it to him, D. Angelo at once declined the proffered honor, and when he was pressed to accept it by the bishop and by his parents, he secretly fled to Nusco, where he hid himself until he heard that the canonry had been conferred on someone else.

His uncle, D. Joseph Latessa, passed into a better life in the year 1722, and his Lordship elected D. Angelo to succeed him, and this time he accepted the honor on the advice of his director Father Julian. No one at Bisaccia felt inclined to murmur at the selection, and D. Angelo fully answered the high expectations which all good people entertained in his regard. His disinterestedness was a subject of edification to all. He observed the canonical laws most rigidly; and he divided the revenues of his canonry into three equal parts, the first of which served for his own maintenance, the second for that of the church, and the third he distributed among the poor. His affection for them was so great, that they were in the habit of calling him their father, and he was always surrounded by them both at the church and elsewhere.

He had been a canon for twelve years, when Father D. Gaetan Julian died in the year 1734. He had nominated D. Angelo as his successor in a chapel built in honor of St. Michael, which he had erected into a benefice: D. Angelo was quite satisfied with this arrangement, and resigned his canonry to his brother, that he might thus be able to labor for the glory of God and the salvation of his neighbor with more facility.

After Mgr. Manerbe was elected bishop of St. Angelo and of Bisaccia, he determined to found a seminary in his diocese, of which D. Angelo was nominated president. The first thing which occupied his attention, after he had been compelled to accept this office, was to establish a spirit of charity among the students, and to make them look upon themselves as being all sons of the same mother. He carefully abolished the use of the words *mine* and *thine*, and he wished that each of them should share what he received from his parents amongst each other, so that they might thus mutually assist each other as if they were really brothers, and he once gave a severe punishment to a seminarist who would not share his portion of chocolate with another. He carefully established the frequentation of the sacraments, he excited all his pupils to the love of meditation, and led them to mortify their senses and passions; and we learn from the testimony of D. Salvadore d' Andrea, the grand-vicar of Nusco, that the young men confided to his care were distinguished for their great piety, in which they were animated by the example of their superior, whose holiness was made manifest to them by God in a striking manner on more than one occasion. One evening when he was visiting the different rooms, he perceived that a seminarist had taken off his stockings before the light was put out. As a punishment for this slight indelicacy, he gave him several blows on the legs; and at the same instant, several other young men who had the same habit, assert that they were struck in a similar manner, although they were not in the same room, and were perfectly ignorant of the correction inflicted on their companion. The seminary of St. Angelo witnessed another prodigy which resembled the miracle of the multiplication of the loaves performed by our Blessed Savior in the desert. One day D. Angelo wished to give the youngest boys a day of recreation in the country; he provided a little roll for each of them, and fruits and cheese in proportion; but when the two head classes heard of this treat they went to their good father, and said that they too were his children, and that it was not fair to deprive them of his favor. "Let all come then," replied the father-president, "and God will provide for them." They therefore took part in the country excursion. When they reached the end, D. Angelo blessed the bread and the rest of the provisions; they were then freely distributed among them all; yet there was not only enough to satisfy every one of them, but to their great astonishment, there was a great deal to spare. This fact has been attested on oath by the grand-vicar of Andrea.

D. Angelo ruled over the seminary for a year, after which he addressed such earnest supplications to the bishop, that although he was very reluctant to do so, he consented to allow him to return to Bisaccia, that he might enjoy that peace and tranquility which were not to be found in the seminary.

We will now relate the mode of life which our Father D. Angelo pursued both at Bisaccia, and at the seminary of St. Angelo. He spent two hours in meditation in the morning, during which he remained prostrate and motionless, shedding torrents of tears; and in the evening he also spent two hours in the same manner, and he allowed nothing to interfere with this. He said Mass in a devotional manner, but without being long; it was preceded by a preparation of half an hour, and he always made a long thanksgiving afterwards. He never ate meat, or drank wine. His dinner consisted of a small portion of vegetables, and in the evening he only took some fruit, or at most an egg. He used the discipline for some time every night with great severity, he always wore a rough hairshirt, and often macerated his body with other instruments of penance, with which he did not dispense even when ill. The seminarists at St. Angelo discovered all this by looking through the crevices of his door. He never slept for more than four or five hours, and his bed was either the floor or a hard plank.

D. Angelo was thus crucified to himself and to the world, and lived in it as if he were separated from it. In imitation of his director D. Gaetan Julian, he too separated from his friends. At first he lived in a solitary cell, and then in two little rooms, which he added to his house to satisfy his brother, canon D. Vito, but no one ever visited him there except a little child, who regularly brought him a small portion of food, which was just enough to preserve life. His whole time was spent between his cell and the church. He did not even know where his own vineyard was situated, nor where the cattle were kept. He was never seen in any public place, except when he accompanied the Blessed Sacrament, or formed part of some procession; and when he went to church, he did so by the most obscure and unfrequented streets. Although D. Angelo lived in such entire solitude, he had many and regular occupations. He daily instructed the country priests in ascetic theology and in morals; and he earnestly exhorted the young to labor for the glory of God and the salvation of souls. His house was a sort of academy of science and religion, and no one ever quitted it without being full of edification, and without having formed many pious designs. He had also a multitude of penitents, on whom he bestowed the most paternal care; he was particularly fond of being surrounded by the poor, who never wearied in listening to his pious exhortations and counsels. The sick and the dying were the objects of his predilection, and if they were poor he used to supply their bodily wants, for which purpose he procured delicacies from the convents in Calitri and Naples, which he kept by him to distribute among them. The dying, however, chiefly occupied his attention, and he neglected nothing which could tend to strengthen them at the hour of their terrible passage. When he was going to assist any of them, nothing could stop him. One night when he was summoned to the bedside of a dying man, an enormous wild boar ran before him, and prevented his passing; his companion was greatly alarmed, but D. Angelo manifested no emotion, and merely said, "It is an evil spirit who wishes to prevent my succoring this soul, but he will not succeed;" and he at the same time made the sign of the cross, upon which the monster instantly disappeared, and the servant of God was in time to succor the dying man in his last extremity.

D. Angelo possessed the most tender devotion towards the Archangel St. Michael, which he inherited from his director D. Julian. Every year during the novena which precedes his feast, he withdrew entirely from the world, even from his spiritual children, and maintained a strict retreat, conversing only with God and his saintly patron. He neglected nothing by which he could honor the saintly archangel, and he spent all the revenues of his living in his honor and for the relief of the poor. In the year 1742, when the town of Bisaccia was afflicted with a grievous scarcity, he gave large alms to the poor in honor of his saintly guardian, as he was persuaded that this would be most pleasing to him. When he entered our Congregation, he gave a last testimony of his devotion towards his angelic patron by erecting an altar in his honor, in a chapel which he embellished with a magnificent pavement and various ornaments in stucco.

Extreme innocence in union with a spirit of penance, were the distinctive characteristics of our Father D. Angelo's life in the world. In recompense for this purity of heart God granted him dominion even over irrational creatures. One day when he was leaving the church with two priests, viz., D. Camillus Ferrarelli and D. Michael

Arminio, who were both his penitents, he perceived two doves which were fighting and quarreling with each other on the tower of the castle. "Stop," said he to the two young priests, "let us see if they will soon give over." After he had looked at them for some time, he said to the doves, "Well, since you will not stop, you must both come down here;" and they instantly obeyed, and presented themselves before him; upon which he told Ferrarelli to catch them. "Go," added he, "and carry them to that poor invalid who is confined to bed." This one anecdote will suffice to show to what an eminent degree of sanctity D. Angelo had attained, and how much he was favored by God.

His was indeed too perfect a soul to be thrown away on an evil world, and so he was taken out of it that he might be brought to still greater perfection in the house of God. We have already said, that Father Angelo highly approved of Father Margotta's entering our Congregation; soon afterwards he himself felt inspired to imitate him. He was too enlightened not to perceive the incontestable superiority of living under obedience to any mode of life in which one preserves one's own will, that is to say, in which one keeps what is dearer to man than aught besides; he also readily acknowledged that one cannot render a more acceptable sacrifice to God than by giving up one's whole being to Him, and thus resigning the tree to Him as well as its fruits. As our fathers Cafaro and Sportelli happened to be giving a mission at Bisaccia at this time, he communicated his wishes to them, although he feared that his great age and many infirmities might prove an insurmountable obstacle to their accomplishment, but it was not so, for they both promised to speak to Father Alphonsus in his favor, and owing to what Father Margotta said about him, he was so far from making any objection to receive him, that he testified the greatest satisfaction in so doing; and though he did not dispense with his observance of rule, he granted him the privilege of making his novitiate privately in the house at Caposele under the direction of Father Mazzini; and he also promised that if he persevered, this time of trial should be abridged in his case by admitting him to make his profession before the usual time. "If he is not strong enough to labor for the public good," said our Father Alphonsus, "I shall be glad to have him in the house, for he will give edification to all who see him." As soon as D. Angelo heard that he was to be admitted amongst us, he hastened to leave Bisaccia, at which the citizens were quite inconsolable, and he reached Caposele at the end of the year 1751, when he was in the sixty-fourth year of his age.

He put on the habit of a novice on the 3rd of the following month, which was the feast of Whitsunday. The first, or rather the only lesson he received from Father Mazzini was, that he must entirely abandon his former mode of life, and embrace that of the Congregation in every particular; he said that he must sleep when he perhaps might desire to watch, that he must talk in spite of his love of being always in a state of silence and meditation, and that he might sometimes have to eat when it was positively repulsive to him to do so. D. Angelo did not require to have this admonition repeated a second time; he never looked back to what he had done, for he devoted himself to simple obedience and entire compliance with the will of his superiors. From the day he entered, he evinced the most admirable simplicity and unexampled humility, joined to a holy ardor, to increase more and more in the paths of perfection. Each stroke of the bell was to him as the voice of God. Although he was so old, he was the first to repair to the choir, and surpassed all the rest in the observance of the most trifling regulations. He looked upon the Congregation as the entrance to heaven, and he said that if we knock at the gate of Paradise by a punctual compliance with rule, it will assuredly be opened to us. He humbly accused himself of what he called his faults at chapter, although they were in reality often acts of virtue; he deplored the years which he said he had wasted in the world, and felt a saintly envy for the young men who had entered the Congregation in their youth. After this, however, he would give vent to a spirit of holy confidence. "Well," he would say to the youthful clerics, "although I am such a poor creature, and although I have begun so late, I will overtake you and become a saint at last."

As soon as he became a novice, he hastened to thank Father Alphonsus for such a great favor. "As I am unable to thank you worthily for such a great boon," he wrote to him, "I will, notwithstanding my great unworthiness, say Mass tomorrow in thanksgiving for your fatherly goodness. I shall thus perform the debt of gratitude I owe you, and I shall also almost compel you to pray for me, a poor sinner, who is already on the brink of eternity. I trust that I shall be able by the aid of your prayers to persevere in the state to which God and your Reverence have called me. In conclusion, I respectfully ask your blessing, and humbly cast myself at your feet," etc.

As he wished to live like a true novice, he begged to have their directory, and it was given to him. After this he was most prompt in complying with all the regulations, especially in going to the kitchen to wash the dishes. He once broke a plate; he instantly ran to the superior with a piece of it hung round his neck to ask for a penance. He used to offer to assist the cook in preparing the soup, and he was equally ready to tender his services to the brother who had the care of the refectory, to clear the table and wash up the plates and dishes. While he was a novice he had the care of the altar, and he used to go and gather the flowers to adorn it with himself; he arranged them in the vases with his own hands, and then devoutly offered them to Jesus in the adorable sacrament. He thus conformed to all that is prescribed in the directory; indeed, had he not been dissuaded from it he would even have learned all the catechism of Bellarmine by heart. He delighted in the retreat which is made among us every Friday, and not only obeyed the least sign from Father Mazzini, but also that of anyone who ordered him to do anything whatsoever.

As he was well known in that neighborhood, all who came to the house were filled with admiration at seeing such a venerable old man become as a little child. When the time of the Jubilee came, Father Margotta thought that he ought to be exempted from going to Caposele with the others on account of his many infirmities, but D. Angelo was so anxious to gain indulgences, that he persuaded him to allow him to accompany the procession, and to join in singing the litanies, and his mere presence in the town had all the effect of a sermon. Someone compassionated him for the fatigue it must have caused him, but he replied, "Nothing is to be gained without suffering." As the devil was envious of his goodness and happiness, he did all he could to disturb his tranquility. He represented to him how hard it was to be obliged to give up all the holy practices he had hitherto observed, but this temptation failed, for he was too well-rooted in virtue to regret his former mode of life; he succeeded however in disturbing his mind, by reminding him of all the good which remained to be done in his native country. The tempter then assumed the guise of an angel of light, and set before him all that he had done in the world, and contrasted it with the little he seemed to be doing in the Congregation, and strove to persuade him that he had embraced an easy and comfortable way of living in exchange for one of austerity and mortification. He reminded him of all the young priests he had instructed, and whose zeal he had excited, of the clerics he had directed in the paths of virtue, and of the numerous penitents to whom his counsels had been of such utility. He also depicted before him the dangers which so many poor creatures were exposed to now that they were deprived of his assistance. This temptation affected him most deeply of all, and when he began to meditate, instead of being united to God, it seemed to him as if He rejected him as a punishment for the error he had committed in entering the Congregation.

When D. Angelo was thus tossed about by the waves of temptation, he wisely distrusted his own judgment. He went to Father Mazzini and with all humility manifested all that had passed within him; and this openness was so pleasing to God, that he immediately recovered his peace of mind; and he used afterwards to tell our young men that a temptation is at least half vanquished after it has been made known to superiors, who hold the place of God in our regard. Another trial however awaited him. Scarcely four months had elapsed since his arrival at Caposele ere he was attacked by a malignant fever. He did not manifest any fear of death, even when the malady was at its height, but he evinced the most anxious desire to receive Extreme Unction. As he went on urging to have it administered to him, Father Margotta at length said, "I forbid you even to speak of Extreme Unction." This answer quite distressed D. Angelo, and he said to his doctor, "I have been in the habit of receiving this sacrament spiritually every evening, and now I run the risk of being deprived of it at the hour of my death." However, as his malady made rapid progress and his life was soon despaired of, it was at length granted to him. When he was on the point of receiving this sacrament he entreated with many tears that he might be allowed to unite himself to God by pronouncing the vows, and that thus a crowning favor might be put to the numerous ones he had already received from God and from the Congregation. His request was granted, and after he had received this great happiness, he did nothing but sigh for the moment when he would be delivered from the prison of the body, and kept repeating with the apostle, "Cupio dissolvi et esse cum Christo."

When our saintly Father Alphonsus heard of the state Father D. Angelo was in, he said, "He will not die; God will leave him amongst us for His greater glory." He at the same time let him know that he must get rid of the fever, and only think of recovery. This confidence on the part of our holy father gave us all the greatest consolation. No sooner had Father Margotta received this message than he went to the bedside of the sufferer, and said to him, "Father Latessa, our father-rector puts you under obedience to recover, and says you must not think anymore about dying." This command threw Father Angelo into the greatest perplexity, for he was agitated by the desire to die on the one hand, and by the fear of disobedience on the other. "Well," said his Dr. Santorelli to him during this dilemma, "how will you be able to reconcile your wish to die with the command of your rector-major?" "There is but one course for me," replied the sick man; "I must obey." And immediately the fever and all the other bad symptoms disappeared.

During his illness, which lasted for six weeks, he received daily visits from priests, gentlemen, and religious. "Let us go," said they, "and see how saints die." He daily received Holy Communion by way of viaticum or devotion; when he was recovering it pained him so much to receive the Blessed Eucharist in his room, that he begged to be assisted in dragging himself to the church. It was indeed a touching thing to see this venerable old man going daily to the choir to receive Holy Communion, supported by one of our lay-brothers. One day he fancied he was strong enough to celebrate Mass, and he sent a message to Father Margotta to ask leave to do so. He was afraid to allow him to make the attempt, but the messenger misunderstood him, and gave a wrong reply to Father Angelo. He therefore said Mass, although he did so with the greatest difficulty, and returned to his room quite satisfied. When Father Margotta heard of it, he went to him and gave him a severe reprimand. "If you choose to put me in prison," replied D. Angelo, "I know I have quite deserved it, but indeed I did not know that I was disobeying you." The correction was too severe, and so Father Margotta laughed and said to Father Gazzili, "See how penitent he is!"

When D. Angelo recovered, he sent our Father Alphonsus a letter full of thanks for all the favors he had received from him. "Most Reverend Father," said he, "would that God would vouchsafe that miracle in my regard which was desired so ardently by holy Job, and that He would engrave all the benefits I have received from your exceeding charity, in enduring characters in my heart, so that they might be always present to my mind during the remainder of my life and for all eternity; but if this cannot be, I wish at least to express my gratitude to you today with all possible humility and sincerity. I am especially thankful to you for having allowed me to become one of your children, for having shortened the novitiate, (with the consent of the other reverend fathers,) and for having put me under obedience to recover when I was dangerously ill. I thank you from the bottom of my heart, and I pray St. Michael, all the choirs of angels, and all the saints, and above all, our most blessed Mother, to reward you for all the signal benefits you have showered down on me. I entreat you, most Reverend Father, to bear me always in your heart, in union with Jesus and Mary, so that I may always remember your goodness to me and never cease to thank you for it; and I conclude by casting myself in spirit at your feet, and humbly ask your holy benediction, and am," etc.

Father D. Angelo was far from being useless while he was in our house at Caposele; in fact, we may even say that he was its soul throughout the whole time he was there. At first he was entrusted with the duties of the confessional; when this was proposed to him, he said, "If I cannot give missions, nor preach, I will at least hear as many confessions as I can." He was the first to go to the church, and he remained there to the latest moment. There is always a good deal to do in the confessional in our church at Caposele, for it is much frequented; but on feast days especially Father D. Angelo's zeal was fully exercised, and he was unable to leave it until long after noon.

When the spiritual exercises were given in the house, he was of immense assistance in hearing confessions, and his ardor was redoubled when he had to do with young candidates for the priesthood. He was however at all times ready to attend to those who came to consult him about their spiritual concerns, and as he had been enjoined to receive such persons, he took pleasure in going with them, and used to take pains to amuse them during recreation.

The Congregation of Artisans was also confided to his care, and at that time it contained three hundred members. He made the most zealous efforts to increase their number and to augment their fervor; he gladly heard the confessions of the associates, addressed very salutary exhortations to them, and never dismissed them without having added fresh ardor to their piety.

Besides this, he was also prefect to our lay-brothers, to whom he used to give regular instructions on the holy mysteries of our religion; he heard the confessions of almost all of them, and unceasingly urged them to love Jesus Christ and to be devout to His blessed mother.

During mission times, when the rector was always absent, he was left in the house almost alone; and then the poor old man was obliged to act as superior. He showed the greatest anxiety for exact observance of rule on these occasions; he carefully watched over the brothers, and was unwearied in striving to maintain good order. It was not easily passed over if anyone arrived too late for any common exercise, or who performed any duty in a negligent manner. When Saturday came round, on which day we accuse ourselves of faults against rule in full chapter, he set forth the gravity of the most trifling breaches of observance, and he was not satisfied if the offender did not make the most sincere resolutions to avoid them for the future; if he therefore relapsed into the same fault again, he gave him a very severe reproof and penance on the following Saturday.

His own conduct was so exemplary that it at all times afforded matter of edification to his brothers. He never absented himself from attendance at the exercises of the community; he was the first to repair to the choir in the morning, even during the severest weather in winter. He was sometimes told that the clock which awakened the rest of the community was not intended for him, and he would immediately answer, "I am very well, therefore why should I require any exemptions, and not join the rest that I may share in their privileges."

He did not confine himself to the meditations prescribed by rule, and although he was at all times recollected and never lost sight of the presence of God, he also consecrated every spare moment to this holy exercise. He passed the day of monthly retreat in entire silence, and generally spent it in a retired corner of the church, and he never omitted to make the spiritual exercises once a year as prescribed by the rule; and he performed them with so much recollection and with such a spirit of retreat, that no one could help admiring him who saw him. In fact, his whole life was a constant union with God, and all his features betokened one whose days were spent in walking in the hidden paths of the interior life. Even during recreation, he only liked to speak of God, or silently to listen to what others said regarding Him. His public mass was rather quick, but this was only because he was afraid of being tedious to the people, for it was quite the reverse when he celebrated in our private chapel. And when he did so, the father-rector and D. Angelo served each other's masses by turns.

Father Angelo had the most tender devotion to the Incarnation of Jesus Christ; he meditated on all the mysteries it contains, and when he did so he shed many tears; indeed this gift was habitual to him. One Christmas night, when the choir sung the words, "Christus natus est nobis," he burst forth into so many tears and sobs that everyone present was deeply affected. He used to meditate on the mysteries of the Blessed Virgin in like manner, and he fasted on bread and water on all the eves of her feasts. "The Madonna," he often said, "is worthy of every homage, and we can never honor her sufficiently."

The love of God and of his neighbor had equal sway over his heart, and he used to say, "He who does not love charity is not a true son of our Congregation." There was no distinction of persons with him; those in suffering were always the special objects of his tenderness, whatever might be their rank in life: the poorest laborer who was afflicted with sickness was sure to be treated by him with the most paternal care.

His nephew was attacked by a deadly malady, which lasted for a whole month, during which he never left him day or night. When he was advised to take some rest, and to think a little about his own health, "I am bound to do what I do through gratitude," he replied; "for he took the same care of me when I was dangerously ill."

His hatred towards himself was as great as his love

towards his neighbor. He never omitted to mortify his senses, and if he could not obtain leave to abandon himself to all his fervor would have led him to desire, he managed to obtain permission for a good deal from the father-rector, who was his director. He kept Wednesdays, Fridays, and Saturdays as days of abstinence, and he never took even the small quantity of wine which is made use of in the community. Although he had a painful hernia, he used often to eat either on his knees or prostrate on the floor, and he generally mingled bitter herbs with his food. He took the discipline every day, and he used it twice on the days when it is enjoined by the rule. Up to the hour of his death he always wore iron chains round his arms and legs, at least three times a week, and he increased these austerities during novenas to Jesus Christ and to the Blessed Virgin. He would have liked to do far more than this, but his director restrained his zeal, as he very reasonably was afraid of his undertaking penances which would have been beyond his strength.

On the 2nd of August, 1755, the Octave of the Porziuncula was commenced in the church of the Conventual Fathers, and D. Angelo eagerly accompanied the father-rector thither in order to gain the indulgences. It is a tedious and toilsome journey, for if the descent is most fatiguing, the ascent is still more painful; yet D. Angelo did not hesitate to undertake it, notwithstanding his many infirmities, but the next day he was unable to leave his bed, whether in consequence of this unfortunate expedition, or through some other cause, we cannot however determine. His illness was a tedious one, for it lasted more than two months. He said Mass on the 6th of August for the last time. "What did Jesus Christ say to you this morning?" asked D. Santorelli. "We took leave of each other," replied D. Angelo; "I said to him, 'This is the last sacrifice which I entreat Thee to offer to Thine Eternal

Father for me, for we shall meet no more at the altar.'"

He received Holy Communion throughout his illness in his own room; he prepared for it with torrents of tears, and his thanksgiving resembled his preparation. He was absorbed in contemplating the goodness of God, and unless when he was interrupted by the doctor or by one of us, he would remain in prayer from morning until night.

When it became noised abroad that he was ill, everyone hastened to come and see him, from the wish to hear his salutary counsels once more. This concourse of strangers was very painful to the humble D. Angelo, but he received them all with kindness, and thanked them for their kind feeling towards him. His mere appearance edified all who saw him, and the words of life which issued from his lips made the most lively impression on every heart. He set the magnitude of their obligations before the priests and religious who came to see him in such a forcible manner, that they went away penetrated with a holy fear. When asked how he was he simply replied, "I am doing the will of God."

His daily anxiety to communicate seemed such a contradiction to his apparent indifference about receiving Extreme Unction, which he did not even name, that his confidential friend, D. Santorelli, could not help saying to him, "How is it that you have never spoken of Extreme Unction since you were put under obedience not to die?" "I will do so when the time comes," he replied. And on the morning of the 3rd of October, 1755, he sent for Father Cajone, the rector of the house, and said, "My father, it is now time to give me Extreme Unction, that I may go and enjoy the presence of God, which I trust I shall do through the merits of my Blessed Savior; I therefore entreat your Reverence to assist me in this extremity." This proves that God had made known to him his last hour, for after he had received Extreme Unction, with entire presence of mind

and with the most tender piety, amid a crowd of priests
and gentlemen, who melted into tears at the sight, he
begged to be left alone, that he might prepare for his
agony. His strength began to fail at about six o'clock in the
evening: before he entered into his agony he kissed his
crucifix and bathed it in tears of devotion; then holding it
with one hand while with the other he embraced the
father-rector, he gave up his pure spirit to God at eight
o'clock, amidst the lamentations of all present. His death
took place on the octave of the festival of St. Michael, the
patron of the dying, for whom he had always felt a special
devotion. At the obsequies of Father Latessa it seemed as
if a solemn fête and gala day were being held at Caposele,
rather than a funeral ceremony. Father Cajone, who was at
that time the superior of the house, invited the clergy, the
chapter, and the Conventual Fathers to be present at the
funeral. Many gentlemen and ladies of high degree were
also present, and crowds of poor people also flocked
thither, full of eagerness to obtain relics of Father Angelo.
The body was placed in the church during the night before
the ceremony. One of our lay-brothers in cutting off his
hair inadvertently pierced the skin, and the blood flowed
from this trifling wound in such quantities that all his
clothes were steeped in it, and we were obliged to tear
them up and distribute the pieces among the Faithful to
gratify their devotion.

The virtues and merits which our Father D. Angelo
Latessa possessed when he entered the Congregation
brought forth tenfold fruit and ripened into perfection ere
he died. We may even confidently assert, that he entered
into a blissful eternity without ever having sullied the robe
of innocence with which he was clad in holy Baptism; for
all the fathers who had the direction of his conscience have
attested that they never found even the shadow of
deliberate venial sin in him. He was betrayed into owning

to D. Santorelli, that the sin for which he felt he had most to reproach himself, and for which he humbled himself most deeply before God, was that he had once played at tennis with his companions whilst he was studying at Acerno. "But, by the grace of God," he added in a spirit of profound humility, "I did not then wear the ecclesiastical dress." On another occasion, when he was conversing familiarly with our Father D. Bernard Maria Apice, the latter laughingly said to him, "I have caught you this time, Father Angelo; you are not telling the truth." "What," he replied, almost weeping through horror at such an accusation, "I do not remember ever having told a willful falsehood since I was born, and can your Reverence think I would begin to lie at my present age?" Such were the innocence and candor of this good father, and yet, as we have already seen, he always felt bound to do penance and to practice the most constant austerity.

Our brother Gerard Majella suddenly entered into an ecstasy eight days after his death in the middle of recreation, and exclaimed in a transport of joy, "Look at our blessed father Latessa, he is just entering heaven!" When we narrate the life of this saintly brother, it will be seen what faith may be attached to his words, and if God could give us a more perfect assurance of the happiness which His faithful servant is now enjoying in heaven.

The Life of
FATHER D. CESAR SPORTELLI,
Of the Congregation of the Most Holy
Redeemer

The life of
FATHER D. CESAR SPORTELLI
Of the Congregation of the Most Holy Redeemer

By Father D. Joseph Landi

 HE FIRST of our fathers who passed from our house at Nocera into the heavenly country, was D. Cæsar Sportelli, who was one of the oldest members of the Congregation. He was born at Mola in the Bari, on the 29th of March, 1702; but his parents belonged to Putignano on the sea coast, which is on the borders of la Pouille, in the kingdom of Naples, where they occupied an honorable rank in society. His mother was celebrated for her great sanctity, and as she died at Naples her body is carefully preserved there. D. Cæsar also went through his studies and became an advocate in that town, and his talents and science caused him to be a shining ornament to his profession. Whilst he was thus engaged he became acquainted with Mgr. Falcoia, who then belonged to the Congregation of Pious Workmen; he chose him for his confessor, and placed himself under his direction, and he also joined the Congregation of Doctors, directed by the same father. When he heard that a new congregation of missionaries had just been founded in the town of Scala, by Father D. Alphonsus de Liguori, a Neapolitan chevalier, who was celebrated for his holiness and for his knowledge, God inspired him with a great love for this Congregation,

and with an ardent desire to become a member of it; however, what made him finally determine to enter it was a dream, in which he saw Jesus Christ in the act of judging the universe; and this made such an impression on him that he at once resolved to leave the world. Mgr. Falcoia was well aware of D. Cæsar's excellence and of his great talents; no sooner then had he ascertained that his vocation was really from God, than he joyfully told him to place himself under the direction of Father D. Alphonsus de Liguori, who at that time had no one with him but Father Vitus Curtius, and who was much consoled by his arrival. D. Cæsar was still clad in the garb of a secular, and was nearly thirty-three years of age when he repaired to Scala. As Alphonsus felt great expectations in his regard from seeing how great were his talents and virtue, he lost no time in sending him to Rome, that he might be ordained priest, and in this he was seconded by Mgr. Falcoia, and not by the bishop of his diocese, who threw many obstacles in the way. As he possessed the requisite age and attainments, D. Cæsar soon received priestly orders, and became one of the first fathers of the new Institute.

Father D. Cæsar immediately devoted himself to a life of mortification and excessive labor, as the Congregation was very destitute of missionaries at the time. He did immense good by his sermons and catechizings, for God gave him a large measure of grace to aid him in these labors of the ministry. I have often heard him, and knew him well, and I can safely assert that he truly excelled in these duties, and that he was loved and admired by all. After some little time he went to exercise his ministry in a great many large towns, such as Salerno, where he gave a retreat to all the clergy, in presence of Mgr. Rossi, the archbishop; he also gave one to the religious at Monte Vergine, and to many other communities, to their great satisfaction, and to the great profit of the souls of those who heard him. Besides the duties in the pulpit and the confessional, in which he was constantly engaged, a great many of his penitents wrote to consult him from all parts. When he gave the spiritual exercises in a convent, they made such an impression on the religious that they could never forget either his sermons or his counsels. He was often superior in a great many of our houses, and he was held in the highest esteem on account of his wisdom and prudence wherever he went; he was especially distinguished by the way in which he established the foundation of our house at Caposele, of which he took possession, and was the first superior. God alone knows all he had to endure there! When he first entered this hermitage, he did not even find forks for dinner, nor food to eat, and he and his first companion, Father Gaspar Corsino, were obliged to find their only sustenance in a little fruit.

He entered this house in the beginning of December in the year 1747; as he had preached to the inhabitants of this place during the preceding Lent with much fruit, they felt the greatest affection for him, and were quite delighted that he was the one selected to be its founder.

This foundation began in the very greatest poverty; on the first evening indeed when he was in the house called Mater Domini, he and Father Gaspar had positively nothing to eat. But when some of his penitents heard of this state of things, they rendered him some assistance. It is true that he had at first received an alms of thirty ducats, but he spent the whole sum in buying the materials required for building the house; the work was carried on by means of further alms received from the poor of the neighborhood, who felt such great love for Father Cæsar, that the very sound of his name was enough to make them eagerly bring him stones, wood, and all other needful materials. Their exertions were also animated by the example of this father, who did the most wonderful things, and spared no personal labor. There was one of his penitents, named Sister Mary Santorelli, at Caposele at this time, who was confined to bed by an affection on the nerves and other serious infirmities; Father D. Cæsar went to visit her, for before we were established in this house, she had often been in it and always felt the greatest interest in it. He asked her how many communions she had lost during her illness. "Five," she replied. "What," exclaimed the father, "five communions lost without my leave!" She then added, that it was to her own great sorrow. "No, no," continued D. Cæsar, "you must not miss any more." Sister Mary then saw that he had given her a command to leave her bed, and so in truth it was, for when she got up the next morning she found that she was perfectly well, and was able to receive Holy Communion. The same sister has related other marvelous things in the life of this father, and said that he had a special and wonderful power in calming troubled consciences.

I will not dwell on the great labors he had again to go through in building our house of Nocera de Pagani, in which undertaking he placed all his trust in Divine Providence, who sent him frequent assistance through friends and benefactors. He had such a wonderful power of gaining over hearts that his demands were always well received, and no one was able to refuse what he asked. Our Congregation was really infinitely indebted to him for the aid he thus obtained. His mortification of sight afforded a perfect model of modesty. Once when he was on a visit with Mgr. Falcoia at Rome, in the house of some nobleman where there were also several young ladies of rank, he never even looked at them or conversed with them, although his stay was by no means a short one. We heard this from the present abbess of the convent of Bauco, who was an eyewitness of what she related.

Amongst his other resolutions he determined never to ask for anything, and never to refuse anything, according to the advice of St. Francis of Sales. Now to test his virtue the superior once forbade anyone to give him snuff, which was a very great privation to him; but God sent an angel to him under the semblance of a young man, who carried a large box full of it, with which he replenished his snuff box, and then instantly disappeared. D. Cæsar had also a great love for prayer, especially for vocal prayers and pious ejaculations, and he was so much in the habit of making use of them that he uttered pious aspirations to God even during his sleep. He was full of charity towards his neighbor. When he was but a secular at Naples, he recommended a young man who was in distress to one in authority; as he found that he had fallen into vicious habits, he unhesitatingly warned him of the evil of his ways. On receiving this reproof and finding himself thus unmasked, the young man had the baseness to try to shoot him one evening; D. Cæsar was not offended at this; but after again succeeding in bringing him back to the paths of virtue, he continued to protect and assist him as before.

After many very great and painful labors, to which he unceasingly devoted himself in the work of the ministry, and after a multitude of cares and obstacles which he had had to experience in the government of our rising congregation, he at length sunk under a weight of infirmities and maladies which caused him to come to a premature end. He was first attacked by a violent apoplectic stroke, which left a trembling in all his limbs and nearly deprived him of speech. In consequence of this fatal blow, he became incapable of all occupation. This infirmity lasted more than a year, during which he never once complained of the decrees regarding him, on the contrary he always manifested the greatest conformity to the will of God. He was submissive to all, attached faith to what he was told, and acted in all and towards all with the simplicity of a child; at length, after he had consumed his life in labor and trial, God deigned to reward him by taking him out of this world to the mansions of eternal bliss. Before he expired, he intoned that glorious hymn of triumph, "In exitu Israel de Egypto," etc., and then resigned his soul into the arms of his Creator. He had several times foretold the day and hour of his death. On the day on which it really took place, he spoke of and would hear of nothing but heaven, and he caused several hymns on the happiness of the saints to be sung to him, and he died in this state of holy joy on the 19th of April, 1750, surrounded by all his fathers. He had from the first been consultor-general of the Congregation, and although he was suffering from the disease of which we have spoken, he was confirmed in this office by the first general chapter which was held after our rules were approved at Rome; which was done as much because of the esteem and respect which was felt for him on account of his virtue and science, as because he was one of the first fathers of the Congregation.

It would be difficult to express what a general sensation was caused by the tidings of his death, so great was his reputation for sanctity. I must however confess before God that we had not such an exalted opinion of his virtue while he was alive as we entertained after his death; for he was a man of simple manners who accommodated himself to everyone; and he had also a way of concealing his virtues and mortifications. On one occasion however he could not hide the singular favors which God conferred on him. He was going to preach at Caposele, where the exercises were being given, and when the lay-brother went to his cell to call him, he found him suspended several inches in the air, and the whole room was filled with a dazzling brightness. His sermon on that day produced the most extraordinary fruit.

When we witnessed the general eagerness to procure something of which he had made use, which took place after his passage to a better life, above all when we heard of the innumerable prodigies and miracles which God everywhere effected through the medium of his relics and images, we were filled with astonishment. Until a more detailed Life of this great servant of God is published, it will be impossible to form a just idea of his merit in the sight of God and of his favor with Heaven. For my part, I will here confine myself to relating a great prodigy which I myself witnessed. As we had not a vault at Nocera at the time of his death, our fathers caused a grave to be made in which he was laid dressed in all his sacerdotal vestments. At the expiration of three years and seven months, we thought it right to take his body out of the damp low grave in which it was at first placed, to put it with the others in the vault which had been constructed for this purpose. It was therefore disinterred, and carried to our chapel of our Lady of Sorrows; and as the miracles which were wrought by him were talked of in all directions, we were anxious to see whether he would work some fresh miracle in our presence, and in what state his body was after the three years and seven months which had elapsed since his death. For this purpose, and by the order of that learned and pious prelate, D. Gerard Volpe, the bishop of Nocera, the keeper of the register, a canon of the cathedral, as well as D. Thomas Cortora, the Abbot of Angri, were sent for, and the coffin was opened in their presence. How great was the astonishment of all when we saw that although all his garments were decayed and almost consumed, yet his body was as entire, flexible, and beautiful, as on the day of his death, and that it also exhaled a sweet fragrance. Our surprise was greatly increased when we saw that his intestines had not become corrupt, and that his stomach had preserved its elasticity. He was bled, and for the further glory of His servant, God permitted bright blood to gush forth after the incision. At this sight we could do nothing but offer up a thousand thanksgivings to Him from whom every good and perfect gift proceeds. The body was then clad in new vestments, and replaced in the coffin; the seals were duly affixed, and all the public records were drawn up according to the requisite forms, so that the cause of the canonization might be commenced at the time appointed by God, and that the state of his body might be duly authenticated.

Two engravings of the portrait of the servant of God were immediately prepared, to gratify the devotion of the people by distributing pictures of him amongst them. Our Father Alphonsus even went the length of petitioning the Holy See to allow his cause to be introduced; but the storms which have agitated the little bark of our Congregation from its very commencement, have prevented his being able to follow up this matter.

The Life of
FATHER D. DOMINIC BLASUCCI
Student of the Congregation of the Most
Holy Redeemer

The life of
FATHER D. DOMINIC BLASUCCI
Student of the Congregation
of the Most Holy Redeemer

By the Rev. Father Tannoja

HE BIRTH of this child of grace, which took place on the 5th of March, 1732, was attended by many surprising prodigies. In the first place he occasioned his mother no inconvenience whatsoever whilst she carried him in her womb, so that she could scarcely believe that she was really pregnant. He came into the world covered with a thick membrane, and surrounded with an equally extraordinary girdle, which caused his mother to exclaim, "Miserable creature that I am! I have given birth to a shapeless mass!" When the midwife however disengaged him from this covering, it was found that his limbs were not only quite perfect, but that he was a most beautiful infant. Scarcely had he entered the world, ere, to the great astonishment of all who were present, he raised his tender arms, and devoutly folded them together on his breast in the form of a cross, as if God thereby wished plainly to foretell the heroic resignation with which he would one day abandon himself to the divine will, and the loving tenderness with which he would unite himself to God to suffer with Him on the sacred wood of the cross. At this sight the midwife consoled his mother and said, "You have cause for joy, for you have not only brought forth a

189

beautiful child, but a saint; the covering in which he was born, the girdle which surrounded him, and the way in which he crossed his arms, are so many manifestations of great holiness."

Dominic began to taste the precious fruits of the tree of the cross very soon after his birth, for his mother had no milk, which caused him to fall into a dangerous illness when he was but two months old. He was one day supposed to be dead, and wept for by his parents as such, so that his eldest brother even went to the parish church and told the sacristan to toll the bell to announce his death; when he returned home to wait for the priest who was to accompany the corpse to the church, he was therefore not a little surprised to find that his brother was miraculously restored to life. The mother was inconsolable at the idea of losing her son, and being animated by a lively faith, she had recourse to God, and poured some drops of holy water into the baby's mouth, after which he was immediately restored to life. When he recovered, he was suckled by Donna Felice Pepe, the wife of D. Peter d' Agostino, who was then the tax-gatherer of the province of the Basilicate. She had been shortly before confined of a little girl, and undertook to nurse little Dominic with great charity and maternal tenderness. It may be said that the bright lily of virginal purity, which he preserved unspotted to the tomb, began to spring up in his heart from his very infancy. He was not five years old when he gave up sleeping in the bed with his mother, who was then a widow. "Mamma," said he, "it is not right for little boys to be in bed with their mother." He loved Jesus in the Blessed Sacrament, and the Blessed Virgin with the utmost ardor from his earliest years. He often received Holy Communion, and never approached the altar without having first made an hour's preparation, which was accompanied by a flood of tears. His thanksgiving lasted until dinnertime, so that when the sacristan went to lock up the church, he found him still kneeling motionless before the Blessed Sacrament. The visit he used to make to this Divine Savior during the day often lasted for three entire hours. Words cannot describe all the tenderness of his love towards the Blessed Virgin Mary, or relate all the fasts, novenas, and devotions he practiced in her honor. It will suffice here to mention that these words were found in his little prayer book: "That he wished to burn and be consumed through love to Mary; that he wished to love her as much as she was loved by the Blessed Trinity;" and he fasted on bread and water every Saturday in her honor.

He caused the sweet lily of his purity to flourish daily more and more, and added intensity to the fire of his devotion by the severity of his penances. Amongst others, he went so far as even to abstain from grapes, although he stayed in his vineyard during the time of vintage, which must have been most trying to one of his age.

God had endowed him with rare beauty and great talents. He was scarcely twelve years of age when he had finished his grammatical studies; and it was not long afterwards when he had perfected himself in rhetoric, philosophy, and canon law, under the direction of his uncle, the archpriest D. Donatus Anthony Carnevale, in which studies he was accompanied by his two brothers Peter and Francis Blasucci, and his cousins Francis Carnevale and Pascal de Paola.

But who can paint the splendor of the virtues which shone forth in him after he entered our Congregation? He was never seen to transgress the least rule, and from the beginning of his novitiate he had formed this resolution: "I would rather give up striving to become a saint, than transgress the most minute portion of my rules." The obedience which he rendered to his superiors was sometimes really miraculous. One day the father-minister said to him, "Brother Blasucci,...go..." and without waiting to hear the rest of the command, he hurried away. When he had got half way, he was called back again to give an account of what he was going to do, "I am going to tell Father N. to go to the confessional," he replied; after which he once more set out to fulfill his orders. The father-minister was quite amazed at his answer, for he well knew that God alone could have revealed his intention to him; and turning towards the fathers who were near him, he said, "Would that I were as far advanced in perfection as brother Blasucci. See to what an extent his obedience is carried." We will now quote some of his maxims with reference to this virtue:

"If a religious does not practice entire obedience, he is worse than lost. The slightest private interpretation is enough to destroy all the merit of obedience. I would not exchange one act of obedience for a hundred hours of mental prayer full of spiritual consolation. If I had virtue enough to perform one action of true obedience, I should think that I had made a great step onwards in the paths of perfection. He who only obeys imperfectly, will never become holy, because he will always be yielding to the impulse of self-love," etc.

It would be impossible to describe the fasts, mortifications, rough haircloths, and bloody disciplines, with which he macerated his innocent body. Suffice it to say that our Father Alphonsus once made this remark, "I only know of one fault in Blasucci, he mortifies himself too much."

Neither would it be possible to give an adequate idea of his virginal purity, his love for Jesus in the Blessed Sacrament, and for the Blessed Virgin, or of his other truly heroic virtues. In a word, Dominic was an angel of innocence, a martyr of penance, and a seraph of love. This love was most ardent towards the adorable Sacrament, most tender towards the Blessed Virgin, and most universal in regard to his neighbor.

But the time soon arrived when God rewarded the virtues of His faithful servant. We may say with the Holy Spirit, that his death was truly precious in the sight of the Lord. During his last sickness, he received Holy Communion daily in the church, except on All Souls' Day, 1752, when the Blessed Sacrament was conveyed to him in bed, and soon afterwards he breathed forth his pure soul into the bosom of his God ere his thanksgiving had ended, while surrounded by all the fathers and brothers of the community, who shed tears of joy. His body remained unburied for twenty-eight hours, and it was as flexible throughout the time as if he had been alive. When it was placed on the bier in the church, he suddenly opened his eyes and fixed them on Father D. Paul Cafaro, the rector of the house at Caposele. At this sight D. Nicholas Santorelli was quite stupefied with astonishment. "Do not be afraid," said Father D. Cafaro to him, "I mentally commanded him to open his eyes to enable his portrait to be drawn." He was taken out of his tomb twenty days after his death, when a vein was opened, and the blood poured forth as if he had been still alive.

A more detailed life of this servant of God, whom with God's blessing we trust we may one day succeed in causing to be honored on our altars, will be published hereafter; however, for the satisfaction of our readers, we will now add some details of great weight and interest.

Let us begin by giving the testimony of the brother infirmarian who attended him during his illness. "If I were to enumerate all the heroic virtues I saw our good Father Dominic practice," said he, "several volumes would not contain all I should have to say; I will therefore only mention some facts which came specially under my notice. It is already known that all the fathers and brothers of our

Congregation unite with one voice in praising and blessing God, for the great favors which He bestowed on him...Suffice it to say that every one called him a second Aloysius of Gonzaga, etc...He specially delighted in exercising charity. When he saw that a brother was in suffering or disquiet, he instantly made it a point to calm and comfort him; and he did this so effectively, that it seemed as if he knew even the interior motions of their hearts. One day Brother Cæsar, as he himself has told us, was tormented by interior trials. Our good Father Blasucci met him while in this state, and as he probably saw by his countenance that he was much agitated, he said a few words of consolation to him, and immediately, and as if by miracle, Brother Cæsar's countenance became serene and tranquil. (We heard this from his own lips.) It seemed as if God wished to manifest to the world the eminent sanctity of this dear and well-beloved son and disciple, even during his lifetime, by the abundant graces with which He favored him, and which were often really miraculous. We may judge of this by the following instance, which our Brother Gerard is ready to affirm on oath; and this brother's evidence is worthy of peculiar deference, as everyone believes him to be a saint; for my part, I am sure he is so. Brother Gerard then was one day suffering more than usual, especially interiorly, and his heart was so dried up within him that he felt almost driven to a state of despair, (these are his own words.) Father Blasucci perceived that something was amiss, and asked him what was the matter. He told him, and at the same time begged him to deliver him from his pain. In reply Blasucci made the sign of the cross on his heart, and immediately Gerard became perfectly free from all his former suffering. He always attributed this sudden change to brother Blasucci, and kept it secret until now. I could also mention a prodigy which happened to myself at the time of his death, but I cannot do so until I have spoken to my director. I feel sure that if I could make this known, it would also contribute to the glory of our deceased brother." And here ends the narrative of the infirmarian.

The archpriest D. Donatus Anthony Carnevale, who was Dominic's uncle, terminates his account in the following terms: "Wherever his death became known, everyone exclaimed with one voice, 'He is blessed! he is a saint!' There were even some gentlemen who wished to obtain possession of his body; and when I announced the death of Father Blasucci to Mgr. de Muro, and the pains which were being taken to collect materials for the composition of his Life, D. Vito Muro replied that he wished these attestations to be made juridically to give them more weight, on account of the numerous prodigies which had been already operated by his intercession." Two of them were attested by the same archpriest in a letter to his nephew D. Peter Paul Blasucci, who is now rector-major of our Congregation. He says, "Mary Caparso, who was dangerously ill and given over by the doctors, was instantly cured by touching his habit. Donatus Anthony Pitocco, who was afflicted with a malignant fever, applied a morsel of his habit towards evening, and was cured next morning."

With regard to his union with God, a member of our Congregation wrote as follows: "In consideration of his bodily infirmities, his director forbade him to think of God. But this command caused Father Dominic the most intense agony; if he thought of God, he was afraid of being guilty of disobedience, and if he did not think of Him he felt as if he must die. In fact, he was so full of divine love that his thoughts and even his senses caused him to become absorbed in God, as it were, in spite of himself. Sad indeed was it then to the heart of our Dominic when thus torn from his God whom he loved so ardently, by the mandate of his director, whose voice was to him as the voice of God Himself. Not being able to bear such intense suffering any longer, he wrote to his Father confessor, saying, 'You wish to sever me from God in order to preserve my bodily life; but it is evident that the violence I have to use in detaching myself from Him will soon kill me; union with God has become natural to me, and in spite of all my efforts, I am with Him, as it were, imperceptibly. I do my best to resist the plenitude of celestial grace, I do violence to myself that I may obey, but how can I fight against God, who kindles this bright flame in my heart, which I have neither courage nor strength to extinguish?' In such a case death alone could give consolation to our Father Dominic. It was a touching spectacle to see him leave the choir: after giving a deep sigh, he would make a profound inclination and get up; then he would make another genuflection; after taking a step or two, he returned to cast a last longing look at Jesus in the adorable Sacrament, when he sighed and genuflected anew, and this he repeated at least three times; if he succeeded in tearing himself away at last, he did so with such regret that it seemed as if his soul would be severed from his body. A companion one day said to him, 'What thanksgivings do you make to Jesus Christ after communion?' 'Ah!?' he replied, one does not know what one does then; one feels as if heaven were in one's heart. Were it possible, I should like my heart to dissolve in divine love as wax melts before a burning flame.' Once when he was walking in the garden with a friend, he said, raising his eyes to heaven, Ah! Lord! when will that happy moment arrive, when I shall be wholly united to Thee!' He always knelt during meditation and the other pious exercises, and never sat down but by the express desire of his superiors. His recollection and devotion in prayer were so great that they even inspired the same sentiments in those who beheld them. One day when the zelator visited him, he found him in such a devotional posture that he could not help saying to another brother, Brother, I visited Brother Blasucci's room today while he was meditating; methought I saw a St. Philip Neri, and I retired in great emotion.' However great might be his infirmities, he used to take the discipline so severely, that the mere sound of the blows was quite appalling."

The following account is also worthy of notice. It is from the pen of Father Picone, who was Dominic's co-novice, and who has since become an excellent father. "The first time I saw him, I felt as if I were looking at an angel," said he, "for his face even then had an air of indescribable sanctity. Even when his health was very bad, whenever he was asked how he was, he replied, 'I am well:' except on the morning of the day he died, when he said, 'I do not feel well.' He used at first to mix bitter herbs with all he ate, but this was afterwards prohibited. The severity of the way in which he disciplined himself, was ascertained by the noise of the blows he gave himself, notwithstanding his great weakness, and by the large drops of blood which were found on the walls of his room. He walked with much difficulty, like a kind of machine, and yet he never said, 'I can do no more.' He never leaned against anything during meditation; but remained motionless throughout the time with his eyes cast down and with the utmost modesty and devotion. He practiced mortification and recollection to such a heroic degree, that he thereby shortened his days. He put us all to confusion by his fervor in the novitiate, and when I went to visit his room, his very appearance was enough to make me recollected."

Father D. Alexander de Meo thus expressed himself in a letter he wrote to me from Nocera on the 9th of November, 1752: "It is said that our dearest, and, alas! for us now too happy Brother Blasucci has taken flight to

heaven, there to plead, as we humbly hope, the cause of
the Congregation, our beloved mother. Everyone calls him
blessed; for my part, I have no doubt whatever that he is
so. The ardor he felt to advance daily in the love of God,
has now obtained a glorious consummation; the sufferings
he loved to endure that he might thus become more
pleasing to Him are terminated. 'Jam dicit spiritus, ut
requiescat a laboribus suis, jam enim hiems transiit et
opera sua ipsum sequuntur,' to produce for him in the
kingdom of the saints, 'æternum glorio pondus.' I earnestly
entreat your Reverence to collect together as many
particulars regarding this holy brother as possible. I could
make the most fervent eulogiums on him, and even attest
them on oath, but only in general terms, because I never
knew him intimately. Yet I would gladly sacrifice my life,
and shed all my blood, and do all in my power to make
known the goodness of God towards the soul of this His
most faithful and most innocent servant. You can consult
Father D. Andrew, and I will speak to Father D. John.
Apply also to his brother, whom I congratulate on having
a brother so dear to God in heaven, for I am certain he
now enjoys the beatific vision, that is to say, if he be really
dead, which however is a fact that we are not sure of; we
received the tidings from Father D. Peter Genovèse, who
says he heard that he died on All Souls' Day. But this was
nine days ago, and how is it possible that we should not
yet have received direct information on the subject?
Whatever may be the case, I place myself at your disposal
in this matter, as I am sure that in any event it is one of
much moment."

In the funeral sermon which the same Father D. Meo
afterwards preached at Nocera on our Dominic, he
mentioned many facts worthy of admiration. We will
content ourselves with quoting the following passages: "He
appeared so calm that he looked as if he were an angel

under the semblance of humanity, so absorbed did he seem in the loving contemplation of his God...But I feel most admiration when I remember how he ceased to act when he was in the room with a companion: he placed himself near the door, and there, with one hand on his breast and holding a book in the other, he stayed motionless as a statue, without resting hand or foot against the table; he did not lean back in his chair, nor open or shut either the door or window, however hot or cold the weather might be; he never spoke to his companion, or moved so much as a book or chair, or even shook the hourglass on the table, which anyone else would have done unthinkingly; but we need not wonder at this, since he had such entire self-control that he never indulged in any thought, movement, or word which was not solely for the glory of God." By this superhuman conduct he gently won over all hearts; even strangers often asked who he was, and everyone looked upon him as a saint. He made such an impression on a gentleman and doctor of Nocera, (whose name I do not however feel at liberty to mention,) during the spiritual exercises at Ciorani, that he not only wrote down his name, but he also asked for his discipline, which he kept as a relic. We were more than once obliged to make him change his cap and other things of the sort in order to satisfy the piety of the Faithful. Strangers however were not the only ones who thus honored him; for those who saw him most frequently, had the greatest veneration for him, which is by no means a usual occurrence. There were some of the novices who secretly kissed his clothes as often as they could, and our father rector-major himself acknowledged that he felt a most peculiar degree of respect and veneration for him. He was as humble as it was possible to be. Although he was very learned, he tried to appear ignorant, and never was heard to utter one word which could display his knowledge. On being once asked if he had run away from his paternal house to enter the Congregation, as all the other novices had done, he replied, "Why should they wish to detain me at home? Nothing could be expected from me." If anyone went up to speak to him, he arose, and with his cap in hand he listened to what they said with all humility. He blushed at either being named or looked at. If his superiors praised him, he said, "O wretch that I am! I am so imperfect that my superiors have to win me over by caresses." He asked his spiritual father for penances with many tears. "I must do penance," said he, "for fear God may abandon me." When he spoke of himself it was plain that he believed himself to be the greatest sinner in the world. On one occasion when a letter of inquiry regarding his health was addressed to him, he replied in tears and confusion at any concern being felt for the health of such a useless creature, who according to him was not as valuable as a little fly. He attained a degree of perfection at which few saints have arrived, for he rejoiced even in his inferior nature at being despised, reviled, and ill-treated. Yet all his directors have assured me, that he always preserved the robe of baptismal innocence without spot, and that they never discovered any deliberate venial sin in him, or even any willful fault. He observed even the most trifling rules, and they were not few in number amongst us. In fact, our Dominic may be called the model, the ideal, and even the soul of our institute.

Devotion towards his beloved Mother Mary, whom he loved more than aught besides, was his most distinctive characteristic, as is plainly evinced by all the novenas he made, by all his familiar conversations in her honor, and by his sedulous care never to commence anything without first asking her permission and saluting her. Though the hand of death was then laid on thee, dear brother, this formidable enemy had no terrors for thee; for thee caresses and tender embraces alone are in store; for thee sadness, tears, and anguish are over in thy regard; and now "neque luctus neque clamor neque dolor erit ultra."

Were there however no other testimony to the sanctity of Dominic than the two letters we are now going to quote, they alone would suffice to cause him to be canonized. One of them was written by Father D. Bernard Maria Apice, who was a celebrated missionary; and the other by Father D. Paul Cafaro, so distinguished for his extraordinary holiness. Let us now quote that of Father Apice:

"R. B. D. Anthony Maria Tannoja, of the Congregation of the Most Holy Redeemer.

"Ciorani.

"My very dear Father Tannoja, I write to inform you of the manner in which our dearest Brother Dominic Blasucci passed from this life into Paradise on All Souls' Day. I say into Paradise, for I feel assured that he did not even go near purgatory, (and our Father Cafaro maintains this also,) and I always have said to those with whom I have conversed regarding the holiness of this angelical young man, that if he has had to endure the pains of purgatory, persons like ourselves have nothing to hope for. I had the consolation of being with him when he died, and assisted him to hold the blessed candle in his hands during the last half hour of his life; and he expired in my arms.

"It would be needless to tell you of the holiness of his life, for I am sure you are well aware of it. But I think it will at least give you consolation if I mention a few things regarding him. I had the happiness of seeing him frequently at Ciorani and at Iliceto, and also in the house at Caposele, where his saintly life terminated. I was commissioned to convey him in a carriage to Iliceto. He left Ciorani on the 3rd of September, and reached Iliceto on the 5th. I learned many a lesson during this journey. Although he was quite exhausted and panting for breath, he never took any recreation, but either remained in silence at the back of the carriage, or conversed on spiritual things; and when the hour of meditation in common arrived, he would say, to my shame and confusion, 'My father, let us make our meditation.' When we reached Ponte di Bovino we could not find any steeds, so were obliged to walk to the town of Bovino, and our brother went up that steep hill, which is more than a mile in length, with the utmost patience and without making a single complaint, although he seemed ready to expire at every step. He gave the most heroic examples of virtue whilst we were at St. Mary's of Consolation. His purity was heroic. He has often owned to me that he had never felt a temptation of the flesh in his life. His obedience was heroic likewise. He not only obeyed his superiors, but also his inferiors, even to the cook, when he assisted him in his work; and he exercised these virtues from morning until night. His humility and self-abnegation were also heroic. As to the renunciation of his own will, he had practiced it throughout his life. No less heroic were his conformity to the will of God and his recollection; indeed this latter virtue might be called his favorite virtue. Whether he were walking, eating, or speaking, his union with God was plainly depicted on his countenance; indeed, I think that even when asleep he might have said with the spouse in the Canticles, 'Ego dormio, et cor meum vigilat.' When obedience compelled him to go out, he walked with his arms folded with an air of angelic modesty, which indeed never left him, from morning until night, and he used softly to sing some pious hymn to excite himself to still greater love for and union with God. He captivated the hearts of all who saw him, by his modesty and recollection;

if one merely looked at him, it was enough to cause recollection. He visited the Blessed Sacrament several times a day, and every evening whilst we were saying Office in the choir he used to perform the Way of the Cross.

"His sanctity made the deepest impression on the bishop of Cedogna, and whenever he came to make his retreat with us, he made it a point to have Brother Dominic to serve his Mass. When he left Pagani he was a model of virtue to all the students, as St. Aloysius de Gonzaga and John Berchmans had been before him. He came to Caposele for change of air about six months before his death. When I think of this period, I feel lost in astonishment and confusion, and I know not where to commence the recital of his heroic virtues. From this time, he did nothing but prepare to welcome his Divine Spouse, as if by some secret presentiment of his approaching death. He was always engaged in meditation either in the choir or in the church; he did not stay long at a time, because his superior had forbidden him to do so, but he repeated it very often in the day, so that he seemed always going to or from the choir and church; hovering round the Blessed Sacrament, like a loving butterfly fluttering around the sweet-scented flower. The fathers accused him of this to the superior, who gave him a sharp reprimand, and ordered him not to think of God more than ten times a day for the future; but on one occasion when this youthful saint was with his companions, he inadvertently said that he could not distract himself from the thought of God, upon which his superior saw that the attempt was only injuring his health, and at once withdrew the command. He was exceedingly anxious to go through the religious exercises like the others, but the superiors dispensed him from them, but from the time he got up he was always trying to do as much as obedience permitted. Only two or three days before his death he still came to the choir after vespers to join with the community in making a visit to the Blessed Sacrament. I will not dwell on the heroic virtues he practiced during his long-continued illness, of his submission to his superiors and inferiors, and especially towards the brother infirmarian, whom he obeyed most punctually; of his patience, which prevented his ever uttering the slightest complaint, and of his constant and unabated fervor, which it is so difficult to preserve during illness. In a word, he daily exercised the most eminent virtues, although they were not displayed before the eyes of men. He was known to God alone, for his life was wholly interior and recollected in God. When he expired, I could not refrain from shedding tears of consolation at having seen a saint die; but this joy was soon turned to bitterness when I examined my own life, and saw all its imperfections. I wept much, especially while I was reciting the prayers in the ritual of our holy Church, 'Occurrite angeli Dei,' etc., O my Father! 'ecce quomodo moritur, justus.' I must now conclude: time fails me; it is night, and I am oppressed with sleep, and I have no more paper or ink, etc. I hope you will read this in public for the consolation of all, and I commend myself to your prayers.

"I am your Reverence's most humble and affectionate servant and brother, in union with the Sacred Heart of Mary of Sorrows,

"Bernard Maria,

"Caposele.

"Of the Most Holy Redeemer."

The letter written by our Father D. Paul Cafaro, who was at that time the rector of the house at Caposele, is no less interesting. It was addressed to our most Reverend

Father D. Alphonsus de Liguori, rector-major of the Congregation of the Most Holy Redeemer, and was as follows:

"Nocera of the Pagans.

"Hail, Jesus and Mary!

"In general terms I may say that our Brother Blasucci, of happy memory, was a saint who is worthy to be canonized, and I asserted this more than once while he was still alive. His virtues strike me as being truly heroic, for he was really dead to all passion, so that every virtue seemed naturalized in him. There was such perfect and universal rectitude in all he did, that the greatest saint could not well have surpassed him. But all his excellence proceeded from his thrice heroic conformity to the will of God, from which proceeded his entire indifference to all things, to suffering or joy, to life or death. How many times was I not filled with holy joy during his illness when speaking to him of death!

"Life and death were the same thing to him; but he often told me, when I asked if he would rather live or die, that if he only consulted his own inclinations, he would give the preference to death. Notwithstanding the painful nature of his disease, for he could not take nourishment or swallow the wine which the doctor ordered for him without the most painful efforts, I never saw him give way to the slightest degree of impatience. Recollection, and a constant sense of the presence of God, were habitual with him up to the last moment of his existence. Everyone can render testimony to the brightness of his other virtues, especially those who saw most of him; I have always said and I still repeat, that Brother Blasucci carried conformity to the will of God to the most heroic degree. Yes, conformity to the will of God, and the most entire perfection in all his actions, both interior and exterior, were his special characteristics.

"He communicated daily in the church, except on All Souls' Day, when I made him receive Holy Communion in bed. After this, and while he was making his thanksgiving, (or very shortly afterwards,) he lost his speech, received Extreme Unction, and died amidst all the fathers and brothers, who were filled with consolation by his precious and saintly death. After he had been buried for twenty-eight hours, his head and arms remained so flexible, that it seemed as if he were still alive. I have not time to enter into any further details, for I am on a mission. What I have said however would be enough to canonize Blasucci. I look upon him as a saint, and have kept a piece of his habit as a relic.

"I beg your Reverence to bless me and kiss your hands. I remain

"Your most humble servant and son,
"Paul Cafaro,
"Of the Most Holy Redeemer.

"Vallata, 15th of November, 1752."

SHORT NOTICE ON THE SAME FATHER
By the Rev. Father D. Joseph Landi.

God has been pleased to raise up models of virtue and perfection in our Congregation, not only among the fathers and missionaries, but also among our simple brothers and youthful students.

Amongst these latter may be numbered young Blasucci, who was born of respectable parents at Ruvo, in the diocese of Muro, in the Basilicate, which is a province which belongs to the kingdom of Naples. He was christened Dominic, although it would have been more appropriate to have called him Angel, since his first appearance in the world, his life, and his death resembled those of an angel.

He led a pure and innocent life from his very childhood; he often went to confession and Communion, did not mix with children of his own age, and spent all his time in his studies and devotional exercises. From the time he began to know God, he also began to love and serve Him, and the regularity of his conduct caused everyone to look upon him as a most devout and well-conducted young man. But God wished him to be still more closely united to Him, and that he should imitate the angelic St. Aloysius Gonzaga in his life, conversation, and death. As soon therefore as Blasucci perceived the vanity and illusions of the world, his only desire was to find a place of refuge wherein he might be sheltered from the storms which so often cause those who live in the world to make shipwreck of their faith. As he heard that a new congregation of missionaries had arisen in Holy Church who made special profession of perfection and holiness, and who spent their lives in working out first their own salvation and then that of their neighbor, and when he also saw that even the most hardened and desperate sinners were converted by the frequent missions they gave in the kingdom of Naples, he wished to devote himself to God in the new institute, both for the sake of his own perfection, and also to satisfy the love with which he was inflamed for God, and his zeal for the salvation of the souls of the poor, which were redeemed by the blood of Jesus Christ. As this desire became daily more and more ardent, he earnestly begged our superiors to receive him into the new institute of the Most Holy Redeemer, and he was the more anxious to enter into this community, as it had been approved in the preceding year (1749) by the Sovereign Pontiff Benedict XIV. Upon his reiterated entreaties, the superiors gave him some hopes of being admitted, as they saw the marks of a true vocation to our Congregation in him, and that he was endowed with many excellent qualifications for the life of a missionary; but as they were afraid that his feeble constitution would be unable to bear the great fatigues and hard study which we have to undergo, they would not at once consent to receive him. Dominic however spoke so plausibly, his manners were so engaging, and he reasoned so eloquently on how God would give him all needful strength, that he at length succeeded in moving the superior, and in the year 1750, on the 2nd of February (the feast of the Purification) he was admitted as a novice to the college at Ciorani, where there was then a most flourishing novitiate.

Young Blasucci was seventeen years of age, ten months, and seventeen days at this time. When he was clothed in the habit of the Redemptorists, and found himself among the many angels we had then in the novitiate, his humility caused him to believe that he was so inferior to all, both in respect to science and to virtue, that he even felt a kind of shame in being amongst them. At every instant he feared that his novice-master would send

him away on account of his faults; in order to prevent such
a misfortune, he was most careful in observing the most
minute regulation in the novices' directory, he devoted
himself to the practice of the most prompt and implicit
obedience, and to entire mortification of the senses and to
a life of the most rigorous penance. When his companions
saw the way in which their Brother Blasucci advanced in
the career of virtue with giant's speed, they were filled
with admiration, and not only despaired of ever making
the same progress, but of even following after him at a
distance. His calm and modest demeanor betokened the
love of God which inflamed his soul. His charity, like a
fire, which burns more and more brightly in proportion to
the amount of fuel within its reach, until it at length
enkindles all around it, unceasingly found fresh fuel in the
good dispositions of his soul, and so its sway became more
powerful and extensive from day to day. Our Brother
Blasucci thus followed in the footsteps of the angelic St.
Aloysius, and lived, as it were, in a continual ecstasy, for
he was always recollected and united to his God. He ate so
little, especially at supper, that what he took scarcely
amounted to a few ounces in the day, and he mingled
bitter herbs with what he took, which he pounded and
carried about with him that he might never be without
them. He was as careful in mortifying all his other senses;
he scourged himself to blood, and fasted on all Saturdays
in honor of the Blessed Virgin, although his habitual
temperance was in reality a perpetual fast. In a word, he
was an object of admiration to all who saw him, and he
shone forth amongst the other novices like the sun among
the stars, for he eclipsed even their brightness by the
dazzling splendor of his transcendent virtues. When
strangers came to the house at Ciorani, I especially refer to
those who came to go through the spiritual exercises, they
were quite delighted whenever he read in the refectory or

in the church, and his reading produced more fruit than the sermons of the preacher; indeed some of them would even cast themselves at his feet and kiss them with veneration. His devotion towards the Blessed Sacrament caused him to communicate almost daily, and he made spiritual communions more than a hundred times in the day. As he was so constantly occupied about spiritual things, and as his mind was always recollected as if in the presence of God, it was observed that he soon became very thin and emaciated. This was not paid much attention to at first, however, as it seemed to be only a natural result of his excessive fervor.

At the expiration of the year's novitiate, he pronounced his vows according to the rule of our institute, on the 2nd of February, 1751, before Father D. Xavier Rossi, by the command of our most reverend father rector-major. He had ardently longed for this happy moment to arrive, and every instant which separated him from it seemed an age, so ardently did he desire to become closely united to his God. He began to study with the others as soon as he left the novitiate, but his first fervor did not therefore suffer any relaxation. He continued to practice all the devotional exercises he had been accustomed to as a novice; he was always recollected in the presence of God, and he did not diminish any of his macerations and penances, so that in a little time he was attacked by consumption, which brought him to the portals of the tomb. When his superiors discovered what was the matter with him by his difficulty in walking and wasted appearance, they immediately forbade him to apply closely to anything; and in order to prevent the continual tension of his mind, caused by the way in which it was always fixed on God, they enjoined him never to make a voluntary act of the presence of God, nay, they even gave him amusing books to read, and required him to give an account of their contents. But all was of no avail, for God drew him more closely to Himself day by day. He was sent into another house for change of air, but this was equally unsuccessful; he was then made to accompany the fathers when they went on missions, but the only effect which this produced was, that he converted more sinners by his modest and recollected appearance, than the preachers could succeed in doing by their sermons. I remember that on one of these missions at Langhusi, our Father D. Blaise Amarante made him kneel in the middle of the church whilst he was in the confessional, and if he met with any hardened and obdurate sinners who would not repent, he said to them, "Go and look at that saintly young man, see how modestly he kneels there, and then return here again." And when these sinners saw this angel in human shape, kneeling motionless and still before the Blessed Sacrament, and perhaps also through the efficacy of his prayers, they returned to his feet full of repentance and compunction,

His superiors thus did all they could to restore him to health for upwards of two years, sometimes sending him to one house, sometimes to another, sometimes causing him to apply to study, and at other times procuring him innocent diversions; but all was in vain; he grew worse instead of better, and no doubts could any longer be entertained that he was in a consumption. For the edification of the house at Caposele, Providence ordained that he should be in it when he became too ill to go about anymore, and was obliged to keep his bed, and be under obedience to the doctor and infirmarian. He was most exact in obeying their most minute directions in all things during his last sickness, and as he knew that he would soon be admitted into the presence of the God whom he adored, he appeared more recollected than ever, and as if he were in an ecstasy of love. His thoughts were of God alone, and he never spoke of anything but of God and heaven.

At length the hour of his rest drew nigh. After he had received all the last sacraments, he gently expired with his crucifix in his hand, and reposing in full confidence in the arms of his dear Mother Mary, on the 2nd of November, 1752, in the twenty-first year of his age. Shortly before this he had succeeded in getting his brother D. Peter Paul Blasucci to enter the Congregation by his prayers to God, and by his persuasive words and letters, which made him say in his last moments, "I die in peace, now that my brother has entered the Congregation." He had indeed much reason to rejoice at it, for he afterwards became the founder of the house of Girgenti in Sicily, and has always been distinguished amongst us for his learning and piety.

Scarcely had Dominic expired, ere crowds of persons flocked to the house to venerate his precious remains, and to recommend themselves to his prayers; no one for a moment doubted that he was already in heaven, and everyone felt happy in being able to obtain possession of anything which had belonged to him. He led the life of an angel, and died with the innocence of a pure spirit; and we hope a time will come when God will glorify His servant throughout the whole Church, if such be in conformity to His blessed will.

The Life of
GERARD MAJELLA
Lay-Brother of the Congregation of the
Most Holy Redeemer

The life of
GERARD MAJELLA
Lay-Brother of the Congregation of the Most Holy Redeemer

By Father Tannoja

Preface

UR BROTHER GERARD would have been honored as a saint long ere this, had not the poverty of our Congregation prevented our being able to introduce the process of his canonization. For his admirable life, and the numerous miracles he wrought during his life and after his death, prevent there being any doubt of our success had we been able to commence it. It was by a fresh prodigy that I was led to compose this little work. Its composition was at first undertaken by Father Cajone, the consultor-general and rector of the house at Caposele, but as he had not time to arrange the materials he had collected together, the undertaking was confided to me; but I also was too busy to finish it. It was to Brother Gerard himself that our readers are indebted for this sketch of his life; and it was brought about in the following manner. On the 26th of August, 1786, I was attacked by a dangerous illness, at St. Angelo of the Lombards, and I went in a state of great suffering to our house at Caposele, where this saintly brother died. I grew worse and worse, when Father D. Januarius Orlando suggested to me to promise Brother

Gerard to write his Life, assuring me that if I did so he would cure me. This happened on the 9th of September. Want of faith caused me to neglect this pious proposition; but when the last struggles, and chill perspiration of death came on the next morning, and I felt that my agony was at hand, I remembered the advice I had received the preceding evening, and addressing our blessed brother with faith, I said, "Brother Gerard, come to my assistance." No sooner had I pronounced these words than a complete change came over me. All my pains left me, and I instantly began to compose this recital of his virtues and of the supernatural graces with which God endowed him. May this blessed brother deign to receive this as a slight tribute of my gratitude. I also offer it in a special manner to the lay-brothers of our Congregation, to whom Brother Gerard is a perfect model. They will learn from him that they ought to unite the activity of Martha to the contemplation of Mary, and will see that they too may become saints amidst their numerous labors, if they will offer them to God, sanctify them by prayer, and strive to attain the perfection of their state with sincerity and ardor.

The above are the words of the author. We are happy to be able to add that several testimonies to the sanctity and miracles of Brother Gerard are to be found in the process of the beatification of our saintly founder, and that after the feast of the beatification of St. Alphonsus, which took place on the 15th of September, 1816, the cause of his illustrious disciple was brought before the Sacred Congregation of Rites. There is every reason to hope that it will be shortly brought to an equally happy conclusion, by the generosity of the friends of religion, and by the exertions of the rector of the house at Caposele, who took a prominent part in the management of this affair.

Part I

CHAPTER I

Birth of Brother Gerard Majella; His Infancy and Favors
He Received from God.

BROTHER GERARD was born at Muro on the 6th of April, 1726. His father was a tailor, by name Dominic Majella; his mother was called Benedicta Galella. They both gained their bread by their daily labor, and were distinguished for their great probity, and brought up their children in the fear and love of God. However, Gerard needed no outward training to cause him to lead a life of virtue, for the Spirit of God assisted and guided him interiorly. He was pious from his very infancy, and never entered into the ordinary amusements of a child. He spent his time during his most youthful days in a hundred practices of devotion. His sisters Anne and Bridget have told us that his only recreation consisted in making little altars, and in imitating the ceremonies he had seen used by priests. D. Alexander Piccolo, a goldsmith at Muro, also says that he arranged divers images of saints on a table, in the middle of which he placed one of St. Michael, and that he used to make little candles out of fragments of wax and burned them in their honor. His great delight consisted in honoring them. He walked up and down before them, making divers inclinations to them, after which he would kneel down and remain there striking his breast. Although he was then apparently too young to understand the meaning of what he did, his conduct was so full of devotion that it excited the admiration of all present. Gerard's childhood also afforded striking proofs that God delights to converse with the sons of men. There are several churches in the neighborhood of the town of Muro which are dedicated to the Blessed Mother of God. In one of them there is a statue, in which she is depicted with the Infant Savior in her arms, which is held in great honor. Once when young Gerard accidentally entered this church, the Infant Jesus went to meet him and gave him a little loaf of very white bread. Gerard was quite joyful at such a gift, and carried it home and showed it to his mother. When asked where he had got it, he replied that a child had given it to him. As his mother only supposed he had received it from some gentleman's son she asked no further questions. As Gerard was attracted by the heavenly graces of the Holy Child, he often went to the same church, and on every occasion the Divine Infant came to play with him, and made him a present of a similar loaf. At a later period, after he had entered the Congregation, his sister Bridget came to see him one day at Caposele, and he said to her with his usual simplicity, "I now perceive that it was the Infant Jesus, and not an ordinary child, who gave me those little rolls." "Well then," replied his sister laughingly, "come back to Muro someday, that you may find the Child again, and get some more bread." "I can now find Him wherever I wish and in all places," replied Gerard.

The favors he received from God were not confined to this however. One day when he was assisting at Mass when he was about seven years old, he went up to the altar, when he saw those around him going to communion, that he too might receive this divine Sacrament. He was much afflicted at being rejected by the celebrant; but as God had determined to be specially united to the soul of Gerard, He found an effectual means of consoling him, for on the following night the glorious St. Michael appeared to him and gave him Holy Communion. Such a signal favor would have remained unknown if Gerard's holy simplicity had not led him to reveal it to D. Alexander Piccolo, the goldsmith, who was his godfather, and to Catherine Zaccardi, his nurse. He also mentioned it to his director after he joined us. This was the origin of the great devotion which this holy brother entertained throughout his life for St. Michael the archangel.

He was sent to school to learn the rudiments of knowledge, and was soon able to read and write and express himself with facility, for he spent all his time there in striving to improve himself. He never liked to enter into the amusements of his companions, but was at all times quiet, silent, and devout. When he was in church, he had the composed and recollected appearance of a grown man, rather than that of a child. He assisted at Mass with great devotion, and at the elevation he used to prostrate himself on the ground and remain thus for some time afterwards. Indeed, his recollection and gravity, and extreme devotion towards this divine sacrament, caused him to be allowed to receive Holy Communion when he was still very young, and he was soon afterwards permitted to do so several times a week. His sisters have told us that, from the time he was nine years of age, he used to discipline himself several times a day, especially after Holy Communion, with knotted cords, which he had tied together. Such was the childhood of Gerard Majella.

CHAPTER II
On the Sufferings Gerard Had to Endure; His Tenderness Towards the Poor; His Devotion and Abstinence.

As Gerard was old enough to work for his bread when his father died, he apprenticed himself to a tailor, that he might learn this business; but whilst he worked hard, he never neglected carefully to correspond to the interior operations of grace in his heart. From time to time, he became ravished into an ecstasy, and would sometimes hide himself under the table, and pour forth his heart before God in loving aspirations. The foreman however was so enraged at all this, that he once dragged him from the spot where he was praying, scolded him for neglecting his work, and struck him into the bargain. Gerard was so far from losing patience, that he only replied by a sweet smile. This made the man fancy he was making game of him. He became still more angry, and said, "What, do you only laugh?" accompanying the words with several blows from a piece of iron which he seized in his fury. Gerard did not even then lose his habitual patience and sweetness, he only threw himself at his feet, and said, "I forgive you for the love of Jesus Christ;" after which he resumed his work without making the least complaint of what had happened to his master, who was very fond of him.

After he had learned his trade and begun to work on his own account, he strove much less to procure a good maintenance for himself than to obtain money to relieve the poor. Their very appearance affected him greatly; he therefore only spent a small portion of his gains on himself, and generously distributed the remainder amongst them on feast days. He often even went without food that he might be able to assist those in distress. He was also most anxious to assist the souls in purgatory; and he often had masses celebrated for them. One week when he made eight crowns, he devoted them all to this holy end, although he was in consequence obliged to eat nothing but a little dry bread himself. He used to say, "They are very poor, and call on us to help them with much earnestness." He was in the greatest distress when business failed, for he was then unable to assist these poor souls. I must here mention an admirable instance of his charity, as it occurred at this period of his life. It so happened that he went to visit his uncle, Brother Bonaventure of Muro, who was a religious amongst the Capuchin Fathers at St. Menna. On seeing how miserably Gerard was dressed, he bought him a great coat; but as he met a poor man all in rags as he was coming out of the convent, he took compassion on him, and he immediately took off the coat and gave it to him. His uncle was much displeased with him for it, and gave him a severe reprimand. Gerard bore the rebuke in silence, and all that he alleged in his defense was, "I gave it to one who needed it more than myself."

When he grew older he never forgot the dear church of St. Mary. Whenever he could spare time, therefore, he used to repair thither with holy ardor, and he would sometimes remain there for two or three days at a time in a kind of retreat, taking no other nourishment than a bit of bread, and enjoying no other rest for his wearied limbs than that which was afforded by the bare ground. This church was a perfect Paradise to him, and he often spent part of the night in it in fervent prayer. At other times he scourged himself most cruelly. We know not all that passed between him and the Blessed Virgin during these retreats, but we do know that he enjoyed celestial peace within its hallowed walls, and found delight in there conversing with God and the Blessed Virgin.

He practiced the greatest mortification of the taste even whilst he was in the world. Eugenia Pasquali, the wife of D. Alexander Piccolo, the goldsmith, says that he practiced this virtue to such a heroic degree, that his existence seemed a constant miracle. She declares that he fasted almost every day, and that when he was pressed to eat, he excused himself by saying that he was not hungry. When he was obliged to accept of some nourishment, he usually gave it all away to the first poor person he met. On one occasion, amongst others, when he had eaten nothing for three days, (his mother attested this fact with many tears,) D. Eugenia sent for him to get him to take something; Gerard replied, "I have no appetite." And this was not to be wondered at, for on searching his pocket she found several roots there, and on asking him what they were for, he replied, "By eating them one loses all sense of hunger."

CHAPTER III

On the Love which Gerard Bore Towards the Passion of Jesus Christ, and Towards the Adorable Sacrament; Snares Which the Devil Lays for Him.

The passion and death of Christ made the most vivid impression on Gerard's heart, even at this early period. It is the nature of love to be incessantly in motion, and never to be at rest until it becomes conformed to the object of its affections. And so it was with this fervent servant of God, who, in contemplating the torments suffered by Jesus Christ, was not satisfied until he became conformed to His likeness. What most affected him in contemplating the passion, was to see the way in which our Blessed Savior was reviled as one beside Himself. He therefore resolved to simulate madness, that he might share in His humiliation. This attempt cost him dear; for the children in the streets not only pursued him with their cries, and cast mud in his face, but threw stones at him. Some young men went so far as to bind him with cords and drag him about the streets. He bore all these injuries with joy, saying, "This is little to endure through love for Jesus Christ, who made Himself of no reputation for my sake." He gave up these practices however in obedience to his confessor, who prohibited him to go on with them.

This fervent young man fell into another excess

through his love towards the suffering Jesus. When he contemplated how He had been scourged, he wished to undergo the same torment. Felix Farenga, who was Gerard's confidant, affirms that he several times tied him to a post at his urgent request, and then scourged his bare shoulders with a wet and knotted rope. Gerard endured all this pain with gladness of heart, and if his friend became anxious to desist, he besought him to go on, until his back at length became one wound, and the blood gushed forth in all directions.

He had another expedient for self-torture; indeed it seemed as if he wished to supply in his own person what was wanting in the passion of our Blessed Redeemer. He caused himself to be suspended from a beam with his head downwards, and ordered old rags steeped in water to be burned underneath. The torment he inflicted on himself must have been excessive, but Gerard only said, "We must suffer, if we wish to please Jesus Christ, who has suffered so much for us."

He had no less tenderness towards Jesus in the adorable Sacrament. His love for the Infant Jesus caused him at first to resort to the church of the Blessed Virgin, of which we have already spoken; but as the Blessed Sacrament was not kept there, he afterwards preferred to go to the cathedral, and whenever he had any spare time he used to go there and prostrate himself before the altar. As he had not time fully to satisfy his pious desires during the day, having to spend part of them in laboring for his bread, he made up for this during the night. As the sacristan of the cathedral was related to him, he willingly consigned the church keys to him, and Gerard used to delight in spending the night there, and in pouring out his soul before the Blessed Sacrament in fervent aspirations of love; he used also to take the discipline there, that he might thus make some reparation for the outrages which are offered to Jesus, especially during the night. When business prevented him from thus fully satisfying his pious desires, he would at least go to the church long before daybreak, receive Holy Communion, and assist at several masses, after which he went away with great reluctance.

The loving intercourse which Gerard held with Jesus in the adorable Sacrament could not fail to be most displeasing to the powers of darkness. In order to make him desist from this holy exercise, the devil one morning presented himself to him when he was opening the door, under the semblance of a fierce dog ready to tear him to pieces. The pious Gerard was in no ways alarmed, and the phantom instantly disappeared on his making the sign of the cross. One night too, when he was kneeling at the foot of the tabernacle, one of the two large wooden angels on the altar fell down on him and wounded him; I know not whether this is to be viewed as an accidental occurrence or not, Gerard, however, had no doubt that it was the work of the evil one. A great many other snares were also laid for him by the devil during the nights he spent in the cathedral.

We have already said that his love for the Blessed Virgin was truly extraordinary. He could think of nothing else on her various feast days, and when he knelt down before one of her images or at one of her altars, he could not tear himself away. He was in the habit of saying, "The Madonna has ravished my heart, and I have willingly yielded it up to her." Once when one of the feasts of the Blessed Virgin was celebrated at Muro, and when her statue was exposed, after Gerard had been kneeling before it for some time, he arose with an inflamed countenance and placed a ring on her finger before a multitude of people; by this act he said he meant to affiance his purity to that of the Blessed Virgin. When marriage was proposed to him, as it sometimes was in a jesting manner, he would enthusiastically exclaim, "I am already married, I am wedded to the Madonna;" and he was so faithful to her, that the lily of his purity shone with its original whiteness up to the hour of his death, and the robe of his baptismal innocence remained unsullied by any spot or stain, for he had never committed a willful sin throughout his whole life.

CHAPTER IV

Gerard Enters into the Service of a Bishop; His Conduct Affords Rare Instances of Humility and Patience.

As Gerard's desire to become conformed to the likeness of Jesus Christ grew more and more ardent, he neglected nothing by which he might become assimilated to His likeness. When he remembered that He had become a servant for our love, he wished to resemble Him in this respect also; for this reason he was submissive to all, and rejoiced in every occasion of humiliation. To obtain these he entered into the service of a bishop, which furnished him with many opportunities of self-denial, for he had such an impatient temper, and it was so hard to bear with his various humors, that no servant would stay even a month with him. Gerard had therefore to endure complaints, scoldings, reproaches, humiliations, excessive labors, and threats of being sent away; but he rejoiced at these sufferings, for he thought that they would make him pleasing to Jesus Christ, who humbled Himself and took upon Him the form of a servant for our sake.

The way in which he was treated excited general compassion, and people marveled how he could go on bearing it. D. Cæsar Peloso said, "While I was in the house of this said bishop on some business, for I was agent to the family of the Orsini, I never ceased admiring his exceeding patience." The same thing was also said by the archdeacon, chanter, and head canon of the cathedral. They said that his silence and humility during the most severe and unjust corrections, and his serene and modest air while receiving them, showed that Christian patience must have taken deep root in his heart, and that from this time everyone looked upon him as a saint. They add, that besides all the bad treatment he received from this prelate, Gerard had also to endure many bodily pains and infirmities at the same time, and yet he was never heard to utter the least complaint, or known to shrink from labor, and he always appeared cheerful, contented, and obedient. During this time he never omitted to practice his daily mortifications. Doctor Dominic Lamorté relates, that one day when he was looking pale and ill, he asked him what was the matter, Gerard quickly replied, "I am very well." As the doctor did not believe this, he began to examine his chest, and found that he had on a rough hairshirt. He was kind to everybody, but especially towards the poor, for whom he felt a particular degree of tenderness. In fact, he hated nothing but himself. His ordinary food consisted in bread and garlic. A plate of vegetables was a magnificent feast to him. If any more savory food than usual were bestowed on him, he gave it away to some poor sick person.

Whilst he was in the service of this bishop, everyone admired the great modesty of his countenance when he went into the town and his recollected demeanor in church. The above-named canons also attest that he sometimes knelt motionless before the Blessed Sacrament for whole hours at a time. When he was not in the palace he was always to be found adoring Jesus in the adorable Sacrament. His example made such an impression, and his advice was so efficacious, that many persons were thus led to repair to the church, and to pay their homage to Jesus in the tabernacle wherein He is imprisoned by His love.

Many celestial favors accompanied the familiar intercourses which Gerard held with his God, and He granted him whatever he asked for. On one occasion a key which he had placed on the edge of a cistern fell into it. As he knew how much its loss would annoy the prelate, he armed himself with holy confidence, and taking an image of the Holy Child, he let it down into the well by means of a cord, saying, "You must recover this, to prevent his Lordship sinning by impatience." And wonderful to relate, when he drew the image of the Child out, it held the key in its hands.

Gerard remained in the service of this prelate for about three years, during which he filled the offices of both valet-de-chambre and cook, so great was the bishop's poverty. He gladly embraced every species of labor, in fact he did all the work of the house. He was so satisfied with his most painful lot that he did not drag his cross, but carried it joyfully and with all his heart; indeed he was so eager for suffering, that nothing but the death of the bishop would have caused him to leave him.

CHAPTER V

Gerard Resolved to Lead an Eremetical Life; His Vocation to the Congregation of the Most Holy Redeemer.

Gerard retired to Muro after the death of the bishop. As he felt a great distaste to leading a secular life, he thought of retiring among the Capuchin Fathers. As he was not able to carry this wish into effect, he resolved to lead a penitential life in some solitary spot. He did not, however, intend to attach himself to any particular church, and to go about the neighborhood begging for his subsistence, as hermits usually do, but retire to the declivity of some mountain and live in the woods, entirely separated from all intercourse with the world, like one of the anchorites of old. He communicated his project to a fervent young man who offered to follow him, but he was the only person who was aware of his intentions.

The plan which Gerard devised on this occasion, and the rule of life which they were to follow together, are enough to fill every mind with astonishment. It was divided into several portions, consisting of different exercises of piety, labors, meditations, and bodily austerities. As they wished to ascertain if they could bear such a severe mode of life, they resolved to begin by trying how far their strength would go. As they knew that the ancient hermits ate nothing but herbs and roots, they resolved to imitate them closely. They did so for three or four days, and would have continued the experiment for a whole week, but their pallid faces betrayed their attempt, and caused them to be compelled to abandon their project.

Gerard was about twenty-two years of age at this time. His design of becoming a hermit was frustrated because it was not the will of God, but it was His will that he should become a lay-brother in our Congregation, so He facilitated his entrance into it. It so happened that D. Francis Garzilli, who was one of our fathers, went to Muro in the August of 1745, with a circular letter from the Archbishop of Conza, ordering a collection to be made in aid of the building of our house at Caposele. Although he knew nothing about our institute previously, from the time Gerard first saw Father Garzilli and the lay-brother who accompanied him, he felt impelled to frequent their society. He questioned the brother as to our way of living, and the penances in use amongst us, and confided to him that he wished to join us as a lay-brother. He replied that our Congregation would not suit him, for that the rule was one of great severity, and the mode of life one of great suffering. To this Gerard joyfully replied, "That is just what I should like." From this time he became most anxious to join us, although he did not then think it expedient to tell Father Garzilli of his wishes.

Through the wise decrees of Providence, matters were so arranged that our fathers went to give a mission at Muro in the following year. This new conjuncture increased the fervor of Gerard's pious desires, and he became so attached to our fathers that he scarcely ever left our house. He then thought it time to manifest his designs to Father Cafaro the superior; but he looked so thin and weak, that he did not think he would be able to fulfill the duties of a lay-brother, and sent him away. The pious suppliant was not discouraged by this refusal, but continued his entreaties; and he had such a firm confidence in God, who called him to enter religion, that he felt sure that he would obtain the favor he so ardently desired.

When his resolution became known, he met with the greatest opposition, especially from his mother and sisters. The following curious scene happened between Gerard and his mother at this time. As the tragedy of the life and death of Jesus Christ were represented at Muro at this season, he was chosen to represent the crucified Jesus. When the cathedral doors were thrown open he appeared fastened on a cross, as if he had just expired in the agonies of death. Although this was a mere representation, it deeply affected all who beheld it. His mother was amongst this number, for when the poor woman saw her son pierced with a lance she fainted away, as if it had been a reality, and it was some time ere she recovered her senses. On finding that Gerard's design of leaving the world remained immovable, his poor mother cast herself at his feet, and as the most moving argument she could use, said, "My son, I conjure you not to cause me this pain by the sword of sorrow which pierced my heart when I saw you transfixed on the cross." The good brother used to relate this anecdote for our amusement during recreation.

When the mission was over, Father Cafaro and his companions set out to give the mission at Rionero. Although Gerard had been rejected, he did not become discouraged. "If they will not take me in," said he, "I will stand with the poor and beg my bread at their door." His mother and sisters did all they could to dissuade him, and never lost sight of him for a moment. As he did not know how else to escape from their watchful vigilance, Gerard secretly got out of a window, leaving a note behind, saying that he had gone away to become a saint, and that they must not think of him anymore.

When Father Cafaro found that Gerard meant to follow him about from place to place, he rebuked him, and tried to persuade him that the Congregation would not suit him. All the fathers were of the same opinion. "Try me," replied Gerard, "and then dismiss me;" and he followed them to Rionero. His firmness was so great, that it at length succeeded in moving Father Cafaro, who consented to send him to the house at Iliceto, rather however for the sake of getting rid of him, than from a wish to receive him. This then was the manner in which Gerard Majella was admitted into the Congregation.

Chapter VI

Narration of Brother Gerard's Virtues While He was in the House at Iliceto.

After Gerard's prayer had been granted, every moment seemed an age to him until he reached our house. He was delighted to find that it was dedicated to our Blessed Lady of Consolation. No sooner had he reached it, than he went to the altar of our Blessed Lady, and protested to her that he meant to live under her protection, and to die in the house which was thus dedicated to her. He wept for very joy, and never could thank God and the Blessed Virgin sufficiently for the great favor they had conferred upon him.

When Father Cafaro returned to Iliceto, instead of finding that Gerard was quite useless, as he had at first imagined, he was surprised to hear all the fathers and brothers uniting in praising his quickness, his diligence, exemplary conduct, recollected demeanor, and prompt obedience. In fact, he gave such general satisfaction that none of the fathers could oppose his reception, and Gerard Majella was therefore numbered amongst our lay-brothers.

Gerard immediately placed himself under the direction of Father Cafaro, who soon perceived that God manifested Himself to him in an extraordinary manner. One day, amongst others, when different theological and ascetical questions were being discussed, Gerard joined in the conversation, and spoke with so much accuracy that he excited the admiration of all who heard him. Father Cafaro was in the habit of proposing questions of various kinds to the brothers; and whenever they were at a loss what to say, Gerard always replied with theological exactness. This sufficed to cause his real worth to become known, and he was soon esteemed among us as highly as he deserved to be.

The life he led in the world was admirable, but that which he led amongst us was far more so. For well did he know how to unite the labors of Martha with the holy repose of Mary. The brothers declare that he did the work of four men, and that he would often labor in their stead, saying, in a cheerful tone, "Go away, and leave me to do that, for I am the youngest." The most servile occupations were the objects of his predilection, and he not only performed them when ordered to do so, but he sought for them and embraced them of his own accord. He was fond of every kind of labor, provided it were sufficiently abject. Thus he really took pleasure in cleaning out the stable, and in performing the most repulsive offices which were required in the house. In fact, fatigue was his beloved spouse, and it grieved him to be deprived of it.

Labor did not interfere however with Gerard's love for meditation, for though he worked hard during the day, he retired to the church at night, and remained in prayer before the Blessed Sacrament, shedding abundance of tears. As he longed to do more than he was enjoined to do by the rule, he made up for this pious want during the night, so that he was to be found in the morning in the very spot where he had placed himself the evening before. And besides this, every moment of his time was spent in meditation; for however distracting the nature of his charges might be, he was always recollected and in the presence of God. His ejaculatory prayers were frequent and like darts of fire. Jesus and Mary were ever in his heart and on his lips, and he was sometimes so absorbed in God that he would stop short in the middle of what he was doing in a kind of ecstasy. He was no novice in the school of Divine love, and this was gradually discovered by the ecstasies and raptures with which he was favored by Heaven. One day some strangers who were going to dinner perceived Gerard in an ecstasy before an image of Mary Immaculate, which was facing the staircase.

He was so sensibly affected by the passion of Christ, that he used to faint when he contemplated a representation of it. Once when there were several candidates for ordination in the house, Gerard was ordered to clean the refectory. Whilst he was thus engaged, another lay-brother came in and found him kneeling before a picture of the "ECC homo," ravished out of himself, with extended arms, holding a fork in one hand and a plate in another. As the brother who found him in this state did not understand this mystery, he ran to call Father Cafaro, who commanded Gerard to come to himself, which he immediately did, and then resumed his work. He was once sent to Melfi to attend Father D. Stephen Liguori, and two of our other fathers who were taking the mineral waters. One day while he was there, Father Liguori began to play and sing Metastasio's well-known air, "If thou wilt find God," etc., upon which he fell into a transport of love, seized on Father Liguori, and danced about with him during his ecstasy, holding him tightly in his arms and carrying him from place to place without the least difficulty, to the great astonishment of all present.

About this time, Gerard one day went to visit Canon D. Leonard Rossi, who purposely turned the conversation on the infinite perfections of God. No sooner had Gerard begun to contemplate them, than he fell into an ecstasy, consumed as it were with the flames of Divine love. As the canon divined the cause, he cooled his breast with cold water, which restored his consciousness, and the brother immediately went away much disconcerted at having been thus discovered. To meditation Gerard united a holy hatred of himself. The instruments wherewith he crucified his flesh were appalling even to look at. The discipline which he used so often and unrelentingly was furnished with twelve steel stars, and with numerous long and sharp points; he used also to scourge himself twice a day with knotted cords, which caused such a great effusion of blood, that his flesh was always covered with wounds, but in common he generally used the former, and he did so with such severity that the place where he took it was watered with his blood.

He made constant use of haircloth round his body, wore sharp-pointed chains round his legs and arms, and daily crucified his body by other cruel instruments of penance. Jesus Crucified was the book which was continually in his hands, and the more he studied it, the more severe did he become towards his own body.

He was at all times most rigorous in mortifying his appetite. He did not take as much as two ounces of bread a day; and if he were obliged to eat the little which was served up at dinner, he took care to season it with aloes and centaury. He used to say, "The love of God cannot exist in a soul if the body be well fed." He seemed to be quite absorbed in God during dinner; he often remained without eating, holding a morsel of bread in his hand, with his eyes bathed in tears in a complete ecstasy. Fathers Januarius Rendina, Francis Juvenal, and Gaspar Cajone, who watched him more narrowly than the others, render their testimony to the same thing.

I cannot here omit to mention an instance of patience which Gerard gave in this house, and which I witnessed myself when I was only a student. A young father, who was afterwards expelled by Alphonsus, was left alone in the house, and therefore became the superior of the brothers; now as he was severe by nature, and had an aversion to Gerard, he could do nothing, indeed he could scarcely even breathe, without this irascible father finding something to complain of. His corrections were harsh and frequent, and his penances were severe; yet Gerard bore them with unruffled patience, never giving way to the least complaint, and never manifesting the slightest repugnance to any order he might receive. He was often obliged to fast on bread and water, and amongst other things, he was enjoined to draw his tongue along the pavement several times a day, or else to make from twenty to thirty crosses of a palm's length with it. This good brother's tongue was quite torn by this, and the pavement was watered by the consequent effusion of blood. This exercise lasted for a month. The other brothers and myself who witnessed this spectacle, felt the greatest admiration for this constancy in suffering, and from that time we began to say, "Brother Gerard is a great saint."

CHAPTER VII
On the pains which Gerard Took to Participate in the Sufferings of Jesus Christ.

When Gerard left the world and entered the Congregation, he brought with him all the instruments which he had invented, that he might imitate the sufferings of Jesus, and become assimilated to His passion. He even redoubled those macerations after he joined us, to which he had been incited in the world by the contemplation of Jesus crucified.

The house which we had at Iliceto is that in which the reform was commenced which the Blessed Felix of Corsaro, of the Congregation of St. John of Carbonara, undertook in the territory of la Pouille. The grotto which this blessed reformer then inhabited is at the foot of this convent, and here it was that Brother Gerard practiced his severest penances. His ardent desires were seconded by a man whom he had converted and in whom he placed great confidence, and by a youth of Lacedogna, named Andrew Longarello, who was anxious to become a lay-brother; for while Gerard acted the part of a victim, they served as his executioners.

As he wanted to imitate the flagellation of Jesus Christ, as he had done at Muro, he caused them to tie his hands together, and was fastened to a beam; after which he made them strike his shoulders with knotted ropes, until the blood gushed forth in all directions and his body was a mass of wounds. As he also wished to imitate the crowning of thorns, he placed a crown of sharp thorns on his head, after the flagellation had ended, and persuaded them to beat them into his head by the blows of a hammer. It is easy to imagine what pain he must then have endured; as a number of these thorns went into his head, the blood flowed in streams, and poor Gerard suffered the most acute torture. He even resolved to imitate the crucifixion of Jesus. He therefore caused himself to be fastened to one of the crosses destined for the calvaries which are erected near the churches during missions; and as he had read in the "Year of Sorrows," that the hands and feet of Jesus did not reach the holes which had been made for the nails until the executioners drew them thither by main force, he determined to share in this suffering also, and had his limbs. stretched until his bones were dislocated. Whilst thus extended on the cross, he caused the crown of thorns, of which we have already spoken, to be placed on his head. This has been affirmed to our Father D. Juvenal by several witnesses. Father Andrew Longarello, lately deceased, has assured me of the same thing. Brother Gerard went on with these tortures for a great part of the time he was at Iliceto, and only left them off in obedience to the commands of Father Cafaro.

All Fridays, as being consecrated to the thought of the passion of Jesus Christ, and specially on those in the month of March, were days of suffering to Brother Gerard, and he tormented himself on them by the use of thistles, chains, disciplines to blood, watchings, and every other mode of penance. He either abstained from all food or took nothing but bread and water on these days, and that he either partook of on his knees or seated on the ground. Holy Week, however, was the season when his sufferings were the greatest; he then seemed like one in his agony, in whom life was nearly extinct; and when our Blessed Lord's entombment is commemorated, he seemed to be buried with Him. Jesus Christ died for me," said he, "and ought not I to die for Him who gave His life to save me?"

This ardent longing for suffering and desire to participate in the sufferings of Jesus Christ was so pleasing to God, that He deigned to grant the prayer of this holy brother, and to favor him with a grace which He only bestowed on a few of His servants, such as a St. Francis of Assisi, and a St. Catherine of Sienna, who experienced in themselves the sufferings endured by Jesus Christ in His passion. Although he appeared to be strong and well on the preceding days, no sooner had the night of Good Friday arrived than he became quite oppressed, as if weighed down with suffering, and his strength forsook him so completely that he seemed as if he were dying. He often spit blood copiously at this season, and his interior sufferings and desolation of spirit were so great then, that he told his directors that they were past description; yet he was quite himself by the night of Holy Saturday, and able to perform all his accustomed duties.

CHAPTER VIII
Ecstasies of Gerard on the Feasts of Our Blessed Lord and of the Holy Virgin; His Anxiety to Cause Them to be Honored by Others.

If the days which are consecrated to the passion of Jesus Christ were days of sorrow to Gerard, it was not so during those glorious seasons which holy Church celebrates by hymns of gladness; he was so full of joy on these days that he communicated it to others. He never failed to get the superior to bestow a double recreation on the community when they occurred. He was in a perfect transport of joy during the Christmas holidays. The arrangement of the crib was entrusted to him, and he strove to adorn the church as beautifully as possible. He prepared for this feast by a novena, which he performed with indescribable fervor; he ate little during its continuance and slept still less, and spent the whole of the last night in praying in the church or in scourging himself in his own room.

What were not his transports of love during the feast of Corpus Christi! The whole octave was a time of jubilee to him. Jesus in the tabernacle was to him as a Lover who absorbed his whole heart. When the blessed Sacrament was exposed to the veneration of the Faithful, he was, as it were, beside himself, and it sometimes even caused him to faint away. It was a touching spectacle to see the struggles which sometimes took place within him in consequence of his love for Jesus Christ and his spirit of obedience, which, however, always had the mastery. Once when I was in the church, but in a place where he could not perceive me, he got up and knelt down before the blessed Sacrament; he then seemed to be struggling to get up; after which, feeling unable to do so, he exclaimed with a loud voice, "Let me go, for I have something to do elsewhere!" After these words, he hastily retired, as if he were tearing himself away from the presence of Jesus Christ by main force.

He made the greatest exertions wherever he went to excite men to visit the Blessed Sacrament. It grieved him to see the churches empty, and public places thronged with people. It was to him that the inhabitants of several districts were indebted for their present assiduity in visiting the Blessed Sacrament. He not only excited many families to frequent communion, but entire populations. The ample privileges which Father Francis Pepe, a celebrated Jesuit, obtained for the distribution of indulgences from his Holiness Benedict XIV., are well known. As Gerard wished to promote frequent communion, he obtained from him a plenary indulgence for all who should communicate every eight days, by the intervention of our Father Margotta. He by this means caused many thousands of souls to be filled with love for Jesus in the Blessed Sacrament, so that Fathers Juvenal and Cajone own that a hundred sermons would not have produced so much good.

He was no less zealous in honoring the Blessed Virgin. He was eager for her feast days to come round, and took the utmost pains in adorning her altars, and instituting processions in her honor, always striving to cause their effect to be increased by discharges of cannon and fireworks. His devotion to the Immaculate Conception was most remarkable, and the greatest portion of the miraculous medals which Father Pepe distributed at Naples passed through his hands. He wished everyone to fast at least on all Saturdays and on the vigils of the feasts of the Blessed Virgin; he used then himself to fast on bread and water, and took the discipline to blood. He always practiced abstinence during her novenas, as well as self-macerations and other good works, and whenever he could he passed the night before the feast in presence of the Blessed Virgin and of Jesus in the adorable Eucharist.

Mary was not insensible to this intense love. We know not all the favors she granted him, but through the attestation of Fathers Petrella, Juvenal, and Cajone, we know that she appeared to him one night in the church, and enriched him with every grace.

Whilst the contemplation of Jesus Christ ravished him into ecstasy, the consideration of the glories of Mary caused him to be absorbed in love. One day when he was at Foggia, in the house of D. Gaetan Sabatelli the priest, and surrounded by several other priests and gentlemen, he began to meditate on the love of Jesus and Mary for us, and on their claims on our hearts, and this affected him so much that he entered into an ecstasy, and became like an inanimate corpse. This ecstasy lasted for three entire hours, to the great astonishment of the spectators.

I will here add another surprising incident. As he was one day returning to Iliceto with two young peasants who had been directed to come to our house, he began to discourse on the mysteries relating to the Mother of God. On reaching the neighborhood of a church which is dedicated to the Blessed Virgin, his countenance suddenly became transformed; he took out his pencil, and after writing something or other, (I know not what,) on a morsel of paper, he made a spring and threw it into the air as if it had been a letter. This was not only followed by an ecstasy but by a flight, and the peasants saw him taken away from their vicinity and carried to a distance of more than half a mile in the direction of our house, that is to say, from the spot where they were, which was near the church, to a field called "The French Field." The two peasants are now dead, but Canon Stramiello assures us that during their lives they never ceased to relate the miracle which they had witnessed with all possible admiration. This is not all. On reaching the door of our house, he found a poor man there whose leg was eaten away by an ulcer. He embraced him and sucked the wound; the next day this poor man found that he was cured, and returned to Iliceto, where he did nothing but extol the holiness of Brother Gerard.

He was also very devout towards his holy patrons, especially towards St. Joseph and St. Michael; but the narrow limits which I have prescribed to myself preclude my entering into further details.

CHAPTER IX
Gerard's Journey to Mount Gargan; Wonderful Events which Occurred by the Way.

As the clerical students in dogmatics at our house of Iliceto expressed a great wish to go and visit the holy grotto of the Archangel at Mount Gargan, the rector gave them leave to go there, and fixed on Brother Gerard to accompany them. The pious brother could not have a greater consolation than that of going to present his homage to his beloved protector in person. Thirty carlins, however, were all the funds which they had to provide for the wants of a party including at least twelve individuals. When the students showed Brother Gerard this small sum, he said, "God will provide for us." The journey was to last for ten days, and their only conveyance consisted in two hired asses.

When they arrived at Foggia, Gerard hastened to accompany the young men on their visit to the hallowed image of the Blessed Virgin, whose frequent apparitions on this spot are so celebrated. Gerard was delighted to be able to honor this miraculous image, and it quite pained him when he had to leave it, so eager was he to pay all possible devotion to his august Mother. Gerard was well known at Foggia for the renown of his virtues and supernatural endowments, which had spread there long ere he visited it in person. As soon as he and the clerics arrived there, several ecclesiastics and gentlemen went to him to enjoy his conversation. They purposely introduced ascetical questions and cases of theology to try him; but Gerard was able to answer all that was started. A religious of the Convent of the Annunziata manifested such a wish to speak to him on matters of conscience that he went to see her. The chief result of this interview was that the religious heard that she must prepare for death. And so it was, for although she was then young and in robust health, in two months she was no more.

Gerard's charity was especially conspicuous on this journey. When he saw that the young men were very tired, he hired a small carriage. "But how shall we manage to pay for it?" asked they. "God will take care of that," he replied. A new difficulty arose, for when they were nine miles from Malfredonia, the two asses could proceed no further, which so disheartened the conductor, who walked alongside of them, that he wanted to leave them when they reached the inn at Candelaro. Gerard only smiled, and gave the asses a blow in God's name, upon which they began to gallop in front of the carriage like two race-horses, and they did not slacken their speed throughout the whole of the rest of the journey. When they reached Malfredonia their purse only contained seventeen grains; but Gerard was so far from being alarmed at this, that he bought a bunch of pinks which he saw at the market, and took them to the church, where he placed them before the tabernacle with these words: "It is for you, dear Jesus, to provide for the wants of my little family." As this devout action was witnessed by the chaplain of the castle, it at once led him to believe that Gerard was a great servant of God. He therefore drew him aside, and asked him to come and stay at the castle, and to bring all his companions with him. And this was not all, Gerard's devotion towards Jesus in the adorable Sacrament made such an impression on another priest that he went to see him, and offered him a silver censer for our church. The gift was most opportune, for the one we had was only made of brass, silvered over. Our clerics were perfectly astonished at this unexpected invitation, as well as at the spontaneous offering made by the priest. He was as good as his word, and soon afterwards sent us a thurible worth sixty ducats.

On the following day they continued their journey towards Mount Gargan. Although Gerard was quite overcome with fatigue, he performed the whole of the ascent on foot in honor of the Archangel. By this time, they had only a few coins remaining, and as the clerics had no provisions, they were in great distress. But Gerard reassured them by saying, "You have a friend who is thinking of you." And so it was, for whilst he was making a meditation in honor of the Archangel, a stranger came up to him, and placed a roll of money in his hand, saying, "Recommend me to Jesus Christ." By this means Providence not only abundantly provided for all their present necessities, but enabled them to pay the expenses of their journey homewards.

Another wonderful occurrence took place at Mount Gargan. In the evening they went to an inn for the night, and next morning the landlord brought them a most exorbitant account. When Gerard saw this imposture, he assumed a tone of confidence, and said, "If you do not repent of your injustice and abandon such unjust claims, your mules will be struck dead." At these words the innkeeper's son came running in with tears in his eyes to tell his father that his best mule was rolling violently on the ground, in a most unaccountable manner. These tidings alarmed and subdued the innkeeper. He protested that he neither wanted to quarrel with the brother, nor with his companions, and he would not have consented to receive anything if Gerard had not forced him to take what was due to him.

The scarcity of water in la Pouille sometimes reduced the inhabitants to extremity. Now there was a public-house keeper who was so avaricious of the water he had, on account of the great drought of the season, that he was so hard-hearted as to refuse it to the pilgrims who wished to refresh themselves. When our young students asked him for some, he positively refused to give it to them. Gerard spoke to him about his inhumanity in an authoritative manner, depicted hell opened at his feet ready to receive him, and even threatened to cause the wells to dry up if he would not change his line of conduct. His tone of voice made such an impression on the innkeeper, that he became quite ashamed of himself, and not only gave the water to the young men, but let the beasts of burden drink also; and what was still more remarkable was, that he never refused it to anyone again.

On their way homewards they passed by Troy. There was a miraculous crucifix in this town which was the subject of great veneration, and which had been sculptured by the order of our Father Alphonsus's maternal uncle, Mgr. Cavalieri of holy memory. The figure is so full of expression, that no one can see it without emotion. Our young men were very glad to be able to visit it, but Gerard's consolation was greater, and the clerics told us that it caused a sensible accession to the beating of his heart and to the transports of his soul.

He also took them to the celebrated sanctuary of the coronation of the Blessed Virgin, which is situated in the environs of Foggia. Gerard became so absorbed in contemplating the glories of Mary while there, that he fell into an ecstasy. When he came to himself again, a cleric asked him what had been the matter with him; "It is nothing," said he, "but an attack of an infirmity from which I suffer."

As this pilgrimage was one succession of prodigies, it was a most agreeable one to our young men; but Gerard well knew how to find means of procuring suffering for himself. While he neglected no means of procuring innocent enjoyments for all the rest of the party, he took equal pains to mortify himself, reserving every difficulty for his own share, and performing almost the whole journey on foot. Although this excursion to Mount Gargan lasted for nine days, instead of having spent the thirty carlins, which was a scanty allowance for even the first day, they returned to the house with a far heavier purse than the one with which they set out.

CHAPTER X

Gerard's Disastrous Encounter with a Guard; His Charity Toward Him; The Miserable Fate of the Latter.

If Gerard was unceasingly seeking for crosses, they also often befell him without any intervention of his own. The Duke of Bovino possesses a great extent of arable land on this side of Castellucci, in the territory of la Pouille, which forms part of the estates of the house of Guevara. The road down the mountain leading to Foggia used to pass through this domain. As Duke John did not like to see his land thus cut up, he ordered his guards to stop any one from passing that way in future. In compliance with this injunction, they not only prevented any one from going that way by words, but even by blows, which led to many fatal accidents, which it is not however our province to relate.

One day when Gerard had to go to Foggia, he went by the accustomed route, as he was not aware of the new regulations. Now the guard who was then on duty was a perfect monster of cruelty. As soon then as he saw Gerard, he rushed upon him and struck him so violently with the end of his musket, that it caused the servant of God to fall; but the ruffian did not therefore cease to ill-treat him, and thrust the point of his gun into his stomach and chest. "I have been long wishing to revenge myself on a monk," said he, "and you have just come and thrown yourself into my power in the most opportune way possible." Gerard got on his knees as well as he could, entreated him to have mercy on him, and made excuses for what he had done. "I do not want either excuses or pretexts," replied the guard more furiously than ever; and went on beating him in the most unmerciful manner. "Strike, brother," said Gerard then, "for you have cause to do so;" and he continued to repeat with clasped hands, "Strike, for you have reason to do so." The guard became softened by his exceeding patience; he repented of what he had done, covered his face with his hands, and threw aside his musket, saying, "O, what have I done! I have killed a saint!" He then cast himself at Gerard's feet, and entreated his forgiveness, who embraced him, and in turn begged pardon for the unintentional offense he had committed. As he was unable to remount his horse, he asked the guard to have the kindness to assist him to do so, and to get up behind him to support him till he reached our house. The guard himself said that he never complained of anything during the ride homewards, except of the way in which he was living at enmity with God, and that he talked a great deal to him about the enormity of mortal sin, and of the danger of offending God, and of thereby meriting hell. Although Gerard was half dead when he reached the house, he only said that he had fallen from his horse. He did not name the injuries he had received. On the contrary, he caused the guard to be kindly treated, as a reward for his charity towards him.

Such was the character of this unfeeling man. He did not escape so easily from a lay-brother of another order whom he began to ill-treat, for he managed to jump down from his horse, and while begging for mercy in the name of St. Anthony and St. Francis, he adroitly slipped below him and seized his musket, and inflicted so many blows on his body with it, that he left him half dead. As the musket was thus broken, the brother flew to the Duke, who was then at his country house, told what had befallen him, and uncovered his mangled shoulders, to let him see how his guard had ill-used him. As this nobleman had a feeling heart, he was moved at the sight, and gave him some money; he also dismissed the guard, and to prevent anything of the sort occurring again, he ordered the road to be left unguarded, so that all might pass by that way as heretofore.

Divine Justice did not allow the cruel guard to go unpunished; for he was soon afterwards killed by a musket shot. Gerard shed tears when he heard of his death, but his chest was so injured by the blows he had received that he never regained his former health.

CHAPTER XI
Divers Resolutions and Vows Made by Brother Gerard to do Always that which is Most Perfect.

The just man is not satisfied with retaining his first fervor. He is unceasingly striving to enkindle it more and more; he is never satisfied with himself, but endeavors to go onwards in the paths of virtue day by day, by a perfect correspondence with every inspiration of grace. As these were the dispositions of our Brother Gerard, he made visible progress in sanctity, under the guidance of the Spirit of God, the great Director of souls. He studied the divers degrees of every virtue, and ardently strove to attain the very highest perfection in all; the spirit of recollection became daily stronger and stronger within him, and he grew more and more assiduous in practicing self-renunciation, so that his example excited a holy emulation amongst the young men, and filled the old with shame.

We should have had no knowledge of what passed between the soul of Gerard and its God, but for Father D. Francis Juvenal. But as his spiritual director, he expressly enjoined him to note down his desires and resolutions, and all that passed between himself and God, adding that he wished to see whether he were animated by the spirit of God or by that of self-love. Gerard obeyed, and wrote the following narration, which he composed in a spirit of holy simplicity:

"May the grace of God ever fill our hearts, and may His blessed Mother watch over and protect us.

"My father, you wish to know all the mortifications I practice, and you also desire me to give you an account of my other desires, sentiments, and good resolutions, together with an explanation of the vow I have made. I am ready to render you an account of all that concerns me, both interiorly as well as exteriorly, so that I may become more closely united to God and walk with more security in the paths of eternal salvation.

"*Daily mortifications.*—Discipline once; a large chain, nearly a palm in length and two palms in width, round my loins. "I draw my tongue along the ground in the form of a cross, every morning and evening; I mix bitter herbs with my portion at dinner and supper; I wear a heart furnished with iron points on my breast, and chew bitter herbs at least three times a day; I say six Ave Marias with my face to the ground in the morning and evening.

"I take my meals on my knees on Wednesdays, Fridays, and Saturdays, and on all vigils, and I also make nine crosses in the refectory with my tongue at dinner and supper, and never eat fruit on these days; I eat only two portions at dinner on Friday, and one at supper; and fast on bread and water on Saturdays.

"I also gird my loins and forehead with a long and double chain during the nights of these days, and I lie on another, which is three palms in length and one in width, and this chain is the one I wear round my waist during the day; I wear one round my arm both night and day; I take the discipline to blood every eight days.

"I practice these mortifications during all novenas, when I also discipline myself twice a day, (once to blood,) besides the extraordinary penances I ask for from your Reverence.

"*Desires.*—I wish to love God very much, to be always

united to Him, to do all things for Him, to practice entire conformity to His will, and to suffer much for Him.

"*Ardent sentiments of my heart.*—I shall have but one opportunity of becoming a saint; if this happiness is not attained by me now, it will be lost forever. But I have every facility for becoming one. I am determined to be a saint then! O how earnestly I ought to labor to attain this end! How great will be my madness if I do not become a saint! Brother Gerard, resolve to give thyself up unreservedly to God. Remember that thou wilt not now become sanctified by devoting thyself only to prayer and contemplation, but that thy best meditation is to be what God pleases. This is what God demands of thee. Do not be a slave either to thyself or to anything else. It suffices to have God alone present to thy mind, and be always united to Him. All that is done for God is meditation; some resolve to do one thing, some another; my only resolution is to do the will of God; no pain is really painful when we act for God alone; nothing is hard.

"On the 21st of September, 1752, I began to understand the following truth better than I had done before: if I had died ten years ago, what pretensions should I have had to the favor of God? Assuredly none. It is a grievous thing to suffer and yet not to suffer for God. No amount of suffering is really painful if borne for God. I wish to act as if the world contained nothing but God and my own soul. Several people say that I deceive the world. What would that signify? The marvel would be if I cheated God! If I am lost, I shall lose God, and if I lose Him, what can I lose more?

"*Resolutions.*—O Lord Jesus Christ, behold me here now with the pen in my hand, going to write down and ratify before Thy Divine Majesty the following good resolutions, which I formed long since, and now confirm through obedience. O Lord, grant me grace to be faithful to them.

Alas! I dare not confide in myself, for I am unable to promise anything of myself; but I trust in Thy goodness and mercy, for Thou art infinite and cannot fail in what Thou dost promise. If I have heretofore sinned against Thee, O God, it was I who did so; from henceforth I desire that Thou shouldst live and act in me; cause me then, O Lord, to keep these promises with exactness. I confidently hope for this, O Lord, for Thy goodness is infinite. Amen.

"*Examination of the secrets of my heart.*—I have chosen the Blessed Spirit of God as my only consoler and protector. May He be my defender and the conqueror of all my passions. Amen.

"And you, my only joy, Mother Immaculate, be also my protector and my consolation under all that may befall me; and intercede for me with God, so that my good resolutions may be crowned with success. I call on you, all ye spirits of the blessed, and implore you to intercede for me with the great God of heaven and earth. I write all this in your presence. Read it from your shining thrones above, and pray God to make me a saint. May your prayers be heard! Behold then what I bind myself to undertake, and which I promise to do in presence of God, of His adorable Mother, and all the saints in heaven. May St. Theresa, St. Mary Magdalene of Pazzi, St. Catherine of Sienna, and St. Agnes assist me in a special manner!

"I will examine my conscience every fortnight, to see if I have failed in the performance of any of these resolutions. But bethink thee, Gerard, of what thou art doing! Remember that all that thou hast here written will be one day brought again before thine eyes; therefore be very careful to observe all that thou hast promised with fidelity and exactness. But who art thou who upbraidest me thus? Thy words indeed are good and true, but art thou ignorant that I never have trusted to myself, and never will do so? As I know my own misery, I have always distrusted myself; had I not acted thus, I should certainly have done evil continually. I confide and hope in God alone, for I have resigned myself entirely into His hands, that He may do with me as He pleases; for although I live, yet it is not I that live, since it is Christ that liveth in me; all my hopes are centered in Him, and it is from Him alone that I expect all the assistance I require to enable me to accomplish all that I have now promised to do. All Hail, Jesus and Mary!

"Observations.—My dear and only Love, I desire to do Thy adorable will from henceforth and forever, and I wish to repeat amidst all the trials and tribulations of the world, 'Fiat voluntas tua.' I will embrace them all from the bottom of my heart, ever raising my eyes to heaven to adore Thy Divine hands, which scatter down on me the pearls of Thy adorable will, which are ever precious, whether they descend in the shape of joy or sorrow.

"Lord Jesu, I will observe all the commandments of Thy holy Church. I will obey my superiors from love to Thee, and I will obey them as if Thou Thyself wert speaking to me. I will so abandon all self-will that I will act as if my judgment and will were only to be found in those of him who commands me. I will forego all pleasure, that is to say, I will never please myself; and my riches shall consist in poverty and trial.

"Amongst all those virtues which are most pleasing to Thee, O my God, purity is that which I love best. O Thou of infinite purity, I confidently trust that Thou wilt deliver me from every thought which could lead me into sin.

"I will only speak in three cases, viz. when the glory of God, the welfare of my neighbor, or any real necessity require it.

"I will never speak during recreation, unless I am spoken to; and whenever I am tempted to say anything contrary to the good pleasure of God, I will make this ejaculation: 'My Jesus, I love Thee!'

"I will never speak of myself, whether for good or for ill, but will act as if I did not exist. I will never excuse myself, however great may be my innocence, unless I should offend against my duty to God and my neighbor by not doing so. I will be silent when reproved, unless commanded to speak.

"I will avoid all singularities. I will not accuse others, nor speak of their defects, even in jest. I will always make excuses for my neighbor when he is not present to defend himself, and I will consider in him the person of Jesus Christ, who was accused by the Jews, although guile was not found in His mouth. I will admonish all who speak ill of others. I will cautiously avoid everything which could irritate others. When I see anyone commit a fault, I will take care not to tell him of it in public, but will do so with all charity, in a low tone of voice, and when we are quite alone. When I see a father or brother in great want of anything, I will leave off whatever I may be doing and go to his assistance, provided holy obedience does not prevent my so doing. I will visit the sick several times a day if I obtain leave.

"I will never meddle with other people's concerns. When I am appointed to assist another in any office, I will implicitly obey him under whom I am placed, and I will never venture to say, 'I do not like that;' or, 'That is not done properly.' However, if I know by experience that a thing is wrong, I will give my opinion in a humble manner.

"When I am sent to discharge any duty in company with others, however mean and lowly it may be, such as sweeping, carrying goods, etc., I will make a point of never taking precedence, or making use of the best tools; but I will give up my own comfort in all things, and take what God will leave for me, and thus we shall all be satisfied. I will never undertake any duty unless I have been previously commanded to do so.

"I will never look about me during meals, unless for the service of others or through duty. I will take the portion which may be nearest to me on the board, without looking at the others.

"I will endeavor not to consent to any interior emotions which are contrary to reason; if then I am reproved or accused, I will say nothing until bitterness of feeling has given place to sweetness.

"*Final resolution of giving myself up wholly to God.*—May these three words be ever in my thoughts—deaf, blind, and dumb! May the words, 'I will,' and 'I will not,' be unknown to me, for my only desire is, 'Thy will, not mine, be done, O Lord.' In order to do the will of God, I must not follow my own inclinations, I desire nothing but God, and if this be so, I must be detached from all besides. I will therefore never seek my own ease in anything.

"I will spend all the time of silence in meditating on the passion and death of Christ, and on the sorrows of the Blessed Virgin. I will offer up my prayers, my communions, and all my actions, in union with the most precious blood of Jesus Christ, for the conversion of poor sinners. If anyone is afflicted with sufferings, who has not patience to bear them as he ought, and asks me to help him, I will pray to God for him, and offer all I do for three consecutive days, that our Lord may grant him a spirit of true conformity to His Divine will.

"When I receive the superior's blessing, I will receive it as if it were given to me by Jesus Christ Himself. My thanksgiving after Holy Communion is to last from the time I communicate until noon, and my preparation for the next day, from noon until six o'clock in the evening.

"I will always show the greatest possible respect to priests, as if in them I saw Jesus Christ Himself, and even when they are not all they ought to be, I will show them respect for the sake of the dignity of their office.

"*Explanation of my vow.*—By this vow I bind myself always to do what is most perfect, that is, to do that which seems to me to be most perfect in the sight of God. This includes all my actions, which I resolve to perform with all possible mortification and perfection; always premising that I have your Reverence's sanction for this, for otherwise I could not act with any safety. I do not consider what I do with distraction or without thought as a breach of this vow. Neither will it be broken by my asking for a dispensation in some particulars when I am absent from the monastery, for otherwise I might be thrown into a state of perplexity and scrupulosity.

"I also reserve to myself power to ask my confessor for a dispensation of my vow, and he can grant me one whenever he pleases."

After this follow many prayers, tender aspirations, and pious practices in honor of the Blessed Trinity and Jesus suffering, as well as of the Blessed Virgin and his holy patrons. I omit them however for the sake of brevity. He held the saint under whose patronage he was born, and him whose name he bore, in special honor, as well as the saint whose feast might fall on the day of his death, although his name was unknown to him.

Chapter XII

On the Fidelity with which Gerard Accomplished His Vow, and of His Perseverance in Virtue.

Gerard was not one of those inconstant souls who make high resolves in time of fervor, and who abandon all in the hour of trial. "God," he used to say in order to excite himself to virtue, "is the same yesterday, today, and forever." And so he used constantly to put in practice what he had resolved, whether in aridity or in fervor, as Fathers Petrella, Juvenal, and Cafaro unite in affirming.

Gerard's spirit of obedience was so heroic and uncommon, that he venerated even the thoughts of his superior. He was so exact in regard to this virtue, that those who commanded him to do anything were obliged to weigh their words carefully for fear of the consequences.

One day Father Cafaro disapproved of his sentiments, and by way of expressing a kind of contempt for him, he said, "Go and shut yourself up in the oven." Gerard instantly obeyed. Soon afterwards the baker came to make the bread; when he began to prepare the fire, he was quite terrified to find Brother Gerard there, and ran to tell Father Cafaro. When he heard it, he struck his forehead and bewailed his thoughtlessness, and, of course, instantly recalled him.

He kept to the letter of the law without either glosses or interpretations. One day when he was at Ciorani, he had to go to Castellamare. Father Rossi told him to take the ass with him. He accordingly led it by the bridle without ever mounting it. As he had to walk thirty miles he was in a most deplorable state when he returned to the house. As Father Rossi suspected the cause, he questioned him as to what he had done. "Your Reverence told me to lead the ass," replied Gerard, "and I did so." His confidence in holy obedience caused him to fear nothing. Once when he was at Carbonara, Father Fiocchi summoned him to Melfi; but as the river Ofante was much swelled by the heavy rains, it seemed impossible for him to get there. He began the journey however, saying, "I must set out, since obedience wills it so." But the current was so swollen, that when he was in the midst of it, an uprooted tree was precipitated against him through its violence. Almost all who saw it gave him up for lost; Gerard however was in no wise disconcerted. He made the sign of the cross over the tree, when its position was instantly changed, and it passed alongside of him without injuring him in the least. He himself related this occurrence to Mgr. Amato when he was at Lacedogna, as a proof of the efficacy of holy obedience.

God indeed gave him most wonderful assistance to enable him to practice this virtue. A sign from his superiors, if given mentally and at a distance, was sufficient to cause him to obey with promptitude. One day at Melfi when Father Fiocchi was boasting to Mgr. Basta of Gerard's heroic obedience, he said to him, "I will show you how far it extends, and how God aids him in its exercise." Upon this he became recollected, and interiorly recommended him to come to him. Although Gerard was then at Iliceto, he instantly told the father-minister of the house, that the father-rector wanted him at Melfi. He therefore set out. When he arrived, Father Fiocchi asked him why he came. "Because your Reverence told me to come," replied Gerard. Many similar instances took place within the knowledge of Father Cafaro, who also made trials of the extent of his virtue.

He exercised the virtue of humility to an equally marvelous degree. He had such a lowly opinion of himself, that there was no degree of contempt or humiliation which he did not feel that he had fully merited. When he met with things of the most humiliating nature, they only afforded him matter for glory and rejoicing. He was at times so impressed with a sense of his own nothingness and ingratitude towards God, that even hell seemed too light a punishment for him. Father D. Vitus Polestra relates that he felt such deep self-abasement, that he used to embrace the earth and entreat it to hide him from the eyes of all men, feeling unworthy even to live. One of our fathers one day asked him what he thought of the state of his soul: "I know," replied Gerard, "that I am so ungrateful, and that I have sinned so grievously against God, that I feel unworthy to appear before Him or to enter into His presence by meditation."

He considered himself as the worst of all the brothers, and was only satisfied when neglected and treated with the contempt he believed himself to deserve. He was wont to say that he was a traitor, and that he deceived the community. It was quite a treat to him to eat the broken scraps left from dinner; for he then felt as if he were one of the paupers who receive the broken victuals of the community.

In order to try his obedience and humility, Father Cafaro one day told him to make his manifestation of conscience to another lay-brother. Gerard did so without repugnance, and performed the duty with more exactness than if it had been to his director himself.

Although D. Camillus Bozio, the canon of Conza, was informed of this holy brother's exceeding virtue by Father Cafaro when he was at Caposele, he did not believe all that he heard about him. It so happened that Gerard was at Atella while he was preaching the Lenten sermons there. One day when he went to the church, he found Gerard in the sacristy surrounded by priests and gentlemen. As soon as he saw him he said to him with an air of supreme contempt, "What are you discussing here? You are only an ignorant lay-brother, and yet you pretend to be a theologian! I am astonished that these gentlemen, who know what you really are, should treat you as they do!" Everyone was amazed at this speech; but the saintly brother received the reproach with all humility. Now as the canon as well as Gerard were both staying with Don Graziola at this time, the preacher happened to go into the brother's room soon after this, when he found him in an ecstasy, and raised to a considerable height from the ground.

This lowly opinion of himself also caused Gerard to practice the virtue of poverty to a heroic extent. He always selected the worst things in the house to himself, and wore the oldest and most tattered clothes and linen. His cell at Iliceto had been a fireplace when the Augustinian Fathers had lived there, and the light of day could never penetrate its gloomy walls. His bed, or rather his rack, consisted in a palliasse, which the fireplace could scarcely hold. Two tiles served for his pillow, and this couch was surrounded by skulls. Father Cæsar says, that he one day had the curiosity to examine his bed, when he found that his palliasse was full of stones and thistles. When Mgr. Basta, the bishop of Melfi, Mgr. Amato, the bishop of Lacedogna, and the auditor Marcante, made their retreat with us, they also visited the hole in which he slept, and were perfectly amazed at the sight. A lay-brother once asked him why he thus ill-treated his body. "I do it because I deserve it," he replied; "I do it for my Creator and my Judge." He afterwards had a room, but he seldom used it, for he always gave it up to the strangers who came when the house was full. If he had been away and found that his room was occupied on his return, he slept on the church floor. When he was at Iliceto on such occasions, he used to get into the old high altar, which was empty inside, and could be entered from behind; and he spent the night there. If he went to one of our houses, and they forgot to assign him a room, he passed the night in the stable, lying on the straw beside the animals.

Meditation and mortification arose and flourished together in Gerard's heart like twin roses on one stalk. Whenever he had any spare time, he spent it before the Blessed Sacrament, or in his own room at the foot of the crucifix. He generally passed the hour of repose after dinner either in spiritual reading, or in praying before the

Blessed Sacrament, and he always passed some hours of the night in church. He was equally assiduous in the practice of mortification. After he had been compelled to use an ordinary kind of palliasse, his director yielded to his earnest entreaties, and allowed him to sleep at least three times a week on a table, with two tiles for a pillow. A stone was then fastened to his feet, and his forehead was bound with an iron chain. When he had to pass the night out of the house, he always slept on the floor. This was discovered by a great many people, although the humble brother strove to conceal the mortification by disarranging the curtains and the bedclothes. He really almost carried mortification of the palate to excess, and that throughout his life. When he was staying at Melfi with D. Stephen Liguori, in the house of D. Mauro Murante the priest, he did not manage so adroitly as to prevent their seeing that he mingled bitter powders with his food. As Father Liguori wished to make sure of this, he put his fork into some macaroni, which he found on his plate, to taste it; but it was so bitter that he could not even swallow it. God also granted His servant a peculiar favor in this respect also. For as he confided to his director, he had prayed to God for three whole years to grant that he might lose his taste, and in the end his petition was heard and answered.

He was also distinguished for his charity. He made himself all to all, and never refused anything he could grant. As he was our tailor, he had to provide for the necessities of all, and he not only kept the oldest and worst clothing for his own share, but he did without what he really required, to provide for the wants of others, to avoid teasing or embarrassing the superiors. During a most rigorous winter at Iliceto, it was observed that he went without his waistcoat to give it to someone else, and contented himself with nothing but his shirt and cassock.

His favorite occupation was to take care of the sick; he

anticipated all their wants, and strove to give them every possible solace. He exercised this virtue towards strangers as well as towards ourselves. D. Francis Anthony Sabatelli, the canon of Melfi, came to our house at Iliceto, and fell dangerously ill there. Although he was a perfect stranger to Gerard, he never left him night or day. As the canon did not see the need of this, he never suspected that Gerard really did it. To his astonishment then one night when he awoke, he saw Brother Gerard standing at the foot of his bed, attentively scanning his countenance. This act made such an impression on him, that he ever afterwards extolled this holy brother's charity and goodness wherever he went.

He attended a hermit who died in our house with most special tenderness, although his illness was most troublesome and revolting. Everyone else was afraid to come near him; but this only caused Gerard to take greater interest in him. But the wretched man did not profit by the care thus lavished on him; for one day when Gerard was praying for him, his lost soul appeared to him, and said, "Pray no more for me; I am damned by a just judgment of God." Gerard was so terrified by the hideous expression of his countenance, that he never forgot it as long as he lived. His charity was not confined to attending on the sick. He was ready to assist everyone, whatever their distress might be. One day when he was going from Melfi to Atella with some candidates for ordination, he met several laborers, who were unable to go to their work in consequence of the overflowing of a river. Gerard was filled with compassion, made them get up behind him on horseback, and carried them across one by one until they had all reached the opposite side. We heard from Don Michael Pinto, that he did this with as much confidence as if there were no danger whatever. When he was cautioned not to expose his life thus, he replied, "The love of my neighbor constraineth me." Then turning to his horse, he said, "My horse, let us please our God." After this, they reached another river, which was also extremely swollen; but Gerard was still full of confidence; he assured the youthful candidates that they would be able to cross it as the others had done, and he carried them across one by one until they were all in safety. His charity, added D. Pinto, cared for no danger when the safety of his neighbor was in question. We could narrate wonderful instances of the compassion which Gerard felt in seeing the sufferings of the poor. One day when he was going to Iliceto, he met a poor man carrying a quantity of wood on his head with great difficulty. He immediately relieved him from his load, and took it on his own shoulders, and did not put it down until he entered the territory of Iliceto. Another time he met an old woman on the steep hill at St. Agatha, carrying a basket of linen on her head, which had been washed at the river. As she was hardly able to accomplish the task, he took it from her and put it on his head, although he was himself on foot. He felt some repugnance to entering the town in this fashion, but he generously surmounted it, walked through the middle of the marketplace, and did not put the basket down until he had left it at its destination. He imitated Brother Curtius in this action, whose manner of life he was well acquainted with, and who used to exercise the like charity towards the street porters at Scala.

He was as solicitous in providing for the wants of others, as he was indifferent regarding his own, which he totally neglected, leaving all concerning himself to Providence. If the superiors did not give him what he required when he left the house, he did not take the pains to remind them of his wants. In this self-forgetfulness he imitated our Father Sportelli, who was a man of great sanctity, and who specially excelled in the practice of this virtue. One day when he was sent to the territory of

Accadia on foot, the father-minister forgot to give him his breakfast, and he therefore arrived there in such a state of exhaustion that he fainted and fell flat on the ground on entering the church. On another occasion he was ordered to go to Ascoli, and as he had no decent shoes to put on, he went in the tattered slippers he was in the habit of wearing about the house. When he reached the town, a group of boys began to mock him when they saw how ill he was shod; but he cared not for what the world thought of him, and bore all with indifference, or rather with joy. Thus fully did Gerard observe and practice his vow.

Chapter XIII
Supernatural Gifts of Brother Gerard; Admirable Conversions Effected by His Means.

The gifts and graces of God are not all alike, and God distributeth them to every one severally as He wills. Yet He was so liberal towards Gerard, that He enriched him with nearly all, for the knowledge of mysteries, the gift of prophecy, penetration of hearts, the gift of tongues, and power over the spirits of darkness, were all united together in this great servant of God.

I will not here enter into a detailed account of his prophecies, because they would fill whole volumes, and besides it is well known to what an extent this gift was bestowed on him. I will not either enlarge on his knowledge of all mysteries. Suffice it to say that it has rendered him most celebrated both in and out of the Congregation. He was everywhere regarded as a great theologian; amongst those who did so, I will specify Bishop Basta, the bishop of Melfi, and Mgr. Amato, the bishop of Lacedogna.

He who entered into controversy with him on any

theological question, was sure to be put to silence. Among many remarkable occurrences which proved the truth of what I assert, I will only cite the following: Father Cajone has told that there was a priest who once began to contend with him, who was really a good theologian, yet he was not long in finding out his own inferiority, for when Gerard asked him for an explanation of the following words in the opening of St. John's Gospel, "In principio erat Verbum, et Verbum erat apud Deum, et Deus erat Verbum," he did not know how to give the proper answer. Gerard then began to speak, and explained the whole mystery in a few words with the utmost clearness.

Gerard had almost a more intimate knowledge of the consciences of others than of his own. A gentleman who came to our house to make a retreat there, was so terrified by the opening sermons by Father Rizzi, that he thought of going away again and giving himself up to despair. Whilst these dark thoughts were passing through his mind, Gerard went into his room and said to him, "What is the matter with you? Banish this infernal spirit of distrust from your mind, for God and the Blessed Virgin have promised to assist you." The gentleman was astonished at the secrets of his interior being thus laid open before him, and at the same instant all his distress vanished.

One day during the general communion of a retreat, Gerard hurried from the gallery to prevent a gentleman who was going through the exercises from making a sacrilegious communion, which he was on the point of doing. When he reached the church, he led him aside and set his crime before his eyes. The gentleman's heart then became filled with compunction, and he hastened to the feet of his confessor, to unburden his conscience fully to him. When he returned to the church, he raised his voice and said, "I was ashamed to confess my sins to the priest; but Brother Gerard has discovered them all, and I now wish to have the confusion of confessing them before you all." And he would really have done so if a priest who was present had not stopped him. The conscience of a priest of Rocchetta was in such an uncomfortable state that he had been led to make a bad confession; Gerard paid him a visit, and spoke to him of the sad state he was in, and told him of several sins which he had not confessed. The priest's heart was touched at this, he entered into himself, and afterwards divulged what had passed between them.

To this gift this holy brother united that of the most ardent zeal. His voice was powerful and persuasive; he did not merely speak, he thundered, and the most hardened hearts could not resist his influence. When he corrected, amendment was sure to follow. When he spoke of sin, it was held in abomination; and an order from Brother Gerard, or even a mere wish, was a command to all. A great prelate once said, "It is God who speaks by his lips. We cannot therefore oppose him, nay we must obey him."

Time would fail me were I to attempt to relate all the conversions of abandoned sinners which were effected by this saintly brother. Fathers Margotta and Cajone did not hesitate to assert that a hundred missionaries could not have done what his zeal and insight into the hearts of men enabled him to effect. For my part I can safely say, that there was not a town or village in the neighborhood of Iliceto, of Caposele, or of any of the other places where he went, which could not render testimony to the prodigious conversions effected by his means. One day he met a man in the neighborhood of Iliceto, whose conscience was burdened with grievous crimes. He stopped him, treated him with great kindness, and laid the whole state of his soul before his eyes, as well as the irregularities of his past life, amongst which he named some sins which were known to God alone. On finding that the most hidden recesses of his heart were thus brought to light, the sinner confessed his guilt, and shed tears of true contrition. Gerard then conducted him to one of our fathers, to whom he made his confession with many sobs and tears; after which he never ceased to extol the sanctity of his deliverer wherever he went.

On another occasion, when he had made a similar conquest, he said to one of our fathers, "I have had the happiness to rescue a great prize from the devil's net. I am sure you will gladly receive it."

One day when he was returning to the house, he met a young man, who said in ridicule at his shabby appearance, (for he was on foot, enveloped in an old cloak, and with a most wretched hat on his head,) "Perhaps you are seeking for a treasure?" Gerard instantly replied, "That is just what I am about, and I also wish to enrich you." Upon this he drew his crucifix from his breast, and said, "Behold a treasure which you have not sought for, and which I wish to restore to you." He then set before him the frightful aspect of the sins which he had never confessed, with all the fire of his zeal, and told him of the number of years he had been living at enmity with God. The young man was filled with compunction; he burst into tears, owned that he had led a most iniquitous life, and that he had not approached the tribunal of penance for six years. Gerard embraced him, and joyfully conducted him to our house, where he kept him for some days. After he was restored to a state of innocence and peace, he went away blessing the happy hour when he had met with this servant of God.

As Mgr. Amato and the archpriest Cappuccio had in vain labored to bring a scandalous sinner to repentance for many years, they sent him to make a retreat in our house, to try what that would do for him. The deceitful man went to confession, but he left out his most serious transgressions. When he was also going to communicate,

Brother Gerard stopped him, and asked what he was going to do. When he told him, Gerard was transported with indignation, and said, "What! are you going to Communion without having confessed all your sins! Go, and do so now, if you do not wish to fall into hell." The heart of the hypocrite was then really softened, he entered into himself, and began to set his accounts with God in order.

There was a relapsed sinner who, although he had fallen back into his evil courses, returned to our house again, through motives of human respect. When Gerard questioned him as to the state of his conscience, he replied that he thanked God for it. But the brother led him into his own room, and told him of the state of his conscience while standing before the crucifix. "What," said he, "have you the heart to offend God thus?" Then pointing to the image of the crucified Savior, he added, "Who inflicted these wounds? Who but thee through thy manifold iniquities? And who but thee drew forth the blood which flows from His sacred wounds?" And at the same time blood gushed forth from all parts of the crucifix. The unhappy man became contrite at the sight, and he instantly went and cast himself at the feet of our Father Petrella, and told him all that had passed, with signs of the most sincere repentance. He gave Father Petrella leave to tell everyone what had taken place between him and this saintly brother, and when he returned home he was quite an altered character.

One day when Gerard was on his way to St. Agatha, he suddenly felt interiorly prompted to stop short. Just as he did so, a man came up to him. The brother accosted him gently, and asked him where he was going. "What business is that of yours?" he replied. "Go away and let me alone." The poor man was in a state of despair, and had abandoned his soul to the devil. Gerard let him see that he knew what was the matter with him, and said to him with an air of winning sweetness, "God has sent me to you, and I wish to help you." The unfortunate man then altered his tone. repented of what he had done, and melted into tears. Gerard reassured and encouraged him, took him with him and consigned him to the care of Father Fiocchi. As he was a tailor, the father-minister kept him in the house where he carried on his trade, and he was afterwards one of those who aided Brother Gerard to perform his most cruel macerations. His conversion was a sincere one. He became a man of prayer and mortification, and after some years he went to Naples, where he entered a hospital and devoted himself to the service of the sick.

Chapter XIV
Torments which the Devils Inflicted on Gerard, and His Dominion Over Them.

This saintly brother's zeal for the salvation of souls, and the wonderful conversions he daily effected, could not fail to enrage the powers of darkness against him. After the devils had once declared war against him they gave him no rest, and were always endeavoring to discourage him and cause him to abandon his pious undertakings. They often appeared to him during the night in great numbers, menacing and ill-treating him, in order to deter him from snatching souls from their grasp. His confessors have attested that they sometimes even dragged him about the corridors. "You will not be quiet," said a devil to him one night, "and I will give you no rest until I have killed you." He was sometimes so tormented and suffocated by these malicious spirits, that he felt as if he must expire upon the spot. One day when he was cooking, several devils fell upon him and tried to throw him into the fire. At other times they appeared before him in the form of furious dogs, ready to tear him to pieces. "You may bark," said Gerard, "but as my Mother Mary and Jesus my Savior are with me, you cannot bite." These combats generally took place on Friday nights, Father Juvenal told us. At these times the devil redoubled his efforts, and did all he could to terrify him, and make him abandon his mode of life, and to quench his zeal for the salvation of souls. Gerard not only preserved his tranquility in the presence of these evil spirits, but he exercised great power over them. How many possessed persons did he not deliver by a word? On one occasion, amongst others, when he was sent for to one of these unfortunate beings, the devil refused to obey him, but he put his cincture round the waist of the person, and the enemy of salvation was put to flight.

One Sunday there were two strange young men kneeling motionless at the side of our church. No one else knew who they were, but when Gerard perceived them he at once said, "What are you doing here? This is not your proper place;" and he commanded them in God's name to cast themselves into hell, upon which the two forms, who were in reality two demons, instantly disappeared. What end they had in view we know not, but the fact is incontestable, for several of our fathers witnessed it.

The following occurrence was still more wonderful. One day when he had to go to Lacedogna, he could not leave Melfi until late, on account of his having previously lost his way in the forests of Ofante. Night was far advanced, and a heavy rain was falling, accompanied by a thick fog. While in this critical position, a demon appeared to him in human shape, and said to him in a tone of fury, "Behold my hour. Thou art now my prey." Gerard knew who he was, but far from being affrighted, he confidently replied, "Monster of hell! I command you, in the name of the adorable Trinity, to take my horse's bridle and to lead me safely to Lacedogna." And no sooner was this said, than it was done. The demon murmuringly bent his head, took the bridle in his hand and led him to Lacedogna without injuring him in the least. The circumstances were most fully related by D. Constantine Cappucci, a gentleman of that town. "At about ten o'clock one night," said he, "I heard someone knock at my door. When I asked who it was, I was surprised to hear the voice of Brother Gerard. I arose, and seeing that he was wet through, I said, 'What brought you here at such an hour and in such weather?' 'My dear Don Constantine,' he replied, with his accustomed candor, "The will of God be done. I have only come from Melfi, but night, the fog, and rain overtook me on my journey, and caused me to lose my way among such precipices on the borders of the forest of Ofante, that I should assuredly have lost my life if God had not come to my assistance. When I was on the brink of one of these ravines, a man, or rather a demon, came up to me; 'Behold the hour and the man,' said he to me. 'Now I am thy master. Hope for nothing now. You have not obeyed your superiors, and God will not forgive you.' I was a little surprised at first, but after I had prayed to Jesus Christ, I perceived that he was not a man, but a demon. 'Fiend that thou art,' I said to him, 'I command thee in the name of the most Holy Trinity to take the bridle of my horse and to lead me straight to Lacedogna without doing me any hurt.' Thus I was saved from the danger which threatened me by the intervention of a demon; for had he not accompanied me I should certainly have either lost my life or remained in the woods of Ofante all night. When we reached the church of the Holy Trinity, the evil spirit turned to me and said, 'You are now in Lacedogna;' upon which he instantly vanished from my sight." Gerard also confided what had taken place to Father Fiocchi, the rector of Iliceto, and to his director, Father Juvenal.

CHAPTER XV
*Gerard is Sent to Corato, Where His Presence Had Been
Solicited; His Sanctity of the Life and the Prodigies He
Worked While There.*

This faithful servant was not like a light hidden under a bushel, but God placed him on a candlestick, that men might see his works, and that souls might thus be led to glorify their heavenly Father. As his sanctity was well known to all the gentlemen and priests who frequented our house, he was sent for to the most distant places. And although his superiors were averse to it, they were often obliged to yield to the solicitations of those to whom they were under obligations.

Among the places to which he was sent was Corato. The holy brother gave proofs of the favor he was in with God even before he entered it; for he met a poor countryman by the way, who complained to him of the manner in which the mice destroyed all his crops, and as he took him for a priest, he asked him to curse them for him. Gerard compassionated the distress of the poor man, and made the sign of the cross upon the land, after which it was instantly covered with the bodies of dead or dying mice.

As his arrival was known beforehand, all the inhabitants of Corato were eager to welcome him. The villager for whose crops he had performed the miracle acted as his herald, and caused everyone to be most anxious to see him, and they soon began to appreciate him adequately. As the fame of his supernatural endowments had preceded him, gentlemen and canons came in crowds to visit him, some from a wish to be instructed, and others in order to test his virtue. Gerard satisfied them all, and everyone was astonished to hear an ignorant and illiterate lay-brother speaking of the mysteries of God in such a sublime manner, and solving the most difficult questions in theology with perfect ease. The house of Mgr. Papale, which was the one in which he was staying, was never empty; some were attracted by his doctrines, others by his sanctity, and some by the marvelous way in which they were both united together in him.

God also confirmed the sanctity of His servant by fresh prodigies while he was at Corato. He laid open the deepest wounds of their souls to some, and set before others the duties of their station, and their own infidelities in the performance of them; and his words were enforced by his own example. He ate sparingly, he slept on the bare ground, and disciplined himself severely during the night. He was always humble, pious, and affable towards all. One day when he was conversing with a gentleman, he fixed his eyes on a crucifix and immediately fell into an ecstasy, which lasted for half an hour. These celestial favors and the holiness of his life caused him to be honored by all as a saint.

He was most zealously anxious for the spiritual welfare of nuns. He visited those of St. Benedict on several occasions, and they consulted him on matters of conscience. He was in their church on a Good Friday evening when the procession of Jesus Suffering entered it; upon which Gerard instantly fell into such a ravishment that he was raised to a considerable height from the ground. The truth of this was affirmed to Father Fiocchi by Canon Giove, and the Abbess Capano and Sister D. Angela Rose Falcioni can attest it also. He was especially earnest in exhorting the religious to frequent communion, to meditation, and detachment from the grate, and from earthly things. The Abbess Azzariti begged him to ask God to release her from the burden of superiority. "It will be taken away from you," replied Gerard, "but you will receive a heavier cross in exchange." And his words were verified, for although her resignation was accepted, a cancer came on in her leg, which caused her to suffer greatly until her death, which did not take place for several years afterwards.

The convent of the Dominicanesses in that neighborhood was in a very relaxed state. Gerard did away with the abuses which existed there, and not only led the religious to fulfill their duties faithfully, but inspired them with a real love of the virtues appertaining to their holy state. His zeal was especially stirred up on account of a window which faced the street, and which was so low that many evils took place in consequence. He had only to express what he felt about it to cause the religious to have it blocked up at once, and to place a crucifix on the outside in its stead.

Many wonderful things took place in this convent at this time. One day when he was speaking in the parlor about Jesus Christ and His claims on our love, he became so enthusiastic that he was carried out of himself by the impetuosity of his feelings, and remained suspended in the air holding on by the bars of the grate for some time. The gift of prophecy was not dormant within him either. There was a young lady in the convent who was so disgusted with the mode of life, that she was impatiently longing for her mother to come, that she might return with her to Naples. She told Gerard how dissatisfied she was with her position, and how anxious she was to leave the convent. "What! do you want to go away?" he replied. "No, No, that will not be. You will stay and become a religious." And when her mother came, instead of coming out, she entreated to be allowed to stay, and consecrated herself to God.

I cannot give a better idea of the good which Gerard effected at Corato than by citing part of a letter to our Father Fiocchi, (who died in the odor of sanctity) from D. Xavier Scoppa, the priest of Melfi, who was an eyewitness of what he related. "Divine Providence willed that Brother Gerard should come to Corato," says he, "for the salvation of many souls was effected through him. His sojourn there and the brightness of his example excited the people to great devotion, and brought about most striking conversions. But I am unable to relate all the marvelous things he did. Your Reverence can form no idea of the concourse of priests and gentlemen by whom he was always surrounded. They treated him as a messenger sent to them from heaven, and often remained conversing with him until midnight. His words penetrated the hearts of all; even high-born lords and ladies were filled with compunction when he spoke, and deep sighs were heard from all around him.

"But it was not only among seculars that he excited a lively horror for sin. A most relaxed convent was entirely reformed through him. Indeed it required but one single discourse from his lips to cause the religious to become perfectly detached from all the indulgences to which they had previously clung, and to make them abandon every abuse, and to become perfectly obedient to the mother-superior. The inhabitants of Corato were so delighted with Brother Gerard, and there is such a general impression in his favor, that more than twenty gentlemen and priests have already determined to make the spiritual exercises in your house; they have also asked to have a mission in November. I hope I shall soon be able to see you and kiss your hand, and tell you of all that has taken place by word of mouth."

Gerard also gave proof of his great obedience while he was at Corato. One evening he suddenly resolved to set out, and no entreaties were able to make him change his mind. "I am wanted," was his reply to all who urged him to stay, "and I must go." And he was right, for Father Fiocchi afterwards told Canon Giove that he had mentally commanded him that very evening to return to the house at Iliceto.

CHAPTER XVI
Wonderful Reconciliation and Other Prodigies which Gerard Effected in the Territory of Castelgrande.

The fame of the spiritual endowments with which God had favored Gerard, and the sway he exercised over the hearts of men, caused him to be sought after in all directions, amongst which was the territory of Castelgrande.

Several years before this time, Martin Carusi, the notary, had killed a young man of twenty years of age, the son of D. Mark Carusi, a gentleman who had property in this territory, in a quarrel. The parents and friends on both sides had ineffectually endeavored to obtain his pardon. As they were most apprehensive about the consequences, they resolved to have recourse to Brother Gerard, and asked Father Cafaro, who was then giving a mission in the territory of Guardia, to send him to Castelgrande.

The devil did not fail to accompany Brother Gerard thither also, and he menaced and insulted him by the way, in order to cause him to give up the journey through fear. Gerard, however, cared little for all his attempts. "I will do all that God commands me to do, through the strength which obedience gives me," said he, "and thou, firebrand of hell, mayst vent thy impotent fury in vain, and then go and cast thyself into that abyss." As he knew what a high opinion the inhabitants of Ruvo entertained of him, he went by another and more indirect route; but as they heard of this, they went out to meet him in crowds, and accompanied him for more than a mile, so that he was forced to pass through their territory, as if he were in a kind of triumph.

He reached Castelgrande at eight o'clock in the evening, and went straight to the house of Doctor Gaetan Frederici, where he was to lodge. His arrival was anxiously expected there by Isabel Sebastiana, who had a daughter who had been possessed by an evil spirit for some time, and her mother instantly told him of the sad state her daughter was in, and he begged her to bring her to him without loss of time. When the possessed reached the door of the house, she cried out, "The wretch has conquered!" Gerard then prayed to God with confidence, and the girl fell to the ground. After having said the litany of the Blessed Virgin with Frederica and the other persons in the house, he caused her to be girded with his cincture; and the devil instantly left her with a loud noise and uttering many murmurs. Gerard then commanded him not to torment the girl anymore, and turning to her, he said, "Go away now; love Jesus Christ, and be not afraid." And I have a written attestation from her mother that Frederica was never again tormented by the devil.

The reconciliation was also brought about most satisfactorily. D. Martin Carusi, the father of the murdered man, was sent for, and Gerard had scarcely spoken to him, ere he became softened and in good dispositions. When his wife, D. Theresa, heard of this, she was most indignant. She loaded her husband with abuse, and took the bloody garments of her son and threw them in his face. "Remember thy son!" she furiously exclaimed. "Look at these clothes steeped in blood, and then be reconciled if you can!" This sufficed to make the husband become more hardened and obstinate than ever. When Gerard heard of this, he said, "God will have the mastery, and not the devil." He then hurried to the house of the Carusi, and spoke to them both with such zeal and winning sweetness that they cast themselves at his feet, repented of what they had done, and freely pardoned him who had injured them so grievously. Instead of keeping up hatred against the murderer of their son, they became reconciled to him, and promised to love him from henceforth. And from that time there was no feeling of animosity or ill-will between the two families, and they were always united together in bonds of strict friendship.

Another marvel of the same kind as the first took place in the church. One day when Gerard was meditating before the Blessed Sacrament, a great noise was suddenly heard. Gerard ran to the spot whence it proceeded, and found a young girl who was possessed by an evil spirit and lying extended on the ground, pouring forth blasphemies against the Blessed Virgin, and against Jesus in the adorable Sacrament. He went up to her, imposed silence on her, and commanded the devil to leave her. She was instantly delivered from her tormentor, and although the holy names of Jesus and Mary could not before be pronounced in her hearing, she from that time frequented the sacraments and led a saintly life.

There was not a sick person at Castelgrande who was not anxious to receive the holy brother's blessing; but I must pass over in silence the numerous and instantaneous cures he effected. One day Doctor D. Gaetan Cianci took him to see a little child of three years of age, the son of Peter di Felice Pace, who was suffering from a contraction of the nerves of his legs and arms. Gerard placed his hand on his head, and made the sign of the cross over him, after which he said to his mother, "Do not be alarmed, your child will not suffer any further inconvenience from his malady." And it was so, for he became quite robust, and grew up without ever having any relapse. As Gerard did not go to Castelgrande for the sole purpose of bringing about the reconciliation of which we have spoken, his sojourn there proved to be a mission of mercy to all the inhabitants. He spoke to a great many of them on the bad state of their consciences, and his words were so efficacious that they effected a number of most marvelous conversions. Among others, he won over fifteen young libertines to Jesus Christ, so that while they had formerly perverted others by their scandalous example, they now became so many models of piety.

Such a sensation was caused when he went away, that more than three hundred people accompanied him on his way for more than a mile, showering down prayers and blessings on his head. He had acquired such a high reputation for sanctity, that when the peasantry saw him pass, they left their work and ran after him to receive his blessing. But the fifteen young men he brought to our house at Caposele, to make their confessions to our fathers, were the most ardent of all. The good he effected at Castelgrande was so durable in its results, that a great many of the inhabitants used from that time to come every Saturday to confession at Caposele, although it was from six to seven miles off, and they had to spend the night away from home in consequence of the length of the journey. The pains these good people took in order to compass their pious end, made such an impression on our Father Cafaro, who was a man of eminent sanctity, that he exclaimed, "It is really wonderful; wherever Brother Gerard goes, he puts the whole country in motion."

CHAPTER XVII

*Gerard Goes to Melfi, Where He is Sent For by Mgr. Basta,
and Works Several Prodigies There Also.*

The town of Melfi was also the scene of many marvels,
by which God deigned to honor Brother Gerard. When
Mgr. Basta heard of all that he had done at Corato, and
how he had induced the religious there to lay aside their
rings and other secular ornaments, he exclaimed, "I now
see that Gerard is really a saint!" He therefore wished him
to come to Melfi, and wrote to ask Father Fiocchi, the
rector at Iliceto, to bring him with him during the novena
to St. Theodore. This visit sufficed to cause Brother
Gerard's merits to be appreciated by all the inhabitants.
His Lordship's esteem attracted that of his diocesans also,
and his transports of love, his ecstasies, and the plenitude
of the science of the saints which he possessed, excited
general admiration, and caused everyone to be eager to see
him.

The priests and confessors applied to him, and
communicated their difficulties in the direction of souls.
Gerard replied to all as one filled with heavenly wisdom.
He at once solved the most intricate doubts, and
manifested such admirable discernment of spirits, that he
enlightened all who came to him, and gave them rules to
guide them according to their various necessities.
Although his Lordship was a man of such great learning,
he had private conferences with him himself, and
submitted to all his decisions.

The conversions he effected at Melfi were most
numerous. The priests and confessors sent the most
hardened sinners to him, for by merely speaking to him
they were converted. As soon as Gerard saw that their
dispositions were good, he joyfully conducted them to

Father Fiocchi. Among this number were several gentlemen, who had been leading irregular lives for years, but who abandoned their evil courses and became exemplary for piety after one conversation with Brother Gerard. The astonishing conversions he effected are spoken of at Melfi to this day.

His penetration of hearts caused the most extraordinary discoveries. One day when he was leaving the bishop's palace, he was accosted by a woman who pretended to be a great saint, and who took delight in conversing with good people, and in deceiving them by her hypocrisy. She was a penitent of Father Martin, who was a distinguished member of the order of the Augustinians. Gerard listened to her in silence. When she had done speaking, he gravely replied, "My daughter, why do you wish to impose on me? You have made sacrilegious confessions and communions for many years, and yet you try to pass for a saint! Go and make a good confession if you do not wish to be damned." The woman was quite abashed, and went to Father Martin at once. She did not, however, tell him of the foul stain within her breast, but contented herself by saying that she wished to make a general confession, because Brother Gerard had advised her to do so. "Nonsense, you are going mad!" replied the confessor. Yet she continued her entreaties on the subject, saying that Brother Gerard had disturbed her peace of mind. Upon this he frowned, and became so angry, that he had the indiscretion to slander the pious brother before several people. Meanwhile his penitent went and cast herself at the feet of Canon Rossi, to whom she confessed that she had been led to make sacrilegious confessions for ten years through false shame. She was so penitent for what she had done, that she allowed the canon to disclose the whole to Father Martin, adding that she wished her guilt to be published in the Life of the saintly brother, to whom she owed so much.

There was also a gentleman who had been guilty of sacrilege for years. One day Gerard happened to be in his company, when he said, "My son, you are living in sin. Do you then wish to die a reprobate? Confess the sin you have concealed so long, that you may make your peace with God." The gentleman's heart was touched, and he lost no time in disburdening his conscience.

On another occasion, when he was conversing with a woman, he said to her, "My sister, how can you be at peace, when you are living at enmity with God? Why do you not confess the sin you have been silent about so many years?" The woman was filled with astonishment, and his pious counsels had such an effect on her, that she went and cast herself at the feet of a good confessor.

The gift of prophecy was also vouchsafed to Gerard at Melfi. I will only, however, cite one out of many instances of the same kind. Our Father D. Michael was still living in the world, and seriously ill, when he received a visit from Gerard, who said to him while feeling his pulse, "What, are you feverish? I think you are quite well." And when the doctor came he was cured. On another occasion Gerard said to him, "You will join us one of these days." "I will when I can touch the heavens with my hands," replied Father D. Michael, who had not the most remote idea of embracing the religious state. Indeed he had almost a horror of the very words; and he particularly disliked our Congregation; however, the prophecy was a true one. "At a later period," said he himself, "I became anxious as to the choice of a state of life. My mind was agitated by a thousand contradictory feelings for six months, and I do not myself know how I came to decide to enter the Congregation, for several religious dissuaded me from doing so, and above all, Mgr. Basta, who had a great regard for me."

CHAPTER XVIII

Mgr. Amato's Anxiety to Have Gerard at Cedogna.

Gerard had been several times at Cedogna, and on each occasion many miraculous results had attended his visits. As Mgr. Amato and that great servant of God D. Dominic Cappuccio the archpriest, were greatly distressed on account of several persons, who not only led scandalous lives themselves, but were an occasion of sin to others, they resolved to send for Gerard, being convinced that he alone could provide an effectual remedy for this great evil.

Gerard therefore repaired to Cedogna. He arrived whilst a public epidemic was raging, and was welcomed not as a man, but as an angel sent down from heaven.

The brother of Don Anthony Saponiero, the canon, was so dangerously ill at this time, that it had been settled that he was to receive the last sacraments. Gerard however was asked to visit him previously, which he did. No sooner did the sick man perceive him than he exclaimed, "God be praised!" and Gerard replied, "Do not be distressed; you will get well." And his words came to pass, for the fever left him and the sick man recovered.

There was another person who had been confined to bed for a long time, with a nervous affection, which had baffled every remedy, so that nothing seemed left but to resign himself to the continuance of the evil. However, when Gerard arrived at Cedogna, he sent for him in a spirit of entire confidence. When he came, he made the sign of the cross on the head of the sick man, and said, "Be of good courage; get up in God's name, and come with me to church and make your confession." He was instantly cured. He went to the church and made his confession, and then returned home in perfect health.

Such astonishing prodigies as these made such an

impression on the minds of all, that he was everywhere regarded as a saint. This produced no change in the conduct of the humble brother. He extended his charity to all, and visited the poorest and most abject as readily as those of high degree. Some he excited to patience, others he prepared for eternity, but most of those he went to see were delivered from all their sufferings. I have not space however to enumerate all the cures he effected.

The hopes of his Lordship and of the zealous archpriest were not deceived; indeed their wishes were accomplished to their fullest extent. Gerard went about from house to house, making the most glorious conquests and winning over souls to Jesus Christ. He neither used stratagems nor guile in order to gain his end; but he attacked the fortress of their souls boldly, and with the weapons of salvation in his hand. Sometimes indeed he found some pretext for going to the houses of those he was in search of, but at others he would stop them in the middle of the street, and adroitly gain their confidence, after which he would immediately begin to speak to them on the state of their conscience. When he saw that they were affected by what he said, he took them to the house where he was staying, told them of all their spiritual necessities, and did not leave them until he had won them over to Jesus Christ. When gentleness proved ineffectual, he assumed an air of severity, and subdued the sinner by the mere sound of his voice. People however were in the habit of saying that he could turn people whither he pleased by a mere glance. Amongst all the erring sheep in the neighborhood, there was not one who had not returned to the fold of the Good Shepherd ere he left it.

Amongst others of a similar sort, I will instance one of a very rich man, who had led a most scandalous life for many years. When his poor wife heard that Gerard was at Cedogna, she came and cast herself at his feet, and told him of the state her husband was in with many tears. Gerard sent for him, represented to him the enormity of his crimes, and how infallibly he would damn his soul if he continued to live at enmity with God. In an instant this wolf became gentle as a lamb. When Gerard saw that his dispositions were really changed, he made him promise to come back with him to our house and go through the spiritual exercises. He kept his word, and the holy brother, who had aided him to set the affairs of his conscience in order, then sent him back to his wife an altered being.

There was another gentleman in the town who was very ill, whose conscience was loaded with crimes, and who seemed quite incorrigible. It was in vain that the best confessors and the archpriest Cappucci himself had exhorted him to go to confession; he was deaf to all their remonstrances. Brother Gerard was therefore sent for; he repaired to his house without delay; he knelt down on entering his room and recited an Ave for the sick man. He instantly became humble and penitent, and earnestly solicited to have a confessor of his own accord.

He also gave many striking proofs of his penetration into the hearts of others while he was at Cedogna, but I will confine myself to citing the two following: Gerard was staying in the house of Signor Cappucci. Now it so happened that one day while D. Emmanuelle, the wife of D. Constantine, was on the ground floor, Gerard was talking to her two daughters and her servant on the first floor. The lady grew impatient at this, as she was in want of her daughters, and said within herself, "Saints have always trembled when they were in dangerous positions, but this man is conversing with my daughters and maid without any fear or restraint whatever." After this she forgot all about it. When Gerard afterwards met her, he looked at her and smiled, and when she asked why he did so, he replied, "I have to thank you for having remembered my weakness. I wish all mothers were as thoughtful." As D. Emanuelle could not make out what he meant, she said, "Tell me what you allude to?" "Do you not remember," he replied, "what you said within yourself only a moment ago?" It may be easily believed how surprised the lady was at her most secret thoughts being thus brought to light.

There was a lady of rank who did not know how to detach herself from a person whom she loved with a passionate affection, and who was thus bringing her to the brink of a most dangerous precipice. She confided what she felt to Gerard, who replied, "It is through your own fault, for you are not really faithful to Jesus Christ." He then showed her that she secretly fomented this passion, and that to a great extent. "Close the avenues of your heart better," he added in conclusion, "and then be of good courage." The fact was, that the poor lady had wished to avoid the snare in a very partial degree. She owned how incautious she had been, put Gerard's advice in practice, and was entirely freed from her temptations from that time.

The good brother had not a moment to himself. An innumerable multitude of people, who might almost be called his penitents, surrounded him even during the night, that they might listen to his edifying conversation. Priests and gentlemen were to be seen amongst them. Even Mgr. Amato himself, the flower of the bishops of his time, was never weary of listening to him. "To converse with Gerard on spiritual and theological subjects," said he, "is the same thing as to declare oneself his disciple, and whoever goes to him as a scholar becomes a good theologian, so great are the lights which one acquires by his teaching." What was specially admired in him was his complete recollection, and his constant remembrance of the presence of God in all places and at all times. He spoke readily to all, it is true, but still he never lost sight of God or of himself. His aspirations were ardent and frequent, and all his actions were referred to God. He was often seen in a state of ecstasy, during which he suspended all exterior occupations, which arose either through the forcible attractions of God's grace, or through his own endeavors to become united to Him.

The fame of all these prodigies naturally spread far and wide. The sick at Bisaccia soon sought his aid also, and Gerard had to go to that town, in compliance with the entreaties of the Canons Céla and Saponiero.

There was a man in this town named Bartholemew Melchione. He had been married for upwards of a year, but ever since the marriage had taken place, he had become dull and heavy, and like a possessed person. He was brought to Campagna while in this state to implore the assistance of St. Anthony, but the journey was unsuccessful. When Gerard saw the sick man, he said, "This is of no consequence, my friend; you are very well." He then recited some prayers over the head of the sufferer, who was instantly restored to his former state. He then took him to the house of the canon, and made him eat with him. He also caused him to sing a hymn, during which there was no trace of his former malady. I pass over the other miracles which Gerard performed at Bisaccia in silence.

When he was returning to Iliceto, he went through Rochetta, where he gained a fresh victory. There was a Calabrian merchant who had settled in this town, who had been living with a mistress for some time, by which he gave great and public scandal. When the holy brother was informed of this, he sent for him, and set before him his most secret offenses. The sinner became humbled, and entered into himself. He burst into tears, and conceived quite a horror for the partner of his guilt. When Gerard saw that he was really penitent, he took him to a prudent

confessor. He was so constant in well-doing, that he used
from that time to be most regular in coming to our church
at Iliceto. He afterwards married, on the advice of Brother
Gerard, and returned to his own country.

CHAPTER XIX

Spiritual Correspondence Gerard Kept up with the
Convents at Foggia and Ripacandida; His Zealous Desire to
See Them Well-Filled.

The most hardened sinners were dear to Brother
Gerard, and he spared no pains in order to rescue them
from their evil condition. But innocent and upright souls
were the very joy of his heart. There were two persons of
the greatest piety living at that time, one of them resided
at Foggia and the other at Ripacandida, and God had
bestowed extraordinary graces on them both. The first was
the Mother-Superior Maria Celeste Castarosa, who gave
such general edification by establishing the convent of St.
Savior at Foggia. The second was the Mother-Superior
Maria of Jesus, who revived the spirit of St. Theresa at
Ripacandida. Gerard became acquainted with these two
religious through our fathers, and their virtues caused him
to love them in Christ. When he went to Foggia, (which
often happened,) the first thing he did was to go and see
Mother Celeste, and she in turn rejoiced at being able to
converse with him. Their conversations turned on nothing
but matters of piety, and they mutually incited each other
to virtue.

He was no less strongly attached to Mother Mary of
Jesus. Gerard had the highest opinion of her, and she felt
the greatest esteem for him. When they conversed together
on spiritual topics, they were as two burning flames
mutually enkindling each other, and seemed transformed

into two seraphs of love. One day when they were both contemplating the love we owe to Jesus Christ, Gerard fell into such a ravishment that he seized hold of the grate to moderate his transports of love, and it bent within his grasp as if it had been of wax. One evening when he was speaking to the nuns at this same grate, he said, "I will today lead you into the storehouse of Divine love." He then went on to speak about the claims our Blessed Savior has on our love, upon which he entered into an ecstasy, and the parlor appeared all on fire, as well as the entrance into the convent.

He even communicated his own spiritual necessities in writing to Mother Mary of Jesus. "My sins are innumerable," he once wrote to her, "pray to God to forgive me. Everyone else is converted, while I remain obstinate. Have the charity to do penance with me, so that God may be induced to look on me with pity and love. I make the same request to all your children. I am full of misery, but no one will believe me. God has so ordered it for my greater good, for I shall thus die without consolation, and deserted by all. And it is thus I desire both to live and die that the good pleasure of God may be accomplished in me." In another letter he turned the picture, and said, "I should like to see you become a seraph, all inflamed with the love of God, so that your children might all be led to love God ardently by your example. Ah! let us love our good God. He alone is worthy of our love. How could we exist without loving such a good God with all our hearts!"

Gerard and these nuns were so anxious to gain souls to God that they felt a holy emulation for each other in this regard also. He thus expressed himself when writing to Mother Mary of Jesus about a soul whom they had mutually assisted in gaining to Jesus Christ: "Our dear D. Louis cannot find rest but in God. He is full of love for

God. He is absorbed in Him, and cannot bear to be separated from Jesus Christ. He looks on the world as a thing of nought, and looks upon all creatures in God alone. In fact, he loves God so much, that he is transformed into His likeness. I cannot say more."

The letters which this servant of God wrote to Mother Mary Celeste have not been preserved.

The high opinion which these two religious entertained regarding Brother Gerard naturally led to his being highly thought of by their children also, so that there was not a nun in the convents at Foggia and Ripacandida, who did not correspond with him about the state of her soul. The superiors rejoiced at the great good which was thus effected, and their respective bishops, Mgr. Basta and Mgr. Simone, were equally delighted at the spiritual advantage which the nuns derived from this intercourse. Gerard often went to the two convents, and when he could not go there in person, he made up for his absence by letters, which cannot be read without admiration, said Father Cafaro, especially when one remembers that he was but a poor lay-brother, who had scarcely been taught how to read and write.

Amongst the number I cannot omit to cite the two following notes: "My sister," he wrote to a religious, "recommend me to God. I have more need of your prayers now than ever. I never forget you, for your very name (of the Holy Trinity) makes me always think of God, and draws me to Him. My sister! God knows how truly I esteem you, because you are a faithful spouse of Jesus Christ. Love God with your whole heart, and become a saint, no matter what it costs you. Have courage. Suffer for God, and then your trials here will be an earnest of heaven hereafter." To another he wrote, "My dear sister in Jesus Christ, I trust you will remember me, by loving me, and praying to God for me. I assure you, you can be of real assistance to me, for you are called the Sister of Divine Love, and I believe that you yourself are filled with that love, and that you are wholly conformed to the adorable will of God. Become a saint without loss of time." By these specimens our readers may judge of the fervor and love of God with which all his letters were filled. What concerned the inmates of these convents, was always near to the heart of Brother Gerard also. When one of the nuns at Foggia was dangerously ill, he wrote as follows to Mother Mary: "I want you to pray very fervently for a sister who is very ill. Tell our good God that I trust she will live, for I am anxious that she should become more holy, and not die until she is of an advanced age, so that she may have the merit and happiness of having passed a number of years in the service of God. Let us have confidence in the almighty power of God; may He grant our desires. In His name I give you obedience not to let her die, and I will begin a novena for her cure." And it was answered, for she recovered.

He was so highly thought of by the respective bishops of these two convents, that he even obtained leave to visit the sisters when they were ill.

There was a pensioner in the convent of St. Savior at Foggia, who was attacked by an illness which had exhausted all the resources of art. As soon as Gerard heard of it, he hastened to go and see her, and making the sign of the cross on her head, he said to her, "Be healed," and the fever instantly left her, and she became quite well. As he was afterwards going into the choir, he was asked to play the organ. He declined, saying that he did not know how to do it, but as they continued to press him, he at last consented, and executed a most beautiful pastorale in the most masterly manner. He made the greatest efforts to cause these two convents to be well-filled, and that a spirit of the greatest piety might reign among their inmates. It was through him that the three daughters of Signor Graziola, the general agent of the Prince of Torella, were placed in the convent of Ripacandida. When he met with a young person who was piously disposed, he managed to persuade her and her parents to do whatever he pleased. He placed as many as twelve cousins of Signor Cappucci of Lacedogna in that of Foggia. He also caused one of his own nieces to enter there as a lay-sister. He took her to the convent himself. When they were crossing the Ofante, he enthusiastically exclaimed, "Do you mean to labor to become a saint? If you have not firmly resolved to do so, I will throw you in the river this very instant." When a young person of good family, but in impoverished circumstances, spoke to him about her vocation, he did all he could to place her in one of these two convents. He even importuned persons of high rank for large sums of money, and never ceased his efforts until he had obtained enough to provide for her dowry. When he could not succeed in obtaining what he wanted himself, he had recourse to others to assist him. Thus in one of his letters to Mother Mary, he said, "Write and ask D. Benedict to give a large alms for Mary Joseph's dowry, and get him to ask the Prince of Torella to give one likewise. Let his gift and that of the prince amount to a hundred ducats each. I feel averse to taking a very prominent part in this affair, but if I can obtain leave from Father Fiocchi, we shall bring the matter to a happy termination. I have also written to Sister Mary Frances of Muro, to get her to ask her brother to contribute something towards this good work."

He also made interest with Father Margotta for another young person. "My father," he wrote to him, "it is three years since Sister Mary Joseph asked me to assist her sister to join the community of the convent at Ripacandida. As I am not a free agent, I can do nothing to help her of myself, but still I feel that God inspires me to aid her.

Father Fiocchi is also most anxious to assist her. He has promised to give me some money towards her dowry, and has told me to collect the remainder. I have obtained fifty ducats already, for God has caused me everywhere to meet with open hands and hearts. Have confidence then, my father, and ask everyone you think can aid you without shrinking through human respect. I shall go on begging without the smallest shame. Apply to Signor Borelli, etc. You can do all I wish if you will."

Gerard was equally partial to the Benedictine convents at Atella and Calitri. Our Fathers Fiocchi and Margotta had established community life there, and restored the rigorous observance of rule. The pious brother was attached to these convents because the Spirit of God dwelt therein, and he caused several ladies of rank to enter them. Many of the nuns there were in correspondence with him, and he often went to see them. Mgr. Basta rejoiced at this, especially with regard to that of Atella, which was in his diocese, for where Gerard went, piety was sure to flourish, and his visits were productive of great good to both these convents. Nothing gave him greater pleasure than to find young persons who corresponded with his own pious desires, and were anxious to consecrate themselves to Jesus Christ. When he was at Cedogna, D. Joseph Panarella the priest asked him to get two poor girls received as lay-sisters either in the convent established by Father D. Francis Pepe, the Jesuit at Naples, or in some other convent. He exerted himself so zealously on the occasion that he succeeded in getting them both admitted. Indeed through his means a great many other young persons were placed in divers convents, either as lay or choir sisters.

CHAPTER XX

Wise Regulations for the Government of a Community,
Which Brother Gerard Gave to the Newly-Elected
Superioress in the Convent at Ripacandida.

Everyone in the diocese of Melfi, and especially the
sisters in the convent at Ripacandida, is aware of the
profound wisdom of Mother Mary Michael of the Holy
Ghost. Yet, after she was elected superioress, she distrusted
her own lights, and asked Brother Gerard to direct her
how to exercise her new office worthily. The good brother
assented to her request, and sent her the following rule,
which he composed himself:

"My dear Mother Prioress,
"Forgive me for the sake of Jesus and Mary, for having
been on this occasion as slothful as ever, and for having
been so tardy in sending you the rule you requested to
have. The will of God be done! I write in great haste, to ask
you charitably to forgive my procrastination.

"In the first place, my dear mother, as you stand in
God's stead, you must perform every duty with the utmost
fidelity, if you wish to please Him who has selected you to
fill His place. You must exercise the greatest prudence, and
always act according to the dictates of the Spirit of God.
You should possess the greatest virtue, and set your
subjects such a good example that they may never have
cause to find fault with what you do. You ought to
resemble a pure vase filled with every virtue, so that you
may be able to communicate them to your subjects, so that
by imitating their mother they may advance day by day in
the paths of perfection. A superior ought never to lose
sight of her own vileness and proneness to evil. Never
forget that God raised you to this high office by His mercy

alone, and not for your deserts, since there are so many others who would fill it so much better. Let humility therefore lead you to feel compassion for the faults of others. Fulfill the duties of your office in a spirit of love, and do not shrink from it as a burden too heavy for you to bear. Remember that God has destined it for you from all eternity, and perform its duties with angelic perfection. Keep close to the Divine will, and remain in this post with entire indifference, without either attachment or repugnance to any duty it entails.

"In difficult cases which you cannot decide by yourself, have recourse to someone who is enlightened by the Spirit of God; but when you have once determined as to the course you ought to pursue, carry it out without human respect, having a single eye to God's glory, were it to cause you to shed the last drop of your blood. The love of God should lead you to despise your own reputation, as if you had none. A superior ought often to say, 'God wills that I should fill this post, and I will do His holy will in all things. I must watch over all my children; I must be the servant of all. It is my duty to counsel them, to instruct them, to comfort them, and to satisfy all their wants. I must give the best of everything to others, and keep the worst for myself, and this from the sole motive of pleasing God. Finally, I must suffer in all things, that I may become conformed to the likeness of my beloved and heavenly Spouse.'

"The mind of a superior should resemble a wheel, and be ever in motion, that she may thus never omit to provide for the wants of her children, whom she ought to love in God alone, and without any distinction of persons. As she knows that her children cannot procure even necessaries but through holy obedience, she ought to forget herself and think only of providing for their well-being. If she receives presents of food, clothes, and such like, she should supply their wants before she satisfies her own.

"She ought to try to inspire them all with confidence, and especially those in whom this sentiment is wanting. For this purpose she should use every method which prudence can suggest in order to gain their affection. She should treat them with kindness, even when she feels disinclined to do so; she should exercise continual violence upon herself in this respect, from the desire of thus becoming pleasing to God. If she does not act in this manner, and does not show maternal affection for those who are tempted, their difficulties will increase, and as they will feel neglected and despised, they may thus be driven to despair. At least this feeling will be as a thorn in their heart, and will prevent their making progress in the love of God, for this proneness to discouragement is a great temptation to women.

"In order to be obeyed, the superior must however unite firmness to gentleness. She must chastise the rebellious, who refuse to listen to the voice of God, but in this she must exercise great prudence. If a reproof be tempered with sweetness, it leaves behind it a kind of peace in the soul, which enables it to perceive its fault. A salutary correction might, for instance, be given in the following manner: 'My daughter, you act in a manner which is unworthy of your high vocation, and it is my duty to reprove you for it. I cannot in conscience put up with your conduct any longer, for it is a source of scandal to all your sisters. My God, what shall I do with this imperfect soul? Alas, my child! if you go on thus, it would have been assuredly better for you to have remained in the world than come to fill a place in God's house, in which anyone but you would have become sanctified. I speak thus, and I must speak to you thus, for I am your mother. God knows how sincerely I love you, and how ardently I desire your welfare and perfection. My child, resolve to give yourself wholly to God, and to correct your faults. Enter into yourself; see if I can assist you in any way, and then come back to me with filial confidence.'

"I think that a correction like that would be calculated to incite an imperfect religious to apply to her superior with confidence, who might thus be able to rescue her from a state of tepidity, and cause her to re-enter the paths of perfection. One always gains more by mildness than by harshness, which leads to distress, temptation, gloom, and discouragement. On the other hand, gentleness is followed by peace and tranquility, and animates the soul to the love of God. If all superiors would follow these rules, all subjects would become saints. It is the want of prudence which causes so much disquiet in some religious houses. Now where there is disturbance the devil must have sway, and where that is the case God must assuredly be absent."

The remainder of this letter is lost, but this will suffice to give the highest idea of Brother Gerard's wisdom to all who are enlightened regarding the direction of others.

Chapter XXI
Respectful Obedience which Brother Gerard Requires Religious to Pay to their Ordinary.

As various innovations had arisen in the convent at Ripacandida, Mgr. Basta determined to put an end to them by forbidding the religious to speak to or write to any other director but their ordinary confessor, not even excepting Brother Gerard. This annoyed them exceedingly, and caused some murmurs to arise, for most part of them had been in the habit of following his advice in all things. As the prioress herself had always acted as if she were his penitent, she sent him a message through a priest to tell him of her sorrow, as well as of the general commotion to which this prohibition had given rise. Gerard was far from being offended at it, or from disapproving of his Lordship's conduct. Indeed, he highly approved it, and praised the wisdom which had suggested it. He wished the religious to submit to it cheerfully, and did all he could to persuade them to do so. We will here give a striking letter which he wrote to the superioress on this occasion: "Dear Reverend Mother, if the illustrious and well-beloved bishop has forbidden you to write letters, he has done well, and it is assuredly in accordance with the will of God. I rejoice that God has sent you so many contradictions, for it is a proof that He loves you, and wishes you to be most closely united to Himself. Be quiet then, and of good courage, for such contrarieties ought to fill you with gladness rather than with sorrow. Everything should be subordinate to the will of God. But you know this better than I can tell you, so what more can I say? I have always spoken to you with all openness, and I ever will do so. You are my mistress on this head. I cannot conceive how one who is consecrated to God can find any bitterness in anything on earth, or how she can cease to find pleasure in entire conformity to His will in all things, for it is the only stay of our souls. Accursed be that self-love which estranges souls from this great treasure, from this foretaste of Paradise, nay, from this possession of God Himself. O how profound must be that ignorance which could make us neglect such a treasure! Although this decision may not seem to us to be God's will, is it therefore not so? Does God deal with us differently to anyone else? shall we be saved by any road peculiar to ourselves? What can be better and more pleasing to God than to do His adorable will always and in all things? And do we not accomplish it perfectly when we do it as He wills, when He wills, and where He wills, being always ready to obey Him in all things from the least to the greatest? Be then wholly indifferent to all but the accomplishment of God's will with that sovereign purity He desires of us. The will of God is the great thing. O thou hidden and invaluable treasure! thou art as holy as the Divinity Himself. Thy excellence is so great that none but God can comprehend it! I assure you it makes me very thankful to feel that your soul, dear Rev. Mother, is one of those which lives in simple dependance on the will of my God, for I well know your heroic virtue on this point. Let your will then be transformed into that of God in all things. What is the sole occupation of the angels in heaven? Is it not to do the will of God? Let us then strive to do on earth what the angels do in heaven. The will of God in heaven makes the Paradise of heaven; therefore, the will of God on earth will turn earth into a Paradise. Let all your children hear these lines, for I think that his Lordship's prohibition extends not only to you, but also to all the sisters. He has acted well, and I trust that no one will complain of what he has done, for that would be the same thing as to murmur against God Himself. May His will be done! I assure you I am quite satisfied that you should cease to write to me, and when I say this I include the whole community. If there is the least shadow of disobedience in sending me messages or remembrances from the sisters, I beg you will not do it anymore, and abstain from so doing for the love of God. I am quite satisfied with all. It will be enough if you will remember me before the throne of grace. I wish things to be as they are, for I know the purity of the intentions of this holy prelate, and that all he desires is to see you wholly united to Jesus Christ. If I come into your neighborhood, I will not even ask leave to see you or write to you. Why need we care to see each other here below, since we shall one day meet in heaven? Whilst we are on earth, therefore, let us labor to sanctify our souls by doing the will of others, and not our own will, since the will of others is what God wills for us."

This letter produced all the desired effect, for the religious at once consented to be as submissive as he wished. Mgr. Basta's prohibition was in truth really called for. The difference of opinions among their various confessors had produced such division amongst the religious, that unity had entirely disappeared from the convent. One followed Cephas, and another Apollo; it was through prudence alone that his Lordship made no exception in favor of Brother Gerard, for when he had succeeded in preventing the nuns writing any more letters concerning the state of their consciences, he told them he wished them all to be regulated by the advice of Brother Gerard, since he was a religious of the same spirit as themselves. His Lordship had such a high esteem for the saintly brother, that when he went to Ripacandida to examine into the virtues of Mother Mary of Jesus, he took Brother Gerard with him as well as Father Fiocchi, who was a man of eminent sanctity, whose body was found incorrupt four years after his death.

CHAPTER XXII

Infamous Calumny Invented Against Brother Gerard: His Exceeding Patience and Silence.

We are now going to see how Gerard comported himself under the greatest suffering. It is well known that the just are usually the victims of calumny, and so it was in the case of this good brother; for as the devil was enraged at finding that all the weapons he had employed against him were of no avail, and that he was daily waging a cruel warfare against him, he had recourse to stratagem, and maliciously succeeded in aiming a dart at him which pierced him to the quick.

It so happened that there was a young girl in a house where the holy brother was in the habit of staying when he was traveling, who had unhappily allowed herself to be seduced. Now the author of the crime persuaded her to attribute it to Brother Gerard; not satisfied with that, he blackened his reputation to our Father Alphonsus himself, and painted the calumny in such forcible and minute terms, that there seemed no possibility of doubting its truth. As this letter was written by a priest, and as the good brother was really intimate with the people of this house, the fact was taken for granted. Gerard of course was not impeccable. And it was by no means an unprecedented thing, for men of eminent sanctity have fallen under similar circumstances. If Alphonsus therefore did not attach implicit faith to what he heard, he at least felt inclined to believe it. Brother Gerard was therefore sent for to Nocera, when the enormity of the crime he was supposed to have committed was set before him, but instead of justifying himself he remained as if he were insensible, without uttering a word in his defense. In consequence of this he was prohibited from receiving Holy Communion, and forbidden under the strictest penalties from having dealings with anyone whatsoever, whether by word of mouth or by letter. Gerard bore all without complaint, and his peace seemed to know no diminution in consequence. Several persons urged him to justify himself, but he replied, "There is a just God. It is for Him to do that."

This calumny made a great sensation in the monastery, but his joyous manner made a still deeper impression on the minds of all. "My cause, O blessed Jesus, is Thy cause," said Gerard; "if Thou willest my humiliation, I cheerfully submit, for Thou Thyself didst tread that narrow path before me." He redoubled his austerities, retrenched his sleep yet more than before, and generally passed the night in the open air on the roof of the house. Whilst contemplating in the glories of the firmament the almighty power of God, his afflicted heart derived strength and comfort by holy meditation. The little rest he allowed himself was only taken in a coffin which had contained the precious remains of our Father Sportelli. So far from complaining of his humiliation, he rather rejoiced at it. His inferior nature no doubt revolted at it, but when feelings of repugnance arose within him, he distrusted his own strength, and had recourse to the prayers of others. He pitied his calumniator on account of the enmity in which he was living with God, offered up his own sufferings to God for him, and was unceasingly praying Him to bestow on him the grace of repentance.

Whilst in this painful situation, Gerard's distress did not arise from his reputation being blackened in the eyes of the Congregation, or of those without, but from being deprived of Holy Communion. However, he did not fail to conform his will to that of God in this point also. When he was pitied for this deprivation, he replied, "It is enough for me to have Jesus in my heart." One day when one of our fathers was urging him to ask our Father Alphonsus to allow him to communicate, he hesitated for a little, but he soon came to a resolution. "No, no," said he. And striking his hand against the windowsill, he added, "We must die under the pressure of the will of God." On another occasion, he joyfully replied to a father who asked him to serve his Mass, "Do not tempt me, I should snatch our Lord out of your hands at the altar."

As Gerard was very intimate with our Father D. Margotta, (so renowned for his sanctity), the saintly brother did not fail to inform him of what had befallen him, and of his own line of conduct in this conjuncture. He received the following note in reply: "My dear Gerard, your letter has given me a double pleasure: first, because you tell me you remember me in your prayers; and next, because your will is united to that of God during the trial He has been pleased to send you. For my part, as I wish you to be filled with heavenly benedictions, I cannot but approve of your resolution to do nothing but what may be suggested to you by holy obedience. Although I am so unworthy, I pray God and our good Mother Mary to give you strength to enable you to be conformed to the Divine will in all things, and to put all your good desires into effect."

Meanwhile, Gerard's silence gave rise to much apprehension. As he had according to all appearances been guilty of sacrilege, Alphonsus sent him to Ciorani, in hopes he might have more confidence in some father in this house. He also told me and Father Rossi the superior, to watch all his actions while he was there as narrowly as possible. But we could find nothing to censure in him. He always seemed cheerful and serene. He was humble towards all, and ready to obey every command. What was most astonishing, was that he never uttered the slightest complaint. When he had any leisure time, he spent it either in his own room, or in praying before the Blessed Sacrament. When he had passed some time in this manner at Ciorani, he was again recalled to Nocera.

The divine attributes were still the subject of his meditations, and it was in this vast ocean that he appeased his ardent thirst to communicate. One day when asked how he could live without communicating, he replied, "I revive my fainting heart by contemplating the immensity of my God." In fact, he always seemed absorbed in the most sublime contemplation. One day Father Cajone witnessed one of his ecstasies, which he thus describes: "As Brother Gerard was ill I attended on him, for I was then prefect over the sick. One evening when I was meditating with him, the subject I chose for our contemplation was the love which we owe to God, and how much He deserves our love. I had scarcely named the points for meditation, when Gerard was ravished out of himself. He was lying on his back, with his head resting against the wall, and his eyes fixed on heaven. I did not at first believe there was anything supernatural in it, but when the meditation was over, although I made a good deal of noise, he remained in the same position, with his eyes immoveable, and clearly ravished out of himself into an ecstasy. He remained in this state for some time, which caused me to feel great astonishment, and made a deep impression on my mind.

Mother Mary Celeste was greatly distressed when Brother Gerard's disgrace became known at Foggia. As she did not know the particulars, she fancied he was suffering for having exercised his works of love too freely. She therefore wrote to him in these terms, "We have heard of your trial with great sorrow. You are always made to suffer for your charity. The devil has effectually prevented your coming to Foggia this time. However, the will of God be done; we trust that the matter will end in the powers of darkness being put to confusion. Let us be united together in God in spirit wherever our bodies may happen to be, and let us love Jesus Christ our only good, who has loved us and given Himself for us." Gerard remained in the crucible of tribulation for about two months. But God was at length satisfied with the extent of his humility, and brought his innocence to light. Some say that the priest fell dangerously ill, which caused him to retract all that he had formerly asserted, and that indeed he was obliged by his confessor to write to our Father Alphonsus and acknowledge that he had written his first letter at the instigation of the devil, and that all it contained was a mere calumny. Others assert that the obligation of making this declaration was imposed on the young woman when she approached the sacred tribunal, and that she told her parents that Gerard was not the author of this great crime, whilst her confessor addressed a letter to Alphonsus to inform him of the innocence of the saintly brother. One thing at least is certain, there were two letters concerning the matter.

These glad tidings caused a general sensation of joy. As for Gerard, calumny had failed to cast him down, so the vindication of his innocence did not make him either vain or elated. Father Alphonsus one day asked him why he had not defended himself; he replied, "How could I, since the rule commands us not to make excuses, but to bear every species of mortification in silence?" On another occasion he said to him, "Were you not very sad at being unable to communicate?" "Never," answered Gerard; "if Jesus Christ did not choose to come to me, what right had I to complain?"

Up to this time our Father Alphonsus had not known much of Brother Gerard, who had been received at Iliceto, where he had been ever since. But when our Father Margotta went to Nocera, he told him of the rare virtues of this holy brother, of the favors he received from on high, and of the ardor with which he strove to obtain the highest possible perfection. Alphonsus was quite astonished at this account; however he himself uttered these remarkable words concerning him, "If he had no other virtues than those he exercised during this time of trial, I should think highly of him." The same father afterwards asked that he might be allowed to go to Naples with him, which was granted without any difficulty.

Part II

Chapter I

*Brother Gerard's Sojourn at Naples; His Exemplary
Conduct in that City.*

Whilst Naples was a new theater for the virtues of
Gerard, it was in itself a novelty to him. But the striking
beauties of this rich capital, which might have caused the
mind of another to become dissipated, only afforded his
piety fresh methods of union with God. As Father
Margotta gave him nothing to do, he spent all his time in
visiting the various churches and in spiritual
contemplation. He preferred going to those where the
devotion of the Forty Hours was being celebrated. As
Father Margotta's feelings had much similarity with those
of Gerard, they always went about together, and often
forgot to return home in proper time. This good father was
also eager to gain all the indulgences he could, which was
a source of great joy to Gerard, who was his constant
companion, and thus shared in the same privileges. Indeed
to be enabled freely to hold converse with his God, formed
a perfect Paradise to the saintly brother. " I am at Naples
with Father Margotta," he wrote to a religious at
Ripacandida, "and I have leisure to pour out my soul
before God."

He one day went to a shop full of images, where some
crucifixes were being made, and his love for Jesus crucified
made him conceive an ardent desire to learn how to make
them himself. As the shopkeeper was a great friend of
ours, he at once acceded to his wishes. After Gerard had
frequented his workshop for some time he became very
expert in the art. He took several models of crucifixes and

"ECC homo" with him when he left Naples, that he might make some like them to distribute amongst the Faithful.

This sojourn at Naples was so far from being a time of ease to Brother Gerard, that it afforded him several opportunities of increasing his mortifications. There was a sort of holy emulation between him and Father Margotta, which caused them to make use of every possible kind of penance. Their only wish seemed to be that which could torment himself the most. Father Margotta never remembered to provide anything for the meals, and as Brother Gerard thought as little about them, they often remained fasting. One day when Father Margotta returned home about noon, he asked what he had prepared for dinner. "Just what you ordered," replied Gerard laughing; that is to say, he had made no preparations at all. The floor served for their bed, and the bodies of both were encompassed by haircloth and iron chains. One thing alone afflicted the heart of Gerard. It was to see the poor all around him, and to have nothing to give them. One day when Brother Tartaglione came to see him, while Father Margotta was absent, he gave him some money to buy provisions. While Gerard was out upon this errand he met a man selling matches and tinder-boxes, who begged him to bestow an alms on him, adding that he was dying with hunger. Gerard was touched with compassion. He thought no more of the meat and fish, and in his simplicity gave him all the money he had in exchange for the trifles in his basket. When Brother Francis saw him, he asked him what he had prepared for dinner. Without replying to his question, Gerard joyfully embraced him, and said, "Why be so careful? Let us think of God alone and nothing more." "That is all very well," responded the brother, "but we must think a little bit about our bodies also." As he then perceived the tinder-boxes and matches on the table, he said, "What is all this for?" "Dear Brother," replied Gerard, "they may be useful to us someday or other. I will candidly own to you that I met a poor starving man whilst I was out who was selling these things, and I could not refrain from buying them with the money you gave me." This answer annoyed Brother Francis not a little, although he admired the good brother's charity, and controlled his mortification as well as he could.

Gerard took great pleasure in visiting the incurables. He felt the most lively compassion for these suffering members of Jesus Christ, and devoted all the time he could possibly spare from his other occupations to administering to their wants. He went about amongst these poor creatures animating some to patience, and preparing others to die. He never omitted to visit them on the days appointed for that purpose by the rules of the hospital, and delighted in procuring them every possible relief, whether spiritual or corporal.

Those bereft of reason were also the objects of his special charity. He collected all who were capable of receiving instruction together in the courtyard, instructed them on the truths of religion as well as he could, and exhorted them to obey those who had the care of them. He spoke to them with such kindness, that the moment they saw him they used joyfully to run to meet him. "My father," they would say, "you are so good to us, we wish you would stay with us, and never leave us anymore. No, you must not go away. No one else tells us such beautiful things as you do. Your lips are the gate of Paradise, and we never weary in listening to the sweet words which you utter." He would sometimes carry them little sweets that he might thus attach them to him, and incline their hearts to receive his instructions.

His zealous efforts were however principally directed to the conversion of sinners, and not a day passed in which he did not save some abandoned soul. He took every opportunity of visiting the librarians, printers, and other tradespeople of our acquaintance, that he might excite their workmen to lead virtuous lives. If he found that the consciences of any of their men were not in a good state, he never lost sight of them until he had caused them to become reconciled with God. Those whom he thus gained over afterwards converted their companions, and thus our house soon became a sort of vestibule of penance.

The holy brother had often to put up with the jeers and insults of the lazzaroni while he was going about the town, for his humble and neglected exterior led them to despise him; but as all his sanctity was within, he rejoiced in all such humiliations.

CHAPTER II
Great Credit Which Gerard Enjoys at Naples; The Marvelous Works He Effects There.

Notwithstanding all the pains which Gerard took to conceal his sanctity, its bright luster was soon spread throughout the town. In Father Margotta's visit to the different religious communities, he was always accompanied by Brother Gerard, who thus soon came to be looked upon as a saint by those who were themselves most distinguished for piety. Father Margotta attests that the brothers of the Congregation of Pious Workmen, the Jesuit Fathers, and those of the Oratory, entertained the highest opinion of him, and unanimously concurred in thinking that he was specially directed by the Spirit of God. His humility, poverty, modesty, and recollection, filled them all with admiration. Father Francis Pepe amongst others, who was himself so renowned for virtue and science, felt the greatest affection for him, and delighted in conversing for hours at a time with him. He also made him his coadjutor in the distribution of the numerous indulgences Pope Benedict XIV. had empowered him to bestow. He placed several thousand plenary indulgences at his disposal, which he allowed him to grant to the Faithful who frequented the altar, or who paid a daily visit to the Blessed Sacrament, as well as to those who honored the Mother of God in some special way, such as by visiting her images, or fasting on Saturdays in her honor. He also gave him faculties to bestow privileged altars on pious and exemplary priests, together with several other favors of a similar sort, too numerous to specify.

The supernatural graces with which Brother Gerard was favored by God, such as the penetration of hearts, the gift of prophecy, and the discernment of spirits, were as manifest in Naples as they had been elsewhere. For brevity's sake I will only mention the most remarkable, however. As it was noised about throughout the town that this illiterate brother knew every doctrine of religion as well as the most profound theologian, many learned men wished to ascertain the truth of this assertion, and came and proposed several theological and moral doubts and difficulties to him. Our Father Celestine de Robertis thus described the discomfiture of one of these theologians, which he himself witnessed: "One day when I was at Naples, a priest began to enter into controversy with Brother Gerard on the mystery of the Blessed Trinity, which he was then studying. He alluded to the difficult mysteries therein contained, such as the generation of the Word, His co-eternity with the Father, and the procession of the Holy Ghost from the Father and Son. Brother Gerard was far from appearing bewildered or at a loss. He replied to every question with such exactness and precision, that I was lost in admiration at the ease and clearness with which he expressed himself on points on which the best theologians have to speak with caution. In fine, the priest had the greatest difficulty in the world to put an end to the discussion without showing that he was vanquished and put to confusion."

On another occasion Gerard and D. Francis Colella went into a shop where rosaries and medals were sold. As the shopkeeper was a man who made pretense of sanctity, he at once turned the conversation on spiritual subjects. He was however far from being what he professed to be. Gerard therefore drew him aside and showed him how full of guilt his soul must appear in the sight of God. Amongst other things he reminded him of one mortal sin which was only known to himself and God. As D. Colella remained in the shop after Brother Gerard left it, the proprietor came back to him again, when he said, "That father who has just gone out must be a great saint." "Indeed he is," replied D. Colella; and the shopkeeper immediately added, "I am quite bewildered. He has just told me of a sin which was known to none but God and me."

The following incident was no less surprising. God had afflicted Father Margotta for some months with such interior desolation and aridity that he was in a most pitiable state. One day, when he was suffering more than usual, he said to Gerard, "Let us go together to St. George's, to ask Father Côme to get our Lady of Power to obtain some relief for me." "Very well, let us go," replied Gerard, "but you will not obtain this favor yet." The prophecy was a true one, and was confirmed by another, as we shall see hereafter. Although Father Margotta went to St. George's and spoke to Father Côme, he returned home in greater suffering than ever.

In this way Gerard's renown for sanctity spread more and more widely, and nothing else was rife in Naples. Crowds came to our house to see him: some came to consult him, others came to enkindle fervor within their own breasts by hearing his pious conversation; whilst others came to expose the sad state of their consciences to him, and to get him to help them to make a good confession. Even chaplains and regulars of distinction came to visit him. Amongst others D. Paul de Majo, that great servant of God, who was so celebrated for his devotion to the Blessed Virgin and for his talent as a painter, entertained the highest esteem for him. Ladies of the highest rank considered it a favor to be allowed to converse with him and to receive him into their houses. Eleonore Sanfelice, the Duchess of Ascoli, who had known him in la Pouille, was the first to publish his virtues. Father Margotta did not know how to get rid of them all, and the holy brother himself was much pained at always being surrounded by such a concourse of people. One morning when he was alone in the house he heard someone knocking at the door. When he opened it he found a servant there. When he asked what he wanted, he replied, "Her Grace the Duchess of Maddalon begs to see Brother Gerard." As he saw that the messenger did not know him, he gave this answer, "I cannot make out why such a fuss should be made about this brother, who is half a simpleton. They are strangely deceived about him at Naples I see. Tell this to her Grace, if you please."

One day he met a lady at the door of the Church of the Holy Ghost, who had met him before at a friend's house, and who thus accosted him, "Brother Gerard, I hope you will do me the favor of coming to my house; I have a son who is ill and in great suffering." To this Gerard wisely and humbly replied, "Madam, what use could my visit be? However, I promise to recommend him to our Blessed Lady." He used always to make similar answers on such occasions.

Gerard had a perfect horror of those vagrants who pretend to be cripples, and lead an idle life by means of the alms they obtain by their roguery. There was one of them who dragged himself about on crutches, and was always sitting near our hospital, with his leg bandaged up in old linen, to excite the compassion of the passersby. Gerard had reproved him on several occasions, but to no purpose. As his patience was at length quite exhausted, he one day gave him a most sharp reprimand, and took off all the hypocritical coverings from his leg, saying, "You cheat! if you wish to save your soul, give over making a mockery of God and man." The abashed impostor ran off as fast as he could on both legs, without bestowing a thought on the crutches he left behind.

The following tale is more tragic. When Gerard went out, he was in the habit of passing through a bystreet which runs between the convent of the Queen and that of St. Joseph. Now everytime he went by, there were two women of bad character, who never omitted to insult his humility and his modesty. One day during the carnival they presented themselves before him as usual. One of them had a tambourine in her hand, and the other had a pipe hung round her neck, and stopping up the path before him, they began to play on their instruments, and to insult him by many indelicate words and gestures. Upon this Gerard gravely said to them, "So you will not desist from this conduct? Do you then wish to experience the judgments of God?" He had hardly pronounced these words when one of them fell down half dead, and had to be carried home.

The incident I am now going to relate is still more remarkable. One day when he was passing by that part of the town called Peter the Fisherman, he saw a great crowd on the seashore who were uttering loud cries and lamentations; for a furious storm had come on, and everyone was watching a bark full of people which could not reach the land, and which therefore seemed in imminent danger of being lost. Gerard was moved with compassion at seeing the danger to which these poor people were exposed, as well as by the cries and tears of those who were gazing at them in unavailing distress. He therefore fortified himself by the sign of the cross, threw his cloak about him, and advancing into the waves, he exclaimed to the bark, "Stop, in the name of the Adorable Trinity!" and he seized hold of it as if it had been a piece of cork, and drew it to the shore. He then issued forth from the waves, before a multitude of spectators, without even having his clothes wet. At the sight of such a prodigy the cry of "A miracle! a miracle!" arose in all directions. In order to escape from the observation of the crowd, Gerard took flight through the streets, as if he had committed some great crime, and never stopped until he reached the house of a shopkeeper who was one of our friends, where he remained until nightfall. When he got to Caposele Father Cajone afterwards asked him to relate the particulars of what had happened on this occasion. Gerard laughingly replied, "O, I caught hold of the bark with two of my fingers, and drew it to the shore!" "I suppose you threw yourself into the sea to cool yourself," added Dr. Santorelli. "In the state in which I was then," replied Gerard, (alluding to his ecstasy,) "I could have flown in the air." This glorious action enhanced the reputation of the servant of God a thousandfold, and is talked of at Naples at the present day.

The recurrence of marvels such as these caused him to be so highly thought of in the capital, that he was an object of general notice wherever he went. As Father Margotta saw that this was a dangerous position for Gerard, for the breath of praise may stir up the spirit of vainglory in the hearts of the most humble, he resolved to send him back to one of our houses. He therefore begged our Father Alphonsus to place him in that of Caposele, which he had himself founded, and for which he always felt a peculiar predilection.

CHAPTER III
Gerard's Sojourn in the House at Caposele; Prodigies which He Effects While There.

Brother Gerard's mode of life at Caposele was just the same as it had been at Iliceto. He was always humble, patient, and laborious; and as he was always recollected and united to God, every charge was agreeable to him. It was a matter of indifference to him whether he had to act as cook, baker, or porter, for, as he himself said, in every employment he felt sure of doing the will and good pleasure of God. Father Cajone could testify that he almost snatched the work from the hands of others, that he might do it himself, although his body was weakened and worn down by penances. Indeed, as this good father says, he was always at work, even when he was really ill.

His residence at Caposele was a sort of succession of prodigies and good works. He was so constantly surrounded by priests and gentlemen, that he could not get a quiet moment for himself. He therefore asked Father Juvenal, the rector of this house, to let him make a day's retreat, which he granted; but as he was wanted in the morning, he sent someone to his room to look for him. As his messenger did not find him, he went to the choir, but there was no Brother Gerard there either. The whole house was then searched, but to no purpose. Meanwhile Dr. Santorelli came in, to whom Father Juvenal instantly said, "We have lost Brother Gerard." Santorelli replied, "Perhaps he is hiding under his bed; let us go and see." And taking a lay-brother with him, he examined the room for himself, but this search was equally ineffectual. There is no cause for alarm," he then said; "when it is time to go to communion he will no doubt reappear." And this was just what took place. The father-rector immediately sent for Gerard, and asked him where he had been. "In my room," he replied. "In your room!" answered the rector, "why we have been twice there to look for you, and could not find you." Gerard smiled and was silent, but on being commanded to explain such an extraordinary circumstance, he replied with the greatest simplicity, "As I was afraid of being distracted during my retreat, I prayed to God to make me invisible." This answer filled Father Juvenal and Dr. Santorelli with astonishment; but the rector replied in a tone of annoyance, "I do not like these mysteries. I will forgive you this time, but take care not to make such petitions again."

Gerard's room was only twelve palms square, and as it only contained a small bed and table, there was nothing to conceal anyone who might be in. We must therefore exclaim with the royal prophet, "God is wonderful among His saints, and can refuse nothing to their prayers." The office of porter was entrusted to him from the time he went to Caposele. When he received this charge, he said, "This key is the key of Paradise to me." What made him specially rejoice in this charge, was that it involved the care of the poor. He was always to be seen at the door, distributing among them the alms which the rector had confided to him for that purpose. They came in crowds every day, and we may truly say that Gerard's tenderness for his cherished poor exceeded that of a mother for her sucking child. He managed to send them all away satisfied, and never got impatient with them for their impertinences or deceit. He was quite aware that they often cheated him by presenting themselves over and over again for relief, but he pretended not to notice it, and as he knew that their wants were really great, he only said, "By bearing such as these we shall become dear to Jesus Christ."

His great charity towards the sick poor, who could not come for relief themselves, was specially to be admired. When they sent their children or relatives with empty basins to fetch them something from the kitchen, Gerard took all possible pains to give them what would nourish them, and would willingly have fasted himself if that would have contributed to their relief. The holy brother's charity was so pleasing in the sight of God, that He assisted him in a miraculous manner on such occasions. One morning when there was a good deal of cooking going on in the kitchen, Gerard kept going in and out to replenish the vessels which the poor had brought. At last the cook said, "What are you about? There will be nothing left for the community?" Gerard only replied, "God will provide for them;" and went on supplying the wants of many other poor people who came after the others. The disconcerted cook did nothing but murmur. "We shall soon see how all this will end." When dinnertime came, he was therefore very much astonished to find that the portions had become miraculously multiplied, so that after the wants of the community had been abundantly satisfied, there was still a great deal left over for the poor.

When Gerard did not find anything else in the kitchen fit to send to the sick, he at least sent them some good bread and cheese to make into panado, which is very nourishing. He used even to ransack the pantry for them, and when he could find any raisins or sweets, he used joyfully to send them to them, often repeating in the most tender accents, "We must sacrifice everything for the poor, for they are the living images of Jesus Christ." Gerard was able to gratify his love for the poor at Caposele in a way he had not been able to do at Iliceto, for as that house was in a less secluded position, Gerard often went to see them when he was sent out, which was frequently the case. He often, however, went on purpose to see them, and his mere presence sufficed to give them consolation, and cause them to become reconciled to the will of God. If he found that they were in want of medicines, he lost no time in procuring them from our dispensary.

One year during the carnival the weather was piercingly cold, and there had been a heavy fall of snow. This excited Gerard's compassion for the poor, and he determined to give them a little feast. He therefore got the other brothers to help him in making macaroni for them. After they had prepared a great deal, he joyfully began to distribute it among them. The number of poor people, however, evidently far exceeded the quantity he had to give them. Gerard was not, however, in the least disconcerted at this. He began to distribute it among them with the utmost confidence, and so far from there being any lack, there was a good deal left over after all had been fully satisfied.

His charity towards the poor was very far from being confined to what he gave at the door. He relieved many respectable but indigent families, who would have been ashamed to come and beg at the door. How many poor widows and married women were assisted by him in all their wants! How many girls were saved from temptation to sin by his zealous efforts to provide for them and set them up in business! and with what promptitude did he not fly to the succor of those who had recourse to him! and Providence never failed to second his pious desires.

Jesus Christ in the sick and Jesus in the adorable Sacrament were the two centers of the affections of Gerard's heart. "The infirm and poor are Christ visible," said he, "and the Blessed Eucharist is Christ invisible." He was constantly going to the church to offer up his heart to Jesus. After Holy Communion his soul seemed a perfect furnace of love. His divine transports were more frequent at Caposele than elsewhere, for no sooner did he approach the Blessed Sacrament than he fell into a ravishment. One morning Father Cajone perceived that he smiled on passing before the tabernacle. He immediately called him to his confessional, and asked why he had done so. "Because my Jesus said that I was mad," replied Gerard, "and I said that that might be more justly said of Him, since He loved me so much as to give Himself for me." When he had to go through the church and to pass before the tabernacle, he always did so with the rapidity of lightning. Dr. Santorelli once asked him why he did this. "What else can I do? Our good God has surprised me so often, that I am always afraid of His doing so again," said Gerard. And this was fully justified by the following occurrence. Sometime afterwards when he was letting Dr. Santorelli out by the sacristy door, the latter went into the church, while Gerard went and prostrated himself before the altar of the Blessed Sacrament. Now just as the doctor was leaving the church, he heard the brother give a loud scream, and on going to see what was the matter, he found him extended on the floor in an ecstasy. When he came to himself and saw the doctor and several others around him, he bent his head in great confusion and went away as quickly as he could. When the doctor saw him next day, he began to laugh. Gerard at once guessed the reason, and said, "Did I not tell you that I have cause to be afraid of Him? Do you not see how He takes me by surprise?"

Time would fail me were I to relate all the miraculous occurrences of this sort which took place in this house. He sometimes gave such deep sighs, that all who heard them were filled with astonishment. One day Father Cajone reproved him for this singularity. In reply Gerard took his hand and placed it on his heart, and Father Cajone was obliged to own that he could not understand how he could bear the violence of its throbs. Another time he said to Dr. Santorelli, "If I were alone upon a mountain, I feel as if I could inflame the universe by my sighs;" and placing the doctor's hand upon his heart, he felt that it beat so violently that it seemed as if it would escape from his breast.

There was a blind musician at Caposele who played the flute and sang most sweetly. One day he came before our door and began to sing the well-known air, "I wish for Thee, my God alone. For Thy good pleasure and not mine own." Gerard was talking to the doctor at the time, but he instantly fell into a transport of love, began to leap and dance with holy exultation, and kept unceasingly repeating, "Thy will, O God, and not mine own."

The enthusiasm of his love for the Blessed Virgin was no less admirable. One day when Santorelli asked him if he really loved our Blessed Lady, he replied, "O doctor! you really torment me! What a question!" And he hurried away to hide the flame which had been stirred up within him. Indeed, Father Cajone said that the mere mention of the sweet name of Mary sufficed to cast him into an ecstasy. One day there was a curious contest between Gerard and our Father D. Andrew Strina, who had a great devotion to the childhood of Jesus. Gerard said to Father Strina, "You do not love the Holy Child;" and the father replied, "And you do not love the Madonna." The feelings of both were aroused, but Gerard's was the most sensibly affected, for he seized hold of Father Strina, held him tightly clasped in his arms, and renewed the scene which had before occurred with Father D. Stephen Liguori.

Gerard knew that there is a time for all things, as saith the Scripture. He therefore never felt any difficulty in leaving Mary at the feet of Jesus to accompany Martha in the active labors about the house. As the foundation at Caposele was a recent one, building was constantly going on, and the saintly brother was appointed to overlook the workmen. Although this was a most distracting occupation he willingly embraced it. He was not satisfied with giving directions and looking on, he set an example by laboring more than all himself, and that without intermission. Sometimes he was at the sandpit, sometimes at the brick kiln, or in the town, and this even during the night. He had an eye to everything, directed all, and was to be found everywhere. One day a horse ran away, and it was manifest that he and his rider would soon rush headlong down a precipice. Everyone looked upon the life of the rider as lost, but Gerard consoled them, saying, "He will fall, but he will not be hurt." And so it was, for the young man was not even bruised by the fall.

Another day when he went to Caposele to get the women to carry faggots, he perceived a cock in the street while he was on the terrace belonging to the lords of Ilario. The sight of this little creature immediately reminded him of the power of God. "Come hither, thou work of the finger of God!" he exclaimed, and the cock instantly ran to his feet, flapping its wings as if it had understood what he said. Gerard caressed it for a long while, and as his thoughts were thus raised to the contemplation of divine things, he fell into an ecstasy for about half an hour. I could cite other instances of the way in which birds came and placed themselves in his hand at his command; but one example will suffice.

He was afterwards appointed cook, and he acquitted himself of this charge in a very astonishing manner, as we shall soon see. One evening, amongst others, after he had been to communion, he retired to make his thanksgiving before a large crucifix in the oratory of the artisans. While he was there he became absorbed in the contemplation of the Passion of Christ, and forgot all about his cookery. When dinnertime came the refectory door was found locked, and he was therefore searched for in all directions. Brother Carmine Santagnello at length met him coming out of the oratory, with an inflamed countenance, and with his spirit still quite absorbed in God. "Oh brother," said he, "do you know what you have done? The kitchen is shut, and the dinner hour has struck!" "O thou of little faith," replied Gerard, "what have the angels to do!" They then went to the refectory, where to the great admiration of all, they found that everything was prepared. A similar prodigy is related in the Life of Brother Buonaventure de Gubbio, a Franciscan lay-brother.

We have already said that he learned to make crucifixes while he was at Naples. He devoted all his spare time to this work. Some of his best specimens are still preserved with veneration. Among others, there is a beautiful "ECC homo" in our sacristy at Iliceto. At an oratory at Montella, there is a crucifix which D. Gaetan Bosco, a gentleman of that neighborhood, had asked him to make. Another crucifix is to be found at Vietry de Potenza, in the house of the lords of Coppola. A third, which was left in an unfinished state, is carefully treasured up in our house at Caposele. All these figures are so full of expression, that one cannot look at them without emotion.

As we have often made mention of Dr. D. Nicholas Santorelli, and as we shall often have occasion to speak of him hereafter, we trust our readers will forgive us for saying a few words regarding this excellent man. His piety and devotion were intense, his love towards the Blessed Virgin was most tender, and he received Holy Communion daily. His constant recollection and union with God were the fruit of meditation, to which he consecrated several hours a day. He loved mortification, never neglected any opportunity of crucifying his flesh, and sought for the will and pleasure of God alone and in all things. When our house at Caposele was founded, he placed himself under

Father Sportelli's direction; after his death he went to Father Cafaro. He went to confession every day, no matter what the weather might be. He always assisted at the sermon and exposition of the Blessed Sacrament, especially on Saturday evenings and during solemn novenas, and performed his daily devotions in our church although he had to walk up a steep hill of more than a mile in order to reach it. After this portrait, it is easy to understand the cause of the great intimacy he contracted with Brother Gerard. In truth, it was a friendship which was purely spiritual and in God, and by means of which they mutually assisted each other in reaching the very highest degree of perfection.

CHAPTER IV
Fresh Prodigies Wrought by Brother Gerard at Caposele.

The gift of prophecy, penetration of hearts, interpretation of mysteries, bilocating, and the power of performing instantaneous cures, indeed all the supernatural favors which God had bestowed on Gerard, were still more profusely showered down on him at Caposele than they had been elsewhere. We have already said that he prophesied to our Father Margotta, that the time of his deliverance was not yet come. Some time afterwards, Dr. Santorelli went into his room and found him writing a letter. On asking what he was doing, Gerard replied, "I am writing to Father Margotta to tell him that his trial is over, and to congratulate him." And so it was, for we soon received a letter from Naples to tell us that Father Margotta's sufferings ceased on the very day when Gerard had spoken to Dr. Santorelli. We also heard that the good father had never felt so happy as he did then in his whole life. This was not the case with Brother Gerard however. He lost his wonted cheerfulness on the day on which he sent his letter to Naples, and he looked quite pale and cast down. As Father Cajone, the rector, was struck by this unaccountable alteration in his appearance, he ordered him to reveal its cause. Gerard replied, "I could not bear to see Father Margotta suffer any longer, so I prayed to God to let me suffer in his stead." He seemed indeed to suffer greatly for some time, but he was afterwards restored to his former state.

He whose conscience was defiled by sin, especially by that of impurity, could never speak to brother Gerard without its being discovered by him. One day when a young woman was leaving the church after having received Holy Communion, the servant of God asked her what she had come there for. "To make my confession," she replied. "I know that," answered Gerard, "but you have not made a good confession." He then specified the sin which she had been ashamed to mention to her confessor. The young person was instantly filled with such sincere compunction that she went back again and became thoroughly reconciled with the God she had offended.

There was a woman who pretended to be possessed by a devil, which several priests had been in vain endeavoring to exorcise for two months. When Gerard heard of it, he felt sure that she was an impostor. He sent for her, and when he had taken her aside, he said, "You are acting as you do for such and such ends. Give over all this hypocrisy, or else I will shame you by making it all public." The woman was alarmed at this, and took good care never to counterfeit possession again.

Fevers and other kinds of sickness, and even death itself, seemed to obey Brother Gerard. D. Emmanuelle Vétromite came to Caposele from Muro, accompanied by her niece, who fell dangerously ill during their stay. She therefore came to our church in a state of the greatest grief, and said to Brother Gerard, "O brother, Ursula my niece is very ill. Take pity on me." "Have confidence," replied Gerard. "Make the sign of the cross on her chest when you return home, and she will be cured." The event verified his promise, for the young lady recovered at the very instant that the condition was fulfillled.

There was a foreigner who was once staying in our house, who was suffering from a severe attack of sciatica, who bitterly deplored his hard fate in being far from all belonging to him, and in such a sad state of health besides. When Gerard heard of his lamentations, he hastened to go and see him, He exhorted him to confide in the Blessed Virgin, and made the sign of the cross over him. The sick man was instantly cured, and all his pains left him; and he said that every hour in the night seemed an age to him, so ardently did he long to tell the community what Brother Gerard had done for him.

D. Januarius Liguori was suddenly attacked by a dangerous illness, which soon brought him to the last extremity. This distressed his parents the more because he had not approached the sacraments for many years. When he was in his agony, Brother Gerard was sent for, and entreated to pray to God that the sick man might recover sufficiently to make his confession. Like a second Elias, Gerard placed his face close to that of the dying man, upon which he regained the use of his senses, made his confession, received the Holy Viaticum and Extreme Unction with every mark of sincere repentance, and passed into a better life some days afterwards. Dr. Santorelli was present when Gerard worked this miracle, which was the fruit of his lively faith and of his unbounded confidence in God.

The infused science which he had received from God rendered him no less famous at Caposele. A great number of learned men determined to satisfy themselves on this subject, and their testimony only served to augment his reputation as a profound theologian. For instance, D. Joseph de Lucia asserts that he once entered into a discussion on theological subjects with Brother Gerard, and that he explained the mystery of the Incarnation and of the Blessed Trinity as perfectly as St. Augustine or St. Thomas could have done.

There was a young priest of the town of Muro who was very proud of his theological attainments, who came to our house and wished to enter into controversy with him; but he was so closely pressed on several points that he was obliged to take refuge in silence, to his great confusion. Gerard then gave him this salutary lesson, "Confess that you know nothing," said he. "You have studied theology it is true, but you are not therefore a real theologian. That science is only acquired by meditation and humility."

"The worldly wise," wrote D. Camillo Bozio, the priest of Caposele, "were put to silence in his presence. He was destitute of instruction, it is true, but he drew forth knowledge from the sources of living water, and not from the troubled cisterns of human wisdom. The first theologians were humbled in conversing with him. The most obscure mysteries became clear as the noon-day when he explained them, and when he became ravished out of himself by the force of divine love, he sounded the depths of the unsearchable things of the Most High in a way in which the most learned men were unable to follow him."

Dr. Santorelli bears testimony to the same thing. "When Brother Gerard began to speak of the things of God," said he, "he seemed rapt out of himself. His words rendered the most abstruse doctrines intelligible, and those which seemed the most obscure became clear and plain when they issued from his lips. His conversation always filled me with admiration, and I could not conceive how a poor lay-brother could penetrate so deeply into the most sublime mysteries of God."

It is not, however, without parallel, that an unlettered man should receive infused science. What is really extraordinary is, that he should be able to communicate it to others when he pleased, and in an instantaneous manner. One day when D. Donatus Spicci, the priest at Muro, entered the room of the servant of God, he found the Life of the venerable Sister Mary of the Crucifix on the table. He immediately took it up and began to read what she says about the solitude around the cross. When Gerard saw what he was doing, he said, "These things are not fit for you." "Are they in Greek or Hebrew?" asked Spicci. "Well," replied Gerard, "read them, and tell me what the saint heard during her ecstasies." The good priest was quite confused at this, for he did not understand anything about them. Gerard then made the sign of the cross on his forehead, and said, "Now begin again." And now he understood everything as distinctly as if someone had explained it all to him. Dr. Santorelli was present when this prodigy happened.

A priest, to whose word implicit credit may be attached, relates that as he could not understand several metaphorical passages in the venerable Mgr. de Palafox's book, called "The Shepherd of Night," Brother Gerard made the sign of the cross on his forehead also, and said to him, "Now read it in the name of the Holy Trinity." He did so, and the passages which had before been so obscure to him, now seemed so plain that he was lost in astonishment.

Gerard received another equally signal favor from Heaven. He was able to multiply himself so that he could be in several places at once. One day when he had not received an answer from Muro about several important matters in which the glory of God was concerned, he said,

"I must go there myself tomorrow." And Laurence de Majo affirms that he was seen at Muro on the following day, whilst on the other hand it is affirmed that he never left our house. Another day Father Margotta said to Dr. Santorelli, "Do you know that Gerard has been in his room all night, and yet he has been in an ecstasy before the Blessed Sacrament in the choir of the Franciscans?"

Prodigies of this sort often occurred. How often was he not seen visiting the sick at Caposele without ever having left the house! "One day amongst others," said Dr. Santorelli, "when I was going my rounds, I felt that Brother Gerard was accompanying me wherever I went. Indeed, I was as sure of this as if I had seen him with my own eyes. After my visits were over, I went to Mater Domini, where he had been all the time. When I met him, I said to him, "What did you mean by following me about all day as you have done?" "What did I mean!" he replied. "Do you not know that I must go away tomorrow, and that I wished to visit all my dear sick beforehand?"

Nothing could be more surprising than what happened to D. Nicholas Fiore, the archpriest of Teora, to whom Brother Gerard's high reputation had given a great desire to make his acquaintance. As he expressed this wish to Dr. Santorelli, he mentioned it to Brother Gerard. "Very well," replied Gerard, "I will go and see him." In a few days afterwards the archpriest came to our house to visit the archbishop of Conza; Santorelli met him there, and said, "I will now introduce you to Brother Gerard." "That is no longer necessary," answered the archpriest. "He came to see me one evening, so I now know him, and I am quite pleased with what I have seen of him." Now as Santorelli knew that Gerard had not been to Teora, he saw that there was some mystery in this. He therefore conducted the archpriest to the place where Gerard and the other brothers were, and said, "Now tell me which of these is

Brother Gerard?" The archpriest at once pointed him out without a moment's hesitation. The fact is, Gerard had appeared to him the very evening he promised to go to see him.

God also revealed to him things which are usually entirely hidden from the sight of man. During recreation one day we were talking of our Father Cafaro, of happy and holy memory, when Gerard suddenly said, "D. Paul is a great saint. He enjoys the sight of God in heaven, and his throne of glory is not far from that of St. Paul the apostle, on account of the thorn in the flesh from which he too suffered." Yet no one in the whole community had had the least idea that Father Cafaro had had to endure any such torment.[8] On another occasion, when we were conversing about the virtues and death of Father D. Angelus Latessa, Gerard suddenly exclaimed in an ecstasy, "Let us rejoice, my brothers, for at this very moment Father Latessa's soul has gone to heaven."

All these extraordinary gifts were far from causing his heart to be puffed up with pride; on the contrary, they were always accompanied by the most profound humility; indeed this was the most precious gift which God had bestowed on him. He never took the slightest pleasure in the honors which were paid him, nor did they ever excite any emotion of vanity in his mind. He could not comprehend how men can be proud, as we have nothing of ourselves but corruption and sin. "A man should not say, 'I humble myself,'" he often said, "because that seems to imply that we are something. None but Jesus Christ can say he humbled himself, because being God He became man, and being so great that the whole world could not contain Him, He abased Himself and became so little that

---

[8] Alphonsus himself, as we have already seen in the Life of this father, only knew of it under the seal of the confessional.

Mary's womb was large enough to hold Him." Gerard had a horror of preferences, and the slightest shadow of esteem made him fly away and conceal himself. The Lords of Filippis de Serino conceived a great desire to see one who had performed so many miracles. Gerard knew this, so one day when he was passing through Serino he went to the inn. As soon as these noblemen heard that one of our lay-brothers was at the inn they instantly sent for him, for they had a particular regard for our Congregation. Gerard accordingly went to their house, but he concealed his virtues and talents so well that they never suspected him to be the brother of whom they had heard so much. This holy brother's humility also caused him to envy the poor, for they, like Jesus, are treated with contempt by the world. One day when a poor messenger came into our house wet through and covered with mud, he exclaimed, "I would give anything to be like that poor man, who exposes himself to the scorn and rebuffs of everybody, for the sake of a morsel of bread, whilst I—." He could say no more, for his utterance was choked by tears.

Chapter V
*Gerard's Anxiety for the Souls He Directed; His Charity
Towards All Who had Recourse to Him.*

The conversions which he effected in the neighborhood of Caposele are quite innumerable. He never went out of the monastery to get what was needful to supply the wants of the community, without having found some new labor of love by the way, so that he was soon surrounded by as large a group of penitents (if I may so call them) at Caposele, as he had been at Iliceto, and they used to follow him about wherever he went. Many whom he had delivered from the bondage of sin and converted to God, led the most edifying lives under his direction. When he could not animate them to virtue by his words, he did so by his letters, and if he heard that any of them had wandered from the right path, he did all he could to bring them back into it again by reproof and correction, without respect of persons.

As he heard that a gentleman was endeavoring to cause a young lady to repent of the resolution she had taken of consecrating herself wholly to the service of God, he wrote to him thus: "Honored Sir, I would have written to you long ago, but such was not the will of God. I now write to tell you that I could not have believed that you could have acted as you have done. No, I could not have imagined you would venture to send presents to Miss N. She is under my protection and that of God. Do you wish to draw down His vengeance on your head? Take care of what you do, and remember that such conduct is unworthy of a Christian. I am far from you, but nothing is impossible with God. Remember that. And more than this; you have dared to curse the deceased parents of her confessor, of him from whom she received the black veil! You know how much I am interested in your welfare, and yet you do such things; but I pardon you, because you have been led to act thus through the fire of youth. When men are young, they think little about sin, nor the infinite loss we sustain when we lose God,..." etc. Gerard wrote a great many such letters, but they have not been preserved.

There was a gentleman who was almost brought to a state of despair by the pressure of trials and temptations, for he had not brought his will into conformity to the will of God. In order to bring peace and patience to his troubled soul, Gerard wrote him the following letter: "I have received your kind letter. Rest assured that God will aid you whilst you are faithful to Him. He alone knows how sincerely I enter into your sufferings. May the Holy Spirit the Comforter teach you how much we should rejoice in suffering for the love of Him who has suffered so much for our sakes. My dear brother in Jesus Christ, have patience amid your tribulations, for God only permits them for your good; for He desires that you should save your soul and become holy. You have but one thing to do; bear all your trials in a spirit of resignation to the divine will, and then they will work together for your eternal salvation. Be constant and firm, for that will enable you to resist temptation. Our good God will give you all you require if you hope in Him with a lively faith."

He also wrote to another person who was leading an irreligious life, and who was impatiently longing to obtain a certain situation. "I entreat you to have patience, even if your wishes are not accomplished at once. Perhaps God is throwing obstacles in your way to punish you. God usually reduces those whom He wishes to bring to a sense of their duty, to a state of great trial, that they may thus be led to enter into themselves, and learn how evil and bitter a thing it is to sin against Him. In such case, the best thing we can do is to bewail our offenses before Him unceasingly, and to beseech Him to grant us time for penance. Why should you be cast down by trials which are a very slight punishment in comparison with that which your sins have merited? Would you not be worse off were you in hell? My son, be vigilant, for the devil is very cunning, and if you do not amend your faults, he will assuredly do you some serious harm. Trust in God, and fight against the devil and yourself with courage, for He will enable you to surmount every difficulty. I have caused you to be again recommended to the duke, who is sorry that he cannot do anything for you at present. Leave all to God; He will aid you in proportion to your fidelity to Him.

The nuns at Foggia, and the Carmelites at Ripacandida, were the principal objects of his solicitude, and a word from him sufficed to console and encourage them. As he heard that one of the novices at Ripacandida was tempted to return to the world, he wrote the following long but admirable letter to confirm her in her vocation: "My dear sister in Jesus Christ, I wish to tell you in God's name that you should banish all your present uneasiness, and let your heart be in unshaken and holy peace. It is the devil who is trying to get you to leave this holy place. Be on your guard, my child. That wicked deceiver is full of cunning and envy; he would like to prevent your becoming a saint, and therefore he cannot bear you to remain where you are. We have all been tempted against vocation, but God sends these temptations to try our fidelity. Let not your heart be troubled, rather let it rejoice. Give yourself up unreservedly to God, and He will not fail to succor you. Can you cease to love God? Can you wish to forget the sweet promises you have so often made to our dearest Jesus, to be His spouse forever? If you once longed for this so ardently, why do you now draw back? My sister, can anyone give you peace but God? Has this dreary world ever satisfied the desires of the human heart, were it that of a princess, a queen, or an empress? We never heard or read of its doing so; but we do know that the hearts of its votaries are thickly strewn with thorns and briars, and that those who are the richest and the most highly honored and esteemed, and surrounded by every pleasure, have the most interior suffering. What more shall I say? Would that I could let you speak to the most contented worldling, and you would then see whether earthly things are really what they appear to be. Believe me, for I speak from experience, it is a miserable thing to live in this bleak and barren world! May God preserve you from such a fate, my sister! It is because He loves you, and because He wishes to strengthen you that He has permitted you to be tempted. Be of good courage then.

Make a vigorous and generous resistance to temptation, by unceasingly resolving to be the spouse of Jesus Christ, our Sovereign Lord and Master. Oh! it is indeed a glorious thing to be the spouse of Jesus Christ! for He is the only source of all lasting felicity, of all true peace, of all solid contentment, of all real good. How vain and transient is the satisfaction the world can give, compared to the celestial and eternal beatitude which the spouse of Christ will enjoy in heaven! I do not say that it is impossible to be saved in the world; but I do assert, that there is continual danger of being lost in it, and that it is far easier to become sanctified in the cloister. Meditate, I beseech you, on the shortness of time and the duration of eternity. Remember that death puts an end to all here below, and that death is but a passage to eternity. He who is now alive will soon cease to remember either its joys or its sorrows. What use is there then in resting on that which cannot support us? Ah! all which does not lead us to God is but vanity, and is of no avail for eternity. Miserable is he who puts his trust in the world, and not in God. Go, my dear sister, I conjure you, to the convent cemetery, where the bones of so many holy nuns are now lying, and reflect on what would now be their portion if they had been numbered amongst the great ones of the world during life! O how it profited them to have been poor, mortified, contemned, and shut up in a severe convent. Perhaps they thereby suffered much trial for a few short years, but what sweet peace did they not experience in their last agony at dying in the house of God! Everyone wishes to be a saint at the hour of death; but there is no time then to become one; on the contrary, each one must then reap what he has sown. It matters not if the storm of temptation has not yet subsided. I have such faith in the most adorable Trinity and in holy Mary, our ever dearest Mother, that I have not a doubt you will one day become a saint in this convent. Crush the head of the infernal serpent, who would snatch you away from this holy spot. Despise him. Tell him you are the spouse of Jesus Christ, and you will make him tremble. Be cheerful, and love God with all your heart. Give yourself up unreservedly to Him, and vanquish the powers of darkness by your unshaken firmness. To conclude, pray for me, for I never forget you in my prayers. It may be easily believed that such a letter answered the desired end. The young lady gave up all thoughts of the world, made her profession, and became an excellent religious. To another religious, who told him of her various trials, he wrote as follows for her encouragement: "Rejoice in the Lord, and never allow yourself to be cast down. Trust in God, and hope for all things, for His mercy is infinite. Mistrust yourself, for when you think all is peace, the enemy is nearest to you. Do not imagine that peace can be enduring. War may break out at any moment. Be on your guard, and unceasingly recommend yourself to the protection of our Blessed Mother, that she may overthrow your enemies by her all-powerful intercession. Your sufferings should not make you sad and downcast; they should only cause you to humble yourself before God and inspire you with increased confidence in His infinite mercy. Rest assured that what you have mentioned to me can only be the work of the evil one, who wishes to occupy your attention and thus cause you to lose time. Be cheerful then. Once more let me exhort you to trust in God, for if you do you will become a saint."

Many persons of high rank, as well as many religious, priests, confessors, and directors applied to Gerard to obtain light amid their difficulties and solace under their trials. Even several of the principal and most learned members of our Congregation were only restored to peace by consulting him. I will only however cite one example. Although Father D. Francis Garzilli, formerly canon of

Foggia, was a good theologian, an enlightened director, and a man of upwards of seventy years of age and full of experience, he consulted him in all his interior afflictions with the utmost humility. The following is a letter which Brother Gerard wrote in reply to certain doubts which this good father had stated to him: "May the grace of God be with your Reverence, and may the most Holy Mary, our Immaculate Mother, have you ever in her holy keeping. I am much consoled and rejoiced, my dear father, at the dealings of God with your soul. I have a firm confidence that He will enable you to triumph over all your enemies. Have courage then, fear nothing, rather rejoice, for God is assuredly with you, and I am certain that He will not abandon you. As for the scruples your Reverence feels about your confessions, they are only a little mortification which God has sent you, that you may have an occasion of suffering. You tell me that you are to blame. Of course, you could not think otherwise; in that the trial consists. It is thus God tries the souls of those He loves, by permitting them to believe that everything is the result of their own negligence. If your Reverence knew that all this came from God, where would your trial be? In such case your sorrows would in reality be a Paradise to you. But, however, supposing that we do commit trifling faults, and that we do stumble and fall, let us remember that the saints were men of like passions with ourselves. Trust then in God, my dear father, and hope in Him, and in charity recommend me to Jesus Christ and to Mary, His spotless Mother, whom I pray to bless us both."

CHAPTER VI
Gerard Goes to Calitri; Prodigies He Works There.

When Father Margotta passed through Caposele, on his

way to Calitri, his native country, he asked Gerard to accompany him thither. Whilst he was occupied with business, the holy brother spent his time in the churches. His virtues and supernatural graces were not known when he first went to this town. One morning however, whilst he was in the church, a woman from Bisaccia knelt down beside him, and when he arose to go away, she threw herself at his feet, and with many tears besought him to cure one of her relations, who was dangerously ill. Gerard listened to her with his wonted sweetness, and did not send her away until he had promised that she should obtain the favor she had solicited. The people of the house where he was staying were astonished at his conduct, and laughingly related it to Father Margotta, who said, "You laugh, because you are not aware of the miraculous gifts with which God has favored him." He then began to relate them, and to pass a high eulogium on his virtues. This sufficed to spread Brother Gerard's fame throughout Calitri, and he was soon surrounded by persons of all classes.

D. John Cioglia, the surgeon, was given over by the physicians, which caused general regret, for he was considered very skillful; but when Gerard was asked to go and see him he refused. When Father Margotta heard of this, however, he expressly commanded him to go. Accordingly, he went, and as soon as he had made the sign of the cross on the sick man's forehead, he instantly recovered his senses. All who were present were astonished at the miracle, but Gerard humbly said, "See what obedience can do!" Cioglia got quite well, and talked of the sanctity of the servant of God wherever he went.

Another gentleman was also confined to bed by a serious illness, and on the point of receiving the last sacraments. Father Margotta was so affected by the tears of his sister, who was a religious, that he commanded

Brother Gerard to go and visit him likewise. After he had made the sign of the cross on him, he too recovered.

There was a lady of high rank who heard so much about the holiness of Brother Gerard, that she determined to go to him and tell him of an interior trial which she had never before dared to reveal to anyone. When she saw him, however, she became so nervous that she had not strength to speak to him. Gerard saw her embarrassment, and said, "You need only listen to me; I will talk for you." He then told her all her most secret thoughts and actions. The lady afterwards attested that no one could have known what Gerard revealed by natural means.

Donna Angela Rinaldi was one day suddenly seized by a violent headache when she was in Signor Borelli's house. As she had heard many marvelous things of Brother Gerard, and as his hat happened to be lying in a corner of the room, she jestingly said, "Let us see whether this brother is really a saint after all." She then put it on her head, and she had scarcely done so ere the pain left her.

Amongst the many prophecies which Gerard made at Calitri, the following is a very remarkable one. Several persons had asked him to try and convert one of the most influential men of the town, who was living at enmity with God, and as if immortality were a dream. Gerard paid him a visit, and endeavored to get him to agree to go through the spiritual exercises which were soon to commence in our house. The gentleman made several frivolous excuses, but Gerard continued to urge him. As he neither wished to assent to the proposition, nor to give a positive refusal, he said, "I will see about it when October comes." "You will not do it now," replied Gerard, "and you will do it in October; but I tell you that you will not live to see October." The gentleman was in good health then, but he was attacked by a malignant fever in August which brought him to the grave.

Gerard was like a kind of extraordinary confessor to the Benedictine nuns, who all wished to confer with him on their spiritual necessities. He exhorted them above all to the exact observance of rule, and to frequent communion, and they united in saying that every word which proceeded out of his mouth was as darts of fire which penetrated the very depths of their heart, and that after having conversed with him, they seemed to be enkindled by the most ardent love for our dearest Lord, and for Mary His holy mother. A novice has herself mentioned that she had become quite disgusted with convent life, and that she had made up her mind to return to the world; but Gerard sent for her, and spoke so energetically to her about the blessings of the religious state, that her feelings were instantly changed, and she was filled with an ardent desire to consecrate herself to Jesus Christ.

Another religious was so disturbed by scruples, that nothing could tranquillize her. She applied to Brother Gerard, who told her all she felt before she had spoken a word. He then gave her such good advice that calm was soon restored to her troubled mind. Although the Benedictines felt the greatest respect for Gerard, they did not always accede to all his wishes. Their parlor was in a bad situation, and what was worse, their entrance was close to the church door, which opened into the street. This seemed a great abuse to Brother Gerard. He spoke to Father Margotta about it, and he told him to mention the evils it might lead to in one of his conferences with the community. Gerard did so, and all the nuns with common consent were of opinion that the entrance should be made where he wished it to be. However, their zeal grew cold that very evening, and they changed their minds. Although Gerard had left them, he saw all that had passed among them in spirit, and suddenly lost his wonted cheerfulness.

When he was asked the reason, he replied, "I am uneasy about the nuns." He went to the convent next morning, at which the abbess was much embarrassed, for she was afraid to tell him of what had taken place, but Gerard anticipated her, and told her every particular with the utmost accuracy. "The entrance has not been changed," said he, "and now it never will be so." The prophecy was true, for although many attempts were afterwards made to change the grate and the entrance, they always proved unsuccessful.

As the family of Borelli observed that his shoes were quite worn out, they gave him new ones and preserved the old ones through devotion. Now a little boy who was in their house was taken very ill, and no remedy succeeded in giving him any relief, but no sooner were these shoes applied to him than he became quite well. D. Joseph Anthony Borelli says that these shoes became so celebrated throughout Calitri that they were always in demand for the sick, amongst whom they worked many miraculous cures. When the religious heard of this, they entreated the family of Borelli to give them one, which he did, so that they became the remedy for every ill throughout the whole neighborhood.

Soon after this our fathers went to give a mission at Calitri, and took Gerard with them, and he worked as many conversions and prodigies during its course as he had done during the missions at which he had assisted before. The gift of prophecy and that of sounding the depths of the heart and conscience caused him to work wonders. In fact, all the fathers had to do was to absolve those whom Gerard converted and brought to repentance.

One day Gerard accidentally dropped a large vessel full of oil in the house where he was staying. A young girl who happened to see him instantly began to reproach him for his awkwardness and carelessness. On hearing her exclamations, her mother ran to stop her; "It does not signify," said she, "the oil is not lost, for I can still use it for the wool." They then began to gather it up as well as they could, but what was the surprise of the woman when she went to pick up the vessel which had been upset, on finding that there was more oil in it than there had been before! She instantly published this miracle far and wide, and it added greatly to the fame the saintly brother had already acquired. Its truth was attested by Father D. Nicholas Mansione, who assisted at this mission.

CHAPTER VII
Great Renown Gerard Acquires at Muro; The Wonderful Works He Performed There.

We are now going to speak of how Gerard acted in his native town of Muro, where he was now venerated in proportion to the neglect with which he had been treated by its inhabitants in his youth. I do not know the object of his visit, but I know that he was at first lodged in the Franciscan monastery, where he was treated with the utmost kindness. As the fame of his virtues and supernatural endowments had preceded him, everyone hastened to make his acquaintance, or to pay their respects to him on his arrival. This was only the fulfillment of a prediction he had before made; for one day whilst he was still at Muro, and when he was loaded with insults and injuries, he said, "You despise me now, but you will one day think it an honor to kiss my hand." In truth, he could not satisfy them all. He received special testimonies of respect from the ecclesiastics and gentlemen. Even the most popular confessors among the regulars came to consult him on the direction of souls, and asked his opinion on many difficult cases of conscience. Gerard discussed all the ascetical and moral questions they proposed with the profound learning of a deep theologian, and solved every difficulty with the wisdom of a learned doctor well skilled in divinity.

When he went out on business, or to visit those who had invited him to their houses, he was always attended by a number of canons and gentlemen. When he went to pay his respects to that distinguished prelate, Mgr. Muojo, the bishop of Muro, he expressed the greatest satisfaction in seeing one of whom he had heard such wonderful things. He was suffering from gout in his feet and hands at the time, and asked Gerard to pray to God to deliver him from his pains. "My Lord, you must bear them with patience," replied Gerard, "for it is not God's will that you should be free from them." During his conversations with him the pious bishop was much struck with the saintly brother's profound humility, and with the plenitude of divine grace with which his heart was filled. He often sent for him to his palace, and always marveled at the precision with which he expressed himself on theological subjects. "His angelical demeanor does me good everytime he comes to see me," said he on one occasion to one of our fathers.

When the Poor Clares heard of his arrival they begged his Lordship to let them see him and converse with him. He not only granted their request, but urged them to profit by his advice. "One talk with Brother Gerard," said he, "is worth more than all the sermons of a Lent." Gerard therefore went there several times, and his burning words and winning eloquence gave the nuns a very foretaste of heaven. He showed them how many dangers might result from frequenting the grate, and from any inordinate attachment; and on the other hand he made them see how inestimable are the advantages of detachment from creatures, love of solitude, interior recollection, and the spirit of prayer. In a private conversation which he had with a nun in this convent, he told her of a sin of which she had never accused herself, either through shame or ignorance, although she had made three general confessions. Another religious of the same convent had an inordinate affection for a little gold heart which she always wore round her neck. Indeed she was so attached to it that none of her confessors had been able to get her to take it off, but one word from Gerard sufficed to make her abandon it forever. The lady abbess, D. Mary Joseph Salines, had been suffering from a tertian fever for some time. She asked Gerard to relieve her, who sent her some dust from the tomb of St. Theresa, which cured her entirely.

The son of D. Alexander Piccolo, the goldsmith, had an apoplectic fit whilst he was out one day, which deprived him of speech and left him half dead. The poor father had not yet heard of the calamity when he and Brother Gerard passed the house where he was lying. When Gerard informed him of the sad state his son was in, the afflicted father did not feel courage to enter it, and begged the servant of God to go in in his stead. Gerard instantly did so, and made the sign of the cross on his forehead, saying, "This is nothing, my son, this is nothing." And he instantly recovered.

The wife of the said Alexander had been living at enmity with God, and in a state of sacrilege for several years. Gerard spoke to her in private, expostulated with her on the evil of her ways, and urged her to make a good confession. "Confess and prepare for death," said he, "for it is at hand." And although she was then a very robust woman, she died within a few months.

Peter Angelo de Rubertis, the notary, has himself told us that he had omitted to confess one sin in his youth through shame, and that one day when he was speaking to Brother Gerard about the state of his conscience, he represented to him what a sad condition his soul was in, and urged him to make a good confession. "Yet," added the notary, "this secret sin was known to God alone."

One day when he was going to the convent with D. Joseph Pianèse, the president of the seminary, they heard a man uttering the most frightful blasphemies against the Blessed Trinity. Gerard turned to the president, and said, "These blasphemies will not remain unpunished, as you will soon see." And so it was, for three days afterwards this man was shot in the public square, and he died without having had time to do penance. The inhabitants were so impressed with Gerard's sanctity, that when he passed along some came up to him to kiss his hands, and others to recommend themselves to his prayers. They even offered him the most precious things they had, as he owned to Father Cajone; the women would have willingly bestowed their earrings on him, and the men would have given him their buttons if he had not had the discretion to refuse all presents.

The splendor of these prodigies however was far exceeded by the depth of his humility. Whilst noblemen and gentlemen would have felt proud to receive him at their tables, and to seat him in the post of honor, the lowly brother daily accompanied the crowd of poor people who went to the seminary door, and received an alms of a morsel of bread and some broth in company with them. The holy brother had learned this heroic practice from our Father D. Francis Margotta, who was in the habit of doing the same thing at the door of the fathers of St. Jerome while he was at Naples. But as our Father Alphonsus forbade him to continue this practice, Brother Gerard was also commanded not to do so if he returned to Muro again.

Chapter VIII

Brother Gerard's Great Charity During a Famine; Fresh Prodigies and Conversions.

Gerard displayed his love for the poor in a signal manner during the winter of 1753, when the severity of frost and snow prevented the laborers from going to work. The mountainous regions suffered the most from the cold, and amongst those who were the most distressed by famine, were the inhabitants of Caposele. More than two hundred starving poor, including men, women, and children, presented themselves at our door every morning. Father Cajone, who was the rector of the house, was so affected at the sight of their distress, that he one day sent for Brother Gerard, and said to him, "I give you full power to supply all the wants of these poor creatures. Their lives are in our hands. If we do not assist them they will die. I therefore give you full power to dispose of anything in the house as you please." These words filled Gerard with joy, and he neglected nothing by which he could assist them in their spiritual and temporal necessities.

He daily assembled them together in the hall or in the open air, and instructed them on the obligations of a Christian. The moral lessons he gave them were always within their comprehension, and he selected the most edifying examples in proof of what he taught them. When it was known that Gerard gave these catechetical instructions, several rich people came to listen to them also, and even ladies of rank mingled amongst the poor to hear him speak of the things of God. As the cold became more and more intense, Gerard lit a large fire before the house, and placed pans of coals in the hall to warm the shivering limbs of the poor of Jesus Christ. He showed peculiar tenderness to the little children, and would point them out to those of riper age, with these words, "It is we who have sinned, and these dear babes are innocent, yet they bear the punishment. He would then take their poor little hands and warm them within his own and burst into tears, for they were to him the living images of the Lamb of God who suffered for sinners.

This charitable brother was specially anxious to dispose the adults to make a good confession. He earnestly begged God to soften the hearts of those who were hardened in sin, and not to deal with them according to His justice. His prayers and labors were so acceptable in the sight of God, that numbers were so touched by grace that they went and cast themselves at the feet of the various confessors when his instructions had ended. Amongst these converted sinners there were several who had not approached the sacraments for years and years.

When he had once begun to open the granary, he bestowed his gifts on all who came with the utmost profusion, and without the least regard to the wants of the community. Dr. Santorelli one day advised him to use a little more discretion in distributing the bread, and only to give it to those who were really in want. "I must give it to all," replied Gerard, "because they all ask for it for the love of God."

It was the general opinion at Caposele, and one of which we ourselves had many proofs, that the bread was miraculously multiplied in his hands. One of our students told Father Cajone that once when he assisted at the distribution of bread, the baskets which he had previously seen empty were refilled without anyone having been near them. Another related that after he had himself given away all the bread contained in a large chest, he unthinkingly reopened it, and to his great astonishment found that it was quite full again. Indeed, if God had not worked these miracles, the provisions in the house must obviously have been inadequate to feed so many; for the famine not only lasted for days and weeks, but for several months.

A person of great respectability was so pressed by hunger, that he entered the hall with the poor, but as he was ashamed to beg he went into a corner, without having courage to present himself before Brother Gerard. After he had sent the others away, he took no notice of this person, never suspecting him to be in want, for it was no rare thing even for pious people of rank to come and witness the beautiful sight which was presented several times a day by the charity of Brother Gerard. Theodore Clef, who was present, and who was well aware of this person's distress, at length told the charitable brother of the situation in which he was placed; but there was nothing then left to give. "Oh, why was I not told before!" exclaimed Gerard with emotion. He paused for some time, and then stepped aside, but instantly retraced his steps, and took a little loaf out of his pocket which was smoking as if it had just left the oven. Signor Clef mentioned this to Father Cajone, who assured him bread was not then being made in the house, that the oven was not hot, and that this little loaf was not the shape of those used by the community. In fact, the marvels which Gerard effected were so well known at Caposele, that gentlemen and ladies of high rank sent their children to mingle amongst the poor, that they might get some of this miraculous bread, which they carefully preserved as a relic.

Gerard was not satisfied with feeding the poor, he also clothed them. Confiding in the general permission the rector had given him, he went to the wardrobe, and took out all the old clothes he could find to give them to the tailors to make up for the poor. Poor girls were the objects of his special solicitude, and he often did without necessaries himself, to save them from dishonor. One day during this severe winter, Father Cajone found that he had nothing on but his cassock and shirt, because he had given away his waistcoat and cloak to the poor. Providence also manifested how well-pleasing His servant's confidence and generosity were in His sight, for we received alms from time to time in the most mysterious and unexpected manner. "Gerard three or four times," said Father Cajone, "brought me a large sum, saying that he had found it in rolls in the keyhole. God and the good brother only know how this came to pass," added the rector; "I do not understand it at all."

About this time he effected a remarkable conversion in the person of a girl who had been for some time living in sacrilege and sin, but she had had the art to deceive our fathers so entirely that they believed her to be most pious all the time. One day when Gerard saw that she seemed in better dispositions than usual, for his instructions had made a great impression on her, he led her aside, and spoke to her about the danger of her state, and then sent her to Father Fiocchi, who was in the house at the time. She made her confession with many tears, and was from thenceforward a model of piety to all the town of Caposele. "She became a bright mirror of perfection from the time of her conversion," said Father Cajone, "and her exemplary conduct is more edifying now than ever. She cannot think of Brother Gerard without shedding tears, on account of the zeal and charity with which he, as it were, snatched her from the brink of hell."

CHAPTER IX
Gerard Converts the Archbishop of Conza's Secretary; The Esteem which this Prelate Entertained for Him.

On one occasion when Mgr. Nicolai, the archbishop of Conza, came to our house, he brought among the members of his suite a certain Roman, who acted as his secretary. He was quite indispensable to the archbishop, on account of his jovial humor, and great talents for business. Gerard soon discovered that all was not right within him, for he dived into the most hidden recesses of the heart by a glance, he therefore showed great interest in the secretary from the first. He noticed his witticisms, laughed at his jokes, and tenderly embraced him in his playful moods, in order to gain his confidence. One day when he seemed in good dispositions, he called him aside, and conducted him to the oratory; when they reached it, he cast himself at his feet, and said to him, with tearful eyes, "My dear friend, I cannot comprehend how you can be so cheerful, while you are at enmity with God. Now you cannot deny that you are married, and that your wife is at Rome. How can you then pretend to be free and lead the life of a libertine?" He then mentioned the exact number of years he had lived thus without bestowing even a thought on God or on his own soul.

The abashed secretary threw himself on his knees and wept in turn, confessed the truth of all he had asserted, and implored him to aid him by his prayers and counsels. Gerard encouraged him by speaking to him of the infinite mercy of God, and when he saw that he was really filled with true compunction, he excited him to make a firm and sincere resolution of amendment. The agitated secretary then hurried to Father Fiocchi, and told him of all that had passed between Gerard and himself. "It must have been either God or the devil who revealed this to him," said he, "but it cannot be the devil, since he has filled my heart with sorrow." The result of his interview with Father Fiocchi, to whom he made his confession, was that he resolved to return to Rome and to take back his lawful wife. Meanwhile, he went to church to receive Holy Communion, but Gerard stopped him and reminded him of a sin he had forgotten to mention in his confession.

Everyone was struck by the sudden change in the secretary. He who had formerly been full of mirthful glee, was now serious and thoughtful. As the archbishop could not account for the change, he inquired into its cause. The secretary burst into tears, and replied, in the words of the Samaritan, "Venite et videte hominem, qui dixit mihi omnia quæcumque feci." And he then told the archbishop of what a sad state his soul had been in, and how he had been delivered from it by the saintly Brother Gerard.

When the archbishop returned to St. Andrew, where he usually resided, equal astonishment was felt at the change which had taken place in his secretary. "There is something mysterious the matter with you," said James Bozio, the president of the seminary, to him; "You have lost all your wonted liveliness and fun. What can be the reason?" "My dear friend, do you not then know what happened to me at Caposele?" he replied. "I am married, and although Brother Gerard did not know me, he told me of all that ever I did." He was so contrite that he told everybody all about himself, as well as the way in which the holy brother had converted him. As the archbishop saw that his dispositions were really good, he sent him back to Rome with letters of recommendation to Mgr. Casone, who was nearly related to him. When the secretary arrived at Rome he at once told all that had happened to Mgr. Casone, who thus became a great admirer of Gerard. One day when this prelate was conversing with some cardinal, he told him all that had taken place in regard to Mgr. de Conza's secretary. The cardinal was so struck with this that he instantly desired to become acquainted with the holy brother, and wrote to the archbishop to send him to Rome; but Gerard was dead when he received the letter. Father Cajone told me that the secretary constantly corresponded with Brother Gerard after his return to Rome, and that he did nothing without consulting him.

Mgr. de Conza's esteem for the holy brother was considerably heightened when he heard that he had worked so many miracles of the same kind, that he might be called the Thaumaturgus of his age.

From this time, he always felt it quite a pleasure to converse with him on pious subjects, and he often wept from emotion when in his presence. His Lordship was naturally cold and reserved, yet when he was going to return to St. Andrew he showed Gerard the most lively testimonies of regard, and urgently entreated him to remember him in his prayers. "My Lord," replied Gerard, "I stand in need of all God's mercy in order to be saved myself. I hope therefore you will remember me at the altar." Gerard had made such a lively impression on this prelate, that the vivid remembrance of his virtues was never blotted out of his mind.

CHAPTER X

Brother Gerard Goes About the Archdiocese of Conza; The Prodigies which Accompany His Labors.

One of the most ardent desires of Mgr. Nicolai, the founder of our house at Caposele, was to see it well and speedily established. The zealous archbishop gave a large sum of money for this purpose every year, and left us three hundred ducats extra after his last visit. In order to obtain funds to complete the building, he sent a circular throughout his diocese to exhort his flock to contribute to this pious undertaking, and he added, that he wished two of our fathers to collect their alms.

Fathers Cajone and Cafaro thought that Brother Gerard was the fittest person they could select for this mission, but as he was ill at this time, they were afraid to risk sending him into unhealthy places and in unfavorable weather. However, Father Cajone, the rector, went up to him, placed his hand on his head, and interiorly said, "In the name of the adorable Trinity, I wish you to recover and to make the collection." Gerard was ignorant of the whole affair, but when the rector placed his hand on his head, he said, "Your Reverence speaks, though you use no words. You wish me to recover, and to make the collection; I will do both." Gerard soon set out, much less, however, with the wish to seek for money than to procure glory to Jesus Christ and good to souls. When he passed through Senerchia, where they were just finishing the parish church, he found the inhabitants in great distress at being unable to convey some large chestnut trees down Mount Acerno, which were intended to serve for the timber work of the roof. On seeing the trouble they were in, Gerard got some peasants to conduct him to the spot. The trees were indeed of extraordinarily large dimensions, but Gerard tied a rope to one of the largest, the weight of which had baffled the efforts of oxen and buffaloes, and drew it to the church without any difficulty, to the great astonishment of all the spectators. On seeing this prodigy, the people took courage and fell to work again, and as the beams had lost all their weight, they were able to transport them to the church with as much ease as if they had been so many sticks.

Once when he was performing his devotions in the church of Senerchia, a number of people came in and surprised him in an ecstasy, which lasted for some time. He also performed many other charitable works while he was in this neighborhood, which I omit for brevity's sake.

As he had to go through Oliveto, he previously gave notice of this to the archpriest Salvatore, in a note which ended thus, "You have long wished to see me the sinner.

You see your prayer is now granted." These last words greatly surprised the archpriest, for though he had felt the most ardent desire to know him, he had never mentioned it to anyone. When Gerard reached his house, he said in a still more explicit manner, "I know that you have for some time wished to become acquainted with me, and now you see God has sent me to you." As the archpriest saw by this that Gerard had penetrated into the very secrets of his heart, he at once concluded he must be a saint. This conviction soon gained new strength, for as the dinner hour had arrived, and Gerard was still in his room, he went to see what he was doing by looking through the keyhole. But what was his surprise and admiration on seeing him ravished into an ecstasy, and raised up about three palms from the ground. When he returned again, he was still in the same state. All thoughts of dinner were then laid aside, and everyone began to shed tears of wonder and emotion. Some time afterwards Gerard left his room with an inflamed countenance; he quietly said to the archpriest when he saw him, "Pray go on with everything as usual, for I do not at all wish to disturb your household." This ecstasy made such an impression on the archpriest, that he marked on the wall the height to which the saintly brother had been elevated in the air, to perpetuate its memory.

Gerard was still at Oliveto when Father Fiore came to join him there, for he was to act as his companion during his journey. When he arrived, however, he was so ill from fever that he was instantly obliged to go to bed in the first room he came to on the ground floor. When the archpriest and Dr. Don Joseph, his brother, informed him of this, he replied, "Tell him from me that he ought to send away the fever through obedience, and come to me here, for I have so much to do in the mission which has been entrusted to me, that I have no time to attend on the sick." D. Joseph began to laugh, but Gerard gravely answered, "I really beg you to go and do what I have said." He went therefore, and found Father Fiore free from fever. When he came to Gerard he said, "How could you go and catch a fever when we are sent here to make the collection?" Then turning to the doctor he added, "Do not be astonished at his speedy recovery; such is the virtue of holy obedience."

As Donna Rose, the archpriest's sister, was also confined to bed with fever, Gerard went to see her. "It is over now," he said, and immediately afterwards her brother the doctor found that the fever had left her.

The priest D. Dominic Sassi had been out of his mind for seven years, during which he had never left his room, where he did nothing but utter screams and blasphemies. The archpriest described the state he was in to Brother Gerard, who only made this laconic answer, "What can I do in the matter?" However, he went to see him about noon, but without telling anyone of his purpose. When the priest saw him, he became furious, and began to utter his usual exclamations. Gerard was in nowise disturbed, but advanced towards him and made the sign of the cross on his head, upon which his frenzy subsided and he became gentle as a lamb. There was a harpsichord in the room, on which Gerard instantly made him play, and they sung the litanies of the Blessed Virgin together. The whole household speedily assembled together and returned thanks to God for such a miraculous restoration. The archpriest shed tears of joy on hearing the glad tidings. As for the priest himself, he was so well that he could have celebrated Mass next day, but Gerard wished him to defer doing so for three days. Whilst Gerard was dining with the archpriest on the third day, he said, "D. Dominic will say Mass tomorrow, and we must all communicate at it." And all took place as he had arranged. When the archpriest went into his room next morning to ask him to assist at the Mass, he found him on his knees in an ecstasy, with his crucifix in one hand and the other crossed on his breast. He instantly ran for D. Joseph, his brother, that he too might see this prodigy. The ecstasy lasted for about half an hour, after which the archpriest again entered his room as if nothing had happened, and asked him to come to church. D. Sassi's Mass was served by the archpriest and by Gerard. A great many of the Faithful assisted at it, and observed that he not only said it with great devotion, but with such exact attention to the rubrics that it seemed as if he had been in the constant habit of attending to them. All the household of the archpriest received Holy Communion at his hands. D. Dominic never had any return of his former malady, and continued to say Mass every day without fail. When the people heard the bell ring for his mass, they used to say, "Let us come and see Brother Gerard's miracle." The fame of this prodigy was spread far and wide, Father Cajone wrote to tell me, and that not only throughout the neighborhood, but even to far distant regions.

Brother Gerard worked another prodigy at Oliveto which was no less remarkable. One day when he saw a large crowd of persons assembled together, he asked the cause. He was told that it was caused by a possessed person who was struggling furiously, and would not suffer anyone to go near him. Gerard, however, approached him without fear and asked who he was. "I am the devil," was the reply, "I am the devil." "In the name of the Adorable Trinity," said Gerard, "I command you to quit this man." "I will go," responded the demon, "but you shall suffer for it." During one of his walks in that neighborhood, Gerard saw a little child who was playing in front of a gentleman's house. He immediately stopped, and exclaimed while gazing at him intently, "Oh what a viper they are rearing up in this house!" This remark made a great impression for the moment, but its meaning was not very apparent. Events however proved a sad commentary on the gloomy forebodings it had aroused; for when this child grew up, he was so vicious that he was more like a devil than a man. Amongst other crimes he committed that of incest, and so far from being contrite when his father reproved him for it, he seized a gun and threatened to kill him. As the father saw that his life was in danger, he took a pistol himself, with which he killed the wretch to whom he had given birth.

The daughter of D. Joseph Mari of Auletta often fell into violent convulsions, and happened to be in one when Gerard entered the house. Her parents asked him to bless her, which he did, upon which the convulsions ceased, and what is still more extraordinary, the girl was entirely freed from them from that time.

One day when he was passing through the marketplace in this city, he met a man, whom he led aside: "My son," said he, "how can you be at peace? You committed a mortal sin at such a time, and you have not yet confessed it. Hasten to a confessor now, and recover the grace of God." At this unlooked-for reproof, the unhappy man confessed his guilt, cast himself at his feet, and promised amendment. He was faithful to his promise, for he instantly went and made his confession, and persevered in virtue from that time.

Whilst he was traveling in this territory, a poor girl was pointed out to him, who had been such a cripple from her birth that she was unable to move either hand or foot. "O it is nothing," replied Gerard, "she is quite cured now!" He then called her, and to the great astonishment of all present, as D. Raphael Abbondati, the priest, can testify, she sprung out of bed and came and kissed her benefactor's hand. A crowd of people were by this time assembled together, who loudly exclaimed, "A miracle! a miracle!" which caused the abashed Gerard to fly to the house of the aforenamed priest to hide himself. The populace followed him there also, and continued to extol him as a saint, upon which the good brother was so distressed that he escaped by a back door, and retreated to the territory of St. Gregory. When Father Francis Fiore was passing through Auletta some years afterwards, he saw this girl, who was pointed out to him as the girl whom Brother Gerard cured.

His marvelous deeds did not cease however by his retiring to St. Gregory. On entering the Archpriest Robertazzi's house, he prostrated himself on the ground saying, "Dearest Jesus! I thank Thee with all my heart, for having delivered me from much suffering." Whilst he was conversing with the archpriest a gentleman came in, who was a great friend of his. Gerard then changed the conversation, and proposed the following question to D. Robertazzi, "If anyone were tempted to commit adultery, nay, had fully resolved to do it, but were restrained from consummating the crime by the influence of grace, would he be bound to mention all these circumstances to his confessor, even though the crime had not really taken place?" The archpriest could not make out what he meant by proposing a question which seemed à propos of nothing. When the gentleman was going away however, he took the archpriest aside, and said in a tone of astonishment, "You have a saint in your house! All that Brother Gerard has just been speaking of, happened to me just before I came in here. Blinded by the temptations of the devil, I had determined to commit the crime in question, but I did not dare to consummate the deed; I confess this as a humiliation to myself and for the glory of this saintly brother." The archpriest was no longer at a loss to understand the drift of the question.

Vietri was also the scene of similar marvels. A woman

of bad character one day came up to Brother Gerard, and asked him for a picture of our Blessed Lady. "There is one," said he. "Think well of how the concerns of your soul stands in the sight of God, and recommend yourself fervently to Mary our holy Mother, for you have only a few days to live." Although she was young and strong, she was seized with a violent attack of fever when she returned home. Owing to the impression which Brother Gerard's warning had made on her, she began to detest her past life and confessed her sins with many tears. Three days afterwards she was no more. We mention this fact on the testimony of D. Onofrio Coppola, the priest, who says that Gerard did many other most wonderful things while he was in this town.

Whole volumes indeed would not suffice were we to relate the incredible prodigies which Gerard effected during his various journeys. Besides, we never took pains to collect them, and those which came to our knowledge were heard, as it were, by accident from the priests who came to our house. Wherever he went he was welcomed as a saint, and when he passed from one place to another, the concourse of people who pressed around him to kiss his hand, and to entreat him to relieve their miseries, is almost incredible. The saintly brother however was so far from becoming vain on account of this applause, and was so full of self-abasement amidst all the honors he received, that he often wept for very shame, and could not comprehend why they should show him such respect. His great sway over the minds of men caused his presence to be, as it were, necessary in the diocese of Conza. He appeased innumerable divisions while there, and made men at peace again; and he had also the art of pleasing everybody. The mere sound of his voice sufficed to bring peace and unity, so that he even succeeded in putting an end to a serious division which had taken place amongst the clergy in a certain neighborhood, and by his influence brought about that for which the authority of the archbishop had been inadequate.

CHAPTER XI

Miraculous Circumstances which Preceded the Death of Brother Gerard.

The year 1755 was a critical but glorious epoch in the life of Brother Gerard. Whilst he was at St. Gregory on business connected with our house, a violent vomiting of blood came on in the month of July, accompanied by a burning fever which weakened him sadly. When the archpriest Salvatore d'Oliveto, and Dr. D. Joseph his brother heard of the state he was in, they made him come to their house. This warning from God of his approaching end did not take Brother Gerard by surprise, for he had predicted his speedy passage to eternity four months before. "Doctor," said he joyfully to Santorelli one day, "do you know that I shall die of consumption this year?" "And how can you tell that?" replied the doctor. "Because I asked my dearest Lord to grant me this favor, and He has promised to do so." "But why do you wish to die of consumption?" replied Santorelli. "Because I shall then be very much left to myself when I am dying, for although the community are so kind towards the sick, one can reckon on very little nursing in that complaint." Some time before this he had also told Father Januarius Rendina, that Jesus Christ had granted his prayer to die alone and in a decline. Let us now see how his petitions were fulfillled.

The spitting of blood which came on at Oliveto was so far from lessening, that it only increased more and more. As he was thus soon quite reduced, he wrote to Father Cajone on the 23rd of August to tell him of the state he was in. His letter terminated thus: "If you wish me to return, I will do so at once, and if you wish me to go on with the collection, I will do so, only send me a command to that effect, and all will be well. I am much distressed at the uneasiness I fear your Reverence will feel on my account. But do not be disturbed, my dear father, this is nothing. Recommend me to God, and pray that I may always and in all things do His holy will and pleasure." Father Cajone could not help being very anxious about him after he had read this letter, and he entrusted the sick brother to the prudent and charitable care of the friends in whose house he was until he was in a state to travel.

In the midst of his sufferings Gerard dispatched a messenger to D. Laurence de Masi, who had written to him from Caposele, to tell him that his father, Stephen de Masi, was given over by the doctors in a malignant fever, and to entreat him to recommend him to Mary our holy Mother. This gentleman attests that the moment Gerard received his letter, his father was free from all fever. As Gerard grew daily worse and worse, he thought it time to return to our house. He arrived there about noon on the 31st of August. He was so reduced, that he seemed more dead than alive. "When I first saw him," wrote Father Cajone, "I had the greatest difficulty in restraining my tears. We all marveled at his exceeding joyousness, and at the unalterable peace he preserved in the midst of all his sufferings. Instead of being cured by coming home the fever only made more rapid progress, and it was soon accompanied by the most alarming symptoms; for a painful dysentery came on, after which he suffered from violent perspirations, frequent delirium, and repeated fainting fits. Whilst he was thus reduced to a state of extreme weakness, the devil appeared to him, and offered him life and health. "Monster!" replied Gerard, " I wish only for what God wills, and I order you not to molest me again."

The father-rector once asked him if his will were wholly conformed to that of God. Gerard replied, "I picture to myself that this bed is the Divine will to me, and that whilst I am fastened down on it, I am also nailed down to the performance of His good pleasure. Indeed, I trust that God's will and mine are synonymous." He afterwards got a paper affixed to his door, on which was written in large characters, "The will of God is done here as God wills, and for as long as He wills." The spitting of blood became at length so copious, that he expectorated several pounds in the course of a few days. During one of his visits, Dr. Santorelli asked him if he would like to live or die. "I neither wish to live or die," replied Gerard; "I only desire the will of God to be accomplished. I should like to die that I might be united to God, but the thought of death afflicts me, for I have suffered nothing for Jesus Christ."

As soon as he came to our house, he placed a large wooden crucifix, in which the wounds of our Blessed Lord were most vividly depicted, at the foot of his bed, and he used if possible to kneel before it for an hour or two a day, to unite his sufferings to those of his Divine Redeemer. His ordinary ejaculation was, "I suffer, my God, because I do not suffer. May I suffer, dear Jesus, and not die." One day when Father Cajone went into his room, Gerard appeared to be in his last agony, but after he had cast his eyes on the crucifix, he seemed suddenly to gain strength and animation. "Ah, my father," said he with a sigh of ardent love, "how greatly do I long to be united to my God!"

When his illness became generally known, not a day passed without priests and gentlemen coming to visit him. The desire to hear once more the salutary counsels which issued from his lips, caused them to come in crowds to the foot of his bed, and they all went away full of admiration at his unalterable conformity to the will of God. Even while in this extremity he wrote a great many letters to those who had been in the habit of being directed by his counsels, to console them and to confirm them in all virtue. The following very remarkable one, which he sent to D. Isabella Salvatore of Oliveto, the niece of the excellent archpriest of the same name, has been fortunately preserved. This letter shows how cautious he was in his intercourse with young females, and how deeply his mind was imbued with the spirit of God.

"Jesus! Mary!

"Blessed forever be the Adorable Trinity, and our dearest and divine Mother Mary.

"My beloved Sister in Jesus Christ, God knows how ill I am, and yet I am enabled to write to you with my own hand. This will prove to you how much He loves you. But how much more will He love you if you do what I am going to entreat you to do. You cannot imagine, my dear child, how much I love you in God, and how ardently I desire your eternal salvation, for God has placed you in a special manner under my care. But my affection for you is exempt from all sensible attachment, or rather, it is spiritualized in God, I love you therefore, in God, and not out of Him; for if your affection for me is not wholly in God also, it is only a firebrand from hell! All those who love God are as dear to me as you are. If I thought that anyone loved me apart from God, I would curse them in God's name; for affection should be pure and chaste as that which filled the heart of Mary, whose Spouse was the beauteous and divine Dove who came from God, and who was God. In fine, we must love all things in God, and not out of Him. Enough of this, however. Let us now speak of ourselves, for I have been too diffuse already. If you will do what I am going to tell you, you will give joy to God and to me. All but the love of God is vanity, my dear child; therefore, put aside every passion and earthly attachment, that you may become wholly united to God. Be courageous, and make a final resolution to consecrate yourself to God. O! how blessed a thing it is to belong to God alone, as those well know who have experienced what it is! Do so likewise, and you will say the same. How can we love a world which has nothing but bitterness and misery to bestow on its votaries! Let your heart belong to God alone from henceforth, and let God dwell therein without a rival. And if you see that any passion or any feeling which is not of God is on the point of entering it, say to yourself, 'My heart is not mine; my Lord has taken it from me, and He fills it all. Flee away then and disappear, all which is not God.' The spouse ought to be jealously anxious to please her divine Lord in all things. She ought to guard against every shadow of vanity in her most insignificant actions with scrupulous attention. She ought to watch over every avenue to her heart, that it may become the temple of God, the house of God, the abode of God, the very dwelling-place of the Most High. For these are the true names of hearts which are consecrated to God. Pray for me, for I need your prayers now more than ever.

"Your unworthy servant and brother in Christ,
"Gerard Majella,
"Of the Most Holy Redeemer."

As the malady grew worse and worse the Holy Viaticum was administered to him. Gerard received it in such a respectful posture, that his mere appearance inspired devotion. Whilst Father Buonamano held the Sacred Host in his hands, he said these words, "Behold the Lord, who is now your Father, and who will shortly be your Judge. Reanimate your faith, and make the preparatory acts." Gerard replied with confidence and humility, "Thou knowest, O my God, that all that I have ever said and done has been for Thy glory. I die at peace, because I trust I have never sought for anything but Thy glory and Thine adorable will." After he had communicated, he wished to be left alone, that he might have time to pray, and to pour forth the affections of his heart into that of Jesus Christ.

When Dr. D. Joseph Salvatore of Oliveto heard that he was so ill, he came to see him, accompanied by Father Abbot D. Prosper d'Aquila, who had come from St. Andrew, and who had a young peasant with him, who was his servant. When Gerard saw him standing at the door, he asked him to play on a harpsichord which was in the room. As the villager knew nothing of music, he wished to be excused, whilst the abbot and the doctor amused themselves at his embarrassment. Gerard, however, insisted on his playing a minuet. As his master pressed him to do so likewise, he began and executed a very sweet symphony. But when he had done, he confessed that whilst he was playing, he felt that his fingers and hand had been guided for him by some unseen agency, and that his skill in playing was attained by no effort of his own.

During this illness Gerard also received a visit from a young libertine, who had by magical arts succeeded in plunging several husbands into misery. The holy brother knew nothing of all this by natural means, yet before he had even had time to speak, he said, "How can you have the face to come here, after having caused so many bitter tears to be shed? And now you wish Jesus Christ to show mercy on you!" D. Laurence de Masi came to consult him, and to manifest his interior to him; Gerard also solved his difficulties, reassured and consoled him, without having heard what he had to say.

On the 6th of September, the day preceding the vigil of

the Nativity of our Blessed Lady, Extreme Unction was just going to be administered to him, when he received a note from Father Fiocchi, in which he commanded him to give up spitting blood and to recover. After Gerard had read this, he respectfully placed it on his heart. When Dr. Santorelli came in, he found him in a state of entire recollection, with the letter in his hand. When he asked him what it was about, Gerard replied, "Father Fiocchi has written to put me under obedience. He says that I am not to spit any more blood." "Well, and what do you think of doing?" asked the doctor. Gerard replied by turning to the infirmarian, and saying, "Take away that basin, take it quite away;" and from that time the expectoration ceased. But as the doctor saw that the dysentery continued, he said, "What is the use of the spitting of blood ceasing, if the dysentery still continues?" Gerard replied, "I have been put under obedience with regard to the former, but nothing was said about the latter." The doctor at once hurried to Father Garzilli, to get him to show Brother Gerard that he had not fully obeyed the command he had received, which signified that he should become wholly cured, and Father Garzilli lost no time in going to the sick chamber of Gerard. "Is this the way you obey, brother?" said he. "Have you no scruple in acting thus? Father Fiocchi not only wishes you to cease to spit blood, but also to send away the fever, and all the other bad symptoms. In fact, he wishes you to get up, and be in good health." To which Gerard humbly replied, "Since this is so, my father, I will obey in all." When Santorelli came to see him in the afternoon, Gerard said, "I shall get up tomorrow." He only laughed; but Gerard again said, "Yes, I must get up tomorrow, and if you like to give me something to eat, I am ready to do so." The doctor hesitated at first, but the confident tone of the sick man reassured him, and he determined to satisfy him. Meanwhile a messenger came from Oliveto with a basket of apricots. When he saw them, the doctor said to Brother Gerard, "If you will promise me to obey Father Fiocchi, I will let you eat one of these." "So be it," answered Gerard. "Let the dictates of obedience be fulfillled, and may God thereby be glorified." After he had eaten the first, a second was given to him, and then a third, and that without any bad effect. Indeed he got so well that he was able to get up and go through his duties as usual. When Dr. Santorelli arrived next morning, he went straight to the sick man's room, and not finding him there, he asked what had become of him. On being told that he was walking in the garden, he exclaimed in a transport of joy and wonder, "Great virtue of holy obedience! What prodigies dost thou not effect!" All the community rejoiced at this miraculous recovery, and their joy was at its climax when the saintly brother resumed his former place in the refectory. There was a joiner, by name Philip Galella, who was a native of Muro, and who was in our house at this time. "My dear fellow townsman," said Gerard to him, "I was to have died on the Nativity of our Blessed Lady; but God has spared my life for a few days longer."

Amongst the innumerable prodigies which happened during this illness, the following is one of the most remarkable: One day, (it was the 24th of September, 1755,) Gerard suddenly turned to another lay-brother, and said, "Mother Mary Celeste of Foggia is now in the enjoyment of the beatific vision." These words seemed of little moment at the time, but we soon afterwards heard, that on that very day, and at the very hour when he had spoken, Mother Mary Celeste had died in the sweet savor of holiness.

Chapter XII
Saintly Death of Brother Gerard; Prodigies which Accompanied it.

Although Gerard recovered, his days were numbered, and his end was at hand. On seeing that our fathers were greatly comforted at his restoration to health, he said, "God has disposed matters thus for His greater glory, to show the efficacy of holy obedience. But I must die, and in a few days I shall be in eternity." The fever reappeared on the 5th of October, and with the same symptoms as before. On the preceding evening he said to his friend Santorelli, "Doctor, I have obeyed, but you must remember, that I have already told you that I must soon die. The time has now come, and there is no longer any remedy." He then took to his bed again, and thought of nothing but of preparing for death. As Gerard had always had an ardent desire to participate in the sufferings our Blessed Savior endured during His dolorous passion, when he saw that his end was at hand, he asked God to grant him the favor of experiencing the interior and exterior sufferings that Jesus suffered during His agony on the cross. Although he carefully endeavored to conceal the graces he had received from God, he could not help some portion of them from being discovered. One day when he was alone, and when he was holding converse with his crucifix, he exclaimed in a loud tone of voice, "O Lord, assist me to bear this purgatory!" As the doctor overheard these words, he asked him, when he went into his room, to tell him what he meant by them. "My dear doctor," replied Gerard, "I earnestly prayed to Jesus Christ to let me satisfy for my sins by suffering for His love, and God has heard my petition; I therefore suffer my purgatory in this world, but I am comforted by thinking that this is well-pleasing to my dearest Lord." Another day he also said, "I suffer a great deal. Indeed I am going through such a positive martyrdom, that I have not strength to speak."

The priest D. Gerard Gisone, who afterwards entered our Congregation, came from the territory of Ricigliano to confer with him on the state of his conscience; but he had only to listen, for the saintly brother exposed his state to him, and gave him good advice ere he had spoken himself. When he was going away he said, "Pray to God for me, for I am suffering greatly." "From what?" asked D. Gisone. "I am hidden in the sacred wounds of Jesus," he replied, "and His wounds are in me. I continually feel all the pains and dolors which Jesus suffered in His adorable passion." This state of torture however gave him joy rather than sorrow. It even gave him pain to see that the community were too uneasy and anxious about him. As the doctor had prescribed some medicine for him which was to be taken at midnight, he ordered a brother to sit up to give it to him. Gerard sighed when he heard this: "O doctor, this is real pain!" and he repeated this several times over with marks of great distress. The prayers which the community offered up for his recovery also made him suffer. "I am useless," said he; "I do not deserve all this." The expense of his remedies was such a bitter addition to his sufferings and anxiety, that he one day sent for the doctor, to ask how much they would come to. "Think of something else," said the doctor; but Gerard replied, "But, doctor, of what use have I been to the Congregation, that it should be put to expense on my account?"

His indifference to every remedy, and his implicit obedience to the orders of the doctor and infirmarian, never left him for an instant. His strength was so exhausted that he was almost unable to take any medicines; yet when the infirmarian presented them to him he made violent efforts to swallow them, and never refused to make the attempt. When overcome by sickness or disgust, he was sometimes heard to exclaim, "My God, I have not strength for it! "but at the word obedience he did violence to every inclination, and forced himself to obey.

He received Holy Communion every morning throughout his illness. On the 15th of October, the feast of St. Theresa, he said to Santorelli, "Recommend me to St. Theresa today, and communicate for my intention." After he had received the Holy Viaticum he asked to have the corporal on which the Blessed Sacrament had rested. When it was given to him he placed it on his breast and held it thus until his agony. "The fathers have recreation today," said Philip Galella. "And they will have another recreation day tomorrow," added Gerard. "Why so?" asked Galella. "Because I shall die tonight," he replied. In the evening he asked Galella what o'clock it was. When he heard that it was six o'clock he replied, "Then I have still six hours more to live." As the doctor was going away, because it was getting late, Gerard, contrary to custom, begged him to remain, for he knew that death was at hand. However, as Santorelli thought that he seemed better, he excused himself, saying that he had other visits to pay. Gerard was then silent, and did not press him further. Next morning, when too late to be of any avail, he understood that Gerard pressed him to stay because he wished him to be with him when his soul passed into eternity.

At about seven o'clock a messenger arrived from Oliveto, with a letter addressed to Brother Gerard, in which he was entreated to recommend to God the success of a building which was destined for a church of the Blessed Virgin, and which was in great jeopardy. The father-minister opened and read the letter without saying anything to him about it. When Gerard saw the messenger, he asked who he was. "Think of yourself alone now," said Father Buonamano. Without knowing the contents of the letter, Gerard said to the messenger, "Let them take courage; the work will not suffer. "He then sent for some of the dust from the tomb of St. Theresa, and told the bearer to have it thrown upon the edifice, and to return instantly to reassure the archpriest, by telling him that there was no danger.

It is impossible to express with what fervor and humility he prepared to appear before the tribunal of Jesus Christ. Although he had preserved his innocence and the whiteness of his baptismal robe unspotted, he sat up in bed, and recited the Miserere with such devotion that all who heard him were affected. After each verse he repeated, "Malum coram te feci;" and when he uttered the words, "A peccato meo munda me," he shed many tears. Indeed, he appeared to be so penetrated by God's justice as well as by His mercy, that all who approached him were affected to tears.

After eight o'clock he several times repeated, "My God, where art Thou? Show me the Light of Thy countenance;" and turning to those around him, he said to them, "Help me to become united to my God. Brother Carminello asked if he had any scruples of conscience; upon this he exerted all his strength, and quickly and emphatically replied, "Why do you speak to me of scruples?" Brother Carminello then added, "We have always loved one another; will you not remember me when you enter the presence of God?" "How could I ever forget you?" replied Gerard. Between ten and eleven o'clock, Gerard became disturbed, and said in an agitated manner, "What are those two wretches doing there? Put them out of the door." (Probably they were two demons.) But he soon regained his usual serenity, and said in joyful accents, "There is the Madonna, let us adore her;" and at these words he fell into a profound ecstasy. Sometime before this he had said that the forty martyrs, towards whom he had great devotion, had promised to assist him in his passage into eternity, but he did not then say anything to show the nature of their assistance. During the two last hours of his life he constantly kept his eyes fixed on the large crucifix, and on a picture of Mary our holy Mother. He made frequent acts of contrition and love, and sometimes was heard to exclaim, "My God, I wish to die to please Thee, I wish to die to accomplish Thy holy will." When his strength had quite failed, he continued to move his lips, and to repeat these acts in a low tone of voice.

As no one imagined that he would die so soon, all the community retired to rest except one lay-brother, who was left to take care of him. He asked for a little water about half an hour before he died. When the brother brought it to him, he found him lying on his side. He at first thought he was asleep, but he soon perceived that he was in his agony. He therefore instantly went to call Father Buonamano, who was the superior. When he came, Gerard gave up the ghost. God no doubt permitted it to be thus, that his own desires and prophecy might receive their accomplishment. At midnight, then, of the 15th of October, 1755, Brother Gerard passed into a better world, amidst reiterated acts of love, resignation, and devotion to Jesus Christ and His holy Mother. He was twenty-nine years of age, six months, and seven days, when he died, of which six years, five months, and fifteen days had been spent in our Congregation. His body emitted such a sweet savor after he expired, that everyone noticed it with admiration.

As soon as the community were assembled together, Father Buonamano ordered a discipline to be taken in common in thanksgiving to Jesus Christ and the most holy Virgin Mary, for the saintly death of this holy brother. Everyone felt so joyous that it seemed as if they already saw Gerard in glory. Amidst these transports a brother went to ring the bell, but instead of tolling it he rang it as merrily as if it announced tidings of joy rather than of mourning. When he was found fault with for it, he said that he had not done it designedly, but as if inwardly impelled to do so. Three hours afterwards it was resolved to draw blood from the holy corpse. "You were always obedient during life," said Father Buonamano, "I now command you to give this proof of your virtue." A vein was then opened in the right arm, and more than two pounds of blood instantly gushed out of the incision as if he had been yet alive. This prompt obedience added intensity to the joy his saintly end had already occasioned; and they hastened to dip their handkerchiefs in his blood, and they were afterwards distributed amongst his friends for their consolation.

As soon as the tidings of his death became public, persons of all ranks hurried to our house, rich and poor, young and old, seculars and ecclesiastics crowded together around his bier. One took pleasure in telling of some prophecy which the brother had made which had been verified in his own person; another mentioned how he had penetrated into the secrets of his heart; whilst a third described the way in which Gerard had led him back into the paths of virtue, and reconciled him to the God he had offended. The poor especially, (to whom Gerard had acted as a father,) caused the church and our house to resound with their sighs and tears. The people not only exalted him as a saint, but began to cut off his hair, and to tear up his cassock, so that it was necessary to send for the guards to surround and protect the body. Our Father Garzilli sung the Mass for the dead in presence of the secular and regular clergy, and Father Buonamano made such a touching panegyric, that it drew tears from the eyes of all who heard it. The body was exposed for two days, to gratify the devotion of the Faithful, who flocked to see it from all parts. Just before the interment Father Buonamano repeated his command to the saintly body to give forth blood, and it gave it as copiously as he had done before. Besides the flexibility of all his members, such an abundant perspiration exhaled from his forehead that handkerchiefs were steeped in it. His tomb is modest and simple, but it stands apart from the others just before the sacristy door.

As the painter was unable to come to take his likeness in time, two casts of his face were made by a statuary. One of them is still kept by the community, and the other is in the possession of the Lords Salvatore of Oliveto, for whom it was taken. We afterwards tried to have a portrait taken from this cast, but the attempt did not succeed. When Father Cajone returned to the house, he addressed the saintly brother, saying, "My dear Gerard, you see the portrait is a failure. Try and teach the artist how to succeed." The painter then found out the secret, for as he declared himself, a voice from heaven told him how he should handle his pencil and what strokes he should put to produce the desired effect. The portrait represents Gerard in the position in which the archpriest Salvatore saw him when he fell into the ecstasy at Oliveto, the crucifix is in one hand, and the other is crossed on his breast, while his body is uplifted to a considerable height in the air. Just after he expired, he appeared to a person of great piety, to whom he was much attached. He looked very joyous, and was clad in his ordinary attire. Soon afterwards he reappeared, but this time he was most richly adorned and resplendent in glory. This person says that he animated him to suffer for Christ, and said to him, "The slight trials which we suffer for God on earth, are amply rewarded by Him in heaven." As soon as he had given up the ghost, he also appeared to Father D. Peter Petrella, and manifested to him the glory he enjoyed in heaven.

CHAPTER XIII

Favors Accorded by Gerard to Those Who Invoke Him; His Miraculous Apparitions.

Whilst the memory of the wicked perishes with them, that of the just lives eternally, saith the Spirit. Soon after the death of the saintly brother, God was pleased to give many proofs of the glory and power he enjoys in heaven. So far from the confidence which people had justly felt in his intercession being lessened by his death, it daily grew stronger and stronger. As soon as his decease became known, everyone had recourse to him, and the favors they received in consequence only proved that his power and charity had been thereby augmented. "Brother Gerard and his friends seem engaged in a sweet contest of love," wrote the archpriest Salvatore. "They are more devoted to him than to any other saint, and he obtains the most signal and abundant favors for them. It would be impossible, dear Father-superior, to tell you all the prodigies which are daily effected in our archdiocese of Conza and in the neighborhood through his intercession." His fame was also widely spread by means of his pictures, which our fathers gave away during the missions, and devotion to Brother Gerard soon became general instead of partial as heretofore.

I cannot here help blaming our fathers for their negligence in not collecting together accounts of all the prodigies he effected. For my part, I will only select a few amongst those which have come to my knowledge.

D. Laurence Gilberti, the president of the seminary at Conza, had for some days been suffering from a most painful complaint, for which several eminent medical men had operated on him without affording him any relief. Whilst he was in this extremity, he said to D. Donatus

Buzio, who happened to call on him, "My dear friend, my case is hopeless" "If you have a picture of Brother Gerard," replied Buzio, "apply it to your body and recommend yourself to him, and you will certainly be cured." D. Gilberti did so, and he obtained instantaneous relief. He always carried the picture about with him from that time, in gratitude for this boon, and never had any return of his malady.

There was a man at Caposele who led a most wicked life. One of his friends went to our Father Petrella to beg him to pray for him. "I will command Brother Gerard to go to him, and make him enter into himself," he replied. Next day the same person returned, and said that Gerard had appeared to the man in question, and that his exhortations had completely changed him. In fact, he soon came running to our church in a perfect terror. He related the vision he had had, and confessed his sins to one of our fathers, with sentiments of the most lively sorrow.

The mule of a gentleman who was riding home to his village was suddenly seized with such violent spasms that it seemed on the point of death. As he was alone, and quite in the country, he had no means of relieving the poor animal, which greatly distressed him. He suddenly remembered however that he had a rosary with him which Brother Gerard had given him. "Brother," said he, "you alone can assist me in this extremity." He then touched the mule with the rosary, and it at once arose quite cured, and thus he was happily enabled to finish his journey.

One of the sons of D. Christine de Rogatis had been suffering from a slow fever accompanied by a bloody flux for some months. One day they believed he was dead, and there was good ground for thinking so, for his uncle, Camillus Bozio, had felt his pulse, and it had ceased to beat. In order to ascertain if he was really dead, he also placed his mouth close to that of the child, and there were no signs of life there either. The inconsolable mother however had recourse to Brother Gerard with confidence, and applied one of his teeth to her son, saying, "Brother Gerard, do not abandon me in my distress. Restore my child to life." And the boy opened his eyes as she pronounced the words, and was free from fever and from every other ailment.

Gerard also restored another corpse to life. D. Thomas Ronco's wife had a premature confinement, and the baby was scarcely christened ere it died. The parents had recourse to Brother Gerard, and touched the infant with his relics, and wonderful to relate, the child was instantly restored to life and seemed quite healthy.

The Marquis of Oliveto's agent was attacked by a malignant fever accompanied with pleurisy, which caused his life to be despaired of. As the marquis had heard of Gerard's numerous miracles, he begged him to have recourse to his intercession. And no sooner had he invoked his aid, than the pleurisy and fever left him.

One day when Brother Gerard was taking leave of Dominic Canillo, who was his intimate friend, he said to him, "Whenever you want me, you have only to call me, and I will come to you." Some years after the death of the servant of God, Canillo was going to the fair at Gravina with a cart full of merchandise. When he reached the bridge of Canosa the vehicle stuck so fast in the mud and ruts of the road, that it was impossible to move it. Canillo then remembered the promise he had received. "Now, Brother Gerard," said he, "it is time for you to keep your word. If you do not assist me, I do not know what will become of me." He had scarcely uttered these words, ere the mules drew the cart out of the mud, as easily as if it had been empty, and without receiving any assistance.

Donna Mary Michael Jourdan, of the territory of Corbara, in the state of Nocera, was in the habit of spending the summer at Caposele. From the time she heard of the numerous prodigies Gerard effected, she often invoked him and placed herself under his protection, although she had never seen him. One day, however, when she was going to church, Gerard came up to her and said, "Prepare for great sufferings; but be of good courage, for God will enable you to bear them." As she was astonished at such a meeting, she went to our Father Augustine, who was then the rector, and told him of what had taken place. The father asked her which of the brothers had spoken to her. "None of those who are in the house now," she replied. As Father Augustine suspected what was really the case, he took her into the hall, where she saw Brother Gerard's portrait and several others which were hanging up. She immediately pointed to it and exclaimed, "That is the very brother who appeared to me!" And his words were fulfilled, for she had afterwards a great many trials to bear, but Gerard consoled her by appearing to her again.

D. Ignatius Cozzo, a canon of the cathedral at Trevico, had been for some years afflicted with a painful hernia, and had found nothing to give him any relief. One day when he was suffering more than usual, he had recourse to Brother Gerard, with whom he had always been very intimate. "My dear Gerard," said he, "if it would contribute to God's glory and the good of my soul, I entreat you to deliver me from this complaint." And so it was, that it entirely disappeared when the words of his prayer had ended, and he never had any relapse, although he often underwent great fatigue in the pulpit and elsewhere.

A nephew of the Signors Ilario, who was a little boy of four or five years of age, came from Naples to Caposele to visit them in 1781. In the July of this year, he was seized with such an alarming fever, that great fears were entertained for his life. They therefore implored the aid of Brother Gerard. On the night of the 15th, the child awoke his aunt, who was asleep beside him, and exclaimed with joyful accents, "O aunt, aunt, look at Brother Gerard! see how beautiful and bright he is. Do, aunt, get up and look at him!" and then he added, "O, but now he has gone away!" Next morning he was perfectly well, and his parents took him to our church, that they might all offer up their thanksgivings at the tomb of Brother Gerard. He himself related this vision and all its attendant circumstances eight years afterwards.

In the month of July, 1785, our Father Mansione was summoned from Caposele to attend D. John Baptist Fungarola the notary, who was on his deathbed. Whilst he was in the room, D. Paschal de Silla, who was a great friend of the sick man, came in. When he saw how ill he was, he said to Brother Gerard with the greatest confidence, "I have heard of all the miracles you have worked; but if you do not cure my friend, I will no longer think well of you." He then laid a picture of the saintly brother on the dying man's chest. At the same moment he ceased to groan, the fever disappeared, and the cure was a radical one. Yet the fever had been a putrid one, and his groans had caused him to be entirely given over, for as Dr. Santorelli said, they are always the precursors of death in that complaint.

Donna Antionette de Vallo of Benevento was so ill during the April of 1776, that she was given over by the physicians; but D. Francis, the priest, who was a relative of hers, placed some relics of Brother Gerard under her pillow while she was asleep, and entreated him to cure her. Gerard appeared to D. Antionette on the night of the 25th, and made the sign of the cross over her. "You are cured," said he. At these words he disappeared. When she awoke, her relative asked her how she felt; she replied, "A religious has been here whom I never saw before, and I have been quite well since then." As they did not know which of the saints they had invoked had granted this favor, they showed her the different pictures which had been put under her bolster; she looked at three, but she said that the likeness of the religious she had seen was not amongst them. That of Brother Gerard was then held up to her, and she immediately exclaimed, "That is the very one who appeared to me." When the doctors came to see her, they found that the fever had entirely left her.

Dominic Anthony Bozio at Caposele, was also attacked by a similar malady in the month of July, 1789, and he too was given over by the doctors. All his household were in the greatest distress at this, for he had a wife and children. Whilst in this state, his uncle, Canon Bozio, told him that before he died, Gerard had promised that he would be the patron of his family in heaven. "If this be the case," replied the sick man, "let us remind him of his promise." After these words he and all his family joined together in invoking his protection. On the seventh day the return of the fever was looked forward to with much apprehension as a most critical time, but the sick man fell asleep before the violence of the attack came on. And the saintly brother appeared to him, and seated himself close to his bed, and with a smiling countenance said to him, "We have done all you wish." When he awoke, he called his family around him, and told them of the vision. The fever had left him, and never recurred again.

In 1795, a lady of noble birth, of the family of the Cocca at Benevento, was so seriously ill that her life was despaired of. She however, had recourse to Gerard's protection, and placed a picture of the saintly brother on her head. During the night he appeared to her dressed in the habit of our Congregation. "Be not afraid," he said to her, "you are healed." And so it was, for when the doctors came to see her, they found her quite well.

The following wonderful cure happened to Sconarde

Miocore. For several months a membrane had grown up in her eye, and covered the interior tunicle so completely that she could not make any use of it. The other was half covered with a similar membrane, so that although she was in good health, she was nearly blind. The poor creature was very sad at this, for the doctor had declared that it was incurable. But after she had recommended herself to Gerard with lively faith, she was instantly cured. When she afterwards met the doctor, she gaily said to him, "You were unable to do me any good, but I have just consulted a doctor who has promised to cure me." "You are only making game of me," replied the oculist. "See if I am not cured," said she, taking her hand away from her left eye, which she had hitherto concealed; "and see who has cured me," added she, holding up the picture of Brother Gerard, which she wore round her neck. The doctor then examined her eyes, and found that they were in as good a state as if nothing had ever been the matter with them.

Gerard's miracles also caused him to become celebrated in Sicily. The following is but one amongst a thousand. A Benedictine nun, called Sister Josephine Pasciuta, of the convent of St. Catherine of Sienna, had such a diseased arm that it was pronounced to be incurable. Our Father Lauria was so full of compassion for her when he heard how much she suffered, that he sent her a picture of Brother Gerard. The nun recommended herself to him with lively faith, and when the surgeon came to dress the wound, he did not even find a trace of where it had been.

The confidence which these innumerable miracles caused men to feel in the protection of this servant of God is almost incredible. He is everywhere called upon as if he were already a canonized saint. His pictures are so eagerly sought after, that it is not possible to satisfy all the Faithful who ask for them. Some kiss them with affection, and press them to their heart or place them on their head through devotion. Others continually carry them about them, or hang them up in their rooms. Some, in fine, fasten them upon ruinous buildings, well knowing that this admirable brother only confers signal favors, and that he effects his greatest prodigies when the danger seems the greatest.

The room in which he died is converted into a chapel, and dedicated to St. Stanislaus de Kostka. The following is the inscription it contains:

Cubiculum
quod eximia innocentia ac pietate vir
FRATER GERARDUS MAJELLA MUZANUS
Congregationis SS. Redemptoris
præsentia quondam usuque cohonestans
sanctorum tandem morte decoravit:
adolescentulorum innocentissimo
angelicarum pulchritudine et odore virtutum
pulcherrimi instar floris inter cœlites nitenti
beato Stanislas Kostka
in sacelli formam redactum
Patres ejusdem Congregationis donum hanc
incolentes
tertio idus julii A.D. MDCCXCVI.
P. P.

All that we have related of this saintly brother, who has justly been called the Thaumaturgus of our Congregation and the glory of his country, is but a short abridgment of his virtues and miracles. Several volumes would scarcely suffice were we to set forth all his heroic actions, and to count up all the prodigies he has effected, and continues to effect, day by day. I will therefore conclude this sketch in the words of St. John, the beloved apostle, "Multa quidem et alia signa fecit in conspectu suorum, quæ non sunt scripta in libro hoc." Joan 20:30.[9]

---

[9] I cannot here refrain from mentioning that the blessed brother especially manifests his power in the case of difficult confinements. At Foggia therefore, and wherever he is best known, every woman who is pregnant has a picture of him, and invokes his name with devotion.

The Life of
JOACHIM GAUDIELLO
Lay-Brother of the Congregation of the Most Holy
Redeemer

The life of
JOACHIM GAUDIELLO
Lay-Brother of the Congregation of the
Most Holy Redeemer.

By the Rev. Father Tannoja.

 OACHIM GAUDIELLO was the first sheaf which our Heavenly Father transplanted from the field of our Congregation to the garners above. He was born on the 20th of August, 1719, in the territory of Bracigliano, the ancient San Severino. He was brought up by an uncle, the parish priest of Ciorani. Our Father Alphonsus had founded a house here some years before; and as Joachim had been in the habit of seeing his aged uncle and his two brothers frequent our house from his very infancy, he imbibed as great an attachment to it himself. He often came to see us, and to pray in our church. He was thus fed with the milk of piety from his very childhood, and grew up without giving sorrow or inconvenience to anyone.

He had scarcely ceased to be a child, ere he resolved to join us as a lay-brother, for grace filled his heart from his tenderest years. When he first proposed it, it was objected to for the sake of his uncle and of his other relations, who could not bear to see him in such a humble condition. But Joachim's fervor triumphed over all their opposition; "I mean to become a saint," said he, "and I wish to follow Jesus who was reviled and despised, and to contemn the world." When one corresponds to grace, every obstacle is sure to give way in the end. And so it was in this case. The

385

uncle changed his mind and went himself to Alphonsus to ask him to receive him. His vocation was well tried, and on the 20th of January, 1758, when he was eighteen years of age, Joachim was numbered amongst our lay-brothers.

He was sent to the house at Scala at the commencement of his novitiate. It may truly be said that Brother Vitus Curzius was his novice-master there, and by his example he was excited to aim at the greatest perfection, and when this house was afterwards suppressed they both returned to Ciorani together.

Joachim began by declaring a cruel warfare against his flesh. He girded himself with haircloth several times a week, and daily wore small iron chains around his legs and arms. He took the discipline once or twice a day, and with such severity that his clothes were wet with his blood. His food was most wretched. At that time a little ill-seasoned soup was quite a luxury amongst us; but Joachim would not take even that without adding bitter herbs to it, such as wormwood and centaury, and he usually partook of it on his knees or extended on the ground. He either took no wine, or so little that it was next to nothing. He always fasted on Saturdays, and on the eves of the feasts of the Blessed Virgin. In a word, Joachim neglected nothing by which he could mortify and subdue his passions. The reader need not however be astonished at hearing of such a young man practicing so many austerities, for all these mortifications were quite in common use amongst us at that time; with such an example before us as that of our Father Alphonsus, we should have been ashamed to treat our bodies with more consideration than he did. Joachim had also another model in Brother Vitus Curzius, but it would be hard to decide which of them edified his brother the most. Fathers Mazzini and Villani united in saying that this holy brother had such a great and sincere desire to become more and more holy, that he turned all the good examples of all the fathers, and all that was said in the conferences, to account for the good of his own soul.

Whilst Brother Joachim was making such rapid progress in the paths of perfection, the enemy of salvation caused him to stumble and fall through envy at his success; but this was so far from stopping his onward career, that it only increased his fervor. One day when he was gathering figs in the garden, he had the weakness to yield to a temptation of greediness or hunger and to eat one. A second followed the first, and then a third. It was then, as it is now, a grievous offense to touch anything except at meals, without the express permission of the superiors. Joachim soon entered into himself and perceived his error, and humbled himself for it before God; the difficulty consisted in bearing the humiliation of confessing it before men. Notwithstanding his extreme repugnance to doing so, he did not allow the devil to get the mastery over him. In the chapter of faults, which was held in the chapel according to custom, he courageously accused himself of this breach of rule before the whole community, and he did so with such sincere sorrow, that it affected all the fathers and brothers who heard it. Our Father Alphonsus thought that this glorious victory over self would be the precursor of the greatest sanctity. And so it really was, for from this time his ardor for the attainment of virtue, his vigilance, and his generosity became even greater than before.

As meditation is closely allied to mortification, it is impossible to neglect the one without neglecting the other also. So Joachim united a most contemplative spirit to an ardent love of labor and mortification. His every breath seemed a prayer, and he never allowed anything that he was doing to interfere with his union with God. He himself owned to Father Mazzini that the meditation in common which was made in the choir seemed to him to last but for a moment. During the most apparently distracting occupations, he was constantly uttering the most fervent ejaculations of love to God. The exercise of the presence of God was so familiar to him, that his heart was at all times recollected, and wherever he was, and whatever he was doing, he never for an instant forgot that God was with him, and that all was present to His sight. He had recourse to Him in all his necessities with the most lively and ardent faith. "Since He is my Father," said he, "I will act towards Him as if I were really His child."

He had a most tender love for Jesus in the adorable Sacrament, and he was so desirous to receive It, that he was allowed to communicate every day. He also made many spiritual communions daily, and whenever he had a spare moment he hurried to the church to pour forth his heart before Jesus in the tabernacle of love.

He had also the most ardent devotion for the most holy Virgin. He was constantly going to salute her image in the church, and he used there to prostrate himself at her feet and to offer her the tribute of his affections with filial tenderness. He never began anything without first saying an Ave to Mary. He seemed in a transport of joy on her feasts, and to be unable to think of anything else whilst they lasted. He celebrated her novenas with incredible devotion. He used then to redouble his austerities and his exercises of piety. He never ate fruit at such times, and disciplined himself to blood, and fasted on bread and water on the vigils of each of her feasts.

Joachim loved meditation, but he did not shun fatigue. He was in the habit of saying that a love of labor is the true test of the virtue of a lay-brother. He always chose the most laborious things for his own share, so that he was always called the fathers' little porter. When he had finished the duties of his own offices, nothing pleased him so much as to be allowed to assist the others in their work; and as his humility always caused him to select the most menial offices, his charity led him to relieve his brothers from what was most fatiguing to them. He was always working, and was quite delighted when he could do a kindness to another. "I work by the piece," he often said, "and my profit increases in proportion to the amount of fatigue I have."

As there was no oven in our house, we were obliged to make use of one in the neighborhood. One of Joachim's offices consisted in carrying the bread thither to be baked, at which he must have felt repugnance, for he had to cross the village in sight of his uncle and brothers with a board full of loaves on his shoulders; and this took place at least twice a week, on account of the number of strangers in our house; but he triumphed over nature. He used also readily to go to the market at San Severino, and come back laden with all the provisions we required. If his nature revolted at this, he said to himself, "Be firm, Brother Joachim, and learn to overcome yourself." He was so free from all love of the world, that he cared for none of its vanities and enjoyments, and found happiness in humiliations and contempt. "What is the world?" he would often say even to gentlemen; "what is it but smoke, and that the smoke of hell?"

He was also a model of exact observance of rule. He never broke silence. He carefully attended to all the signs in use amongst the community, and he was always the first to repair to the various exercises.

Father Villani declared that none of the fathers who had watched him most narrowly had ever discovered any voluntary fault in him. He was never actuated by human respect, and when duty was in question he was afraid of no one. The following is a proof of this. D. Andrew Sarnelli, the priest, who was the son of the baron of that name, who was a great benefactor of ours, happened to be one day in the court of our house with Joachim's brother, the priest, when a heavy shower suddenly came on. They both ran into the kitchen for shelter; but as Joachim knew that it was contrary to rule to admit anyone there, he turned them out most unceremoniously. Signor Sarnelli was not however offended, for when he reached his mansion all dripping with rain, he said to the priest, "I now see that Joachim is a real saint."

Joachim was also distinguished for his love for holy obedience. The voice of his superior was to him as the voice of God. He was always humble and submissive, and ready to obey the most trifling order. It was a beautiful thing to see his prompt obedience to everyone. "I must obey," said he, "for God has called me to be a servant. It is not for me to inquire whether I receive a command from a stupid brother, or from a learned father. My day's work is done when the sun sets." He never put his own meaning on what he was told, but scrupulously adhered to the letter of the command. As the cook one day told him to go and wash the endives in the garden pond, Joachim went and threw all the leaves into the middle of the pond, which of course instantly floated about hither and thither on the surface of the water. As he was a long time away, the cook went in search of him, and found him fishing out the leaves one by one with a long rod. When he was reproved for his awkwardness, he artlessly replied that he had been told to do so. This was not the only adventure which his simplicity gave rise to; indeed Father Mazzini told me that it was necessary to be most prudent in giving him any directions, for fear of the consequences of his literal obedience.

His modesty charmed everyone. Indeed, he imitated St. Aloysius in regard to his exterior deportment as well as by his interior recollectedness. No one knew what color his eyes were, Father Villani told me. He kept such custody over his eyes, that when he was sacristan he walked about the church without knowing whether there was anyone in it or not. When anyone gave him a commission, he stood at a distance and at one side while receiving the order. "It is the ear, and not the eye which must act," said he. Brother Tartaglione has assured me, that once when he was speaking to his mother by the rector's order, (it was almost the only time he consented to see her,) he never even raised his eyes to look at her. Joachim was no less heroic in regard to the virtue of holy poverty. He could not bear to have even a book in his room which he did not really require. If he had a pious picture beyond the number enjoined by the rule, he instantly got rid of it. The more shabby his clothes were, the more pleased he was, and he was not ashamed to appear before his relations in a habit which was covered with a hundred patches. His predilection for old clothes caused him many bodily mortifications, but he bore them all with pleasure, for he said that such was the will of God. The very semblance of an offense against this virtue caused him to tremble. He once made use of some scraps of waste paper, but he afterwards looked upon this as such a want of the spirit of holy poverty, that in the chapter of faults he exaggerated his offense, so as even to accuse himself of having given scandal by appropriating property which was not his own. He also always reproached himself for having once used a bit of packthread which he found on the ground. These are the two great sins for which Brother Joachim was always accusing himself in his confessions and at the chapter for faults. His detachment from his relations was also very remarkable. Although his two sisters were constantly in our church, and although he was sacristan, he never spoke to them or looked at them. His two brothers, (of whom one was a priest,) also often came to our house, but he never stopped to speak to them. One day when he was going to Bracigliano to recreate with the fathers there, he happened to meet his mother. He either did not see her or pretended not to do so, for he passed her by without noticing her. His mother however, in a very natural transport of maternal love, or from happiness at having such a virtuous son, ran back to embrace him. When Joachim saw her he got out of her way, and he would not even have looked at her if the father who presided had not told him to converse with her for some time. Joachim did so, but modestly kept his eyes down while speaking to her.

Every virtue seemed to be united together in this holy brother, and all his actions were so actuated by the Spirit of God, and carried on with such perseverance, that he caused the most virtuous to envy him. "Joachim gives us many a lesson," our Father Alphonsus often said. As he gave so many proofs of his constancy in well-doing, no difficulty was felt in allowing him to make his profession on the 21st of July, 1740. Joachim soon began to feel the effects of such a constant conflict between the flesh and the spirit. His exhausted strength at length quite failed; but he did not therefore abandon his mortifications, although a slow fever came on, which was followed by spitting of blood which caused his life to be despaired of. These sufferings formed a new school of perfection to Joachim, for while his body wasted away, his virtues only acquired fresh vigor. He lovingly embraced his cross, and thanked God for having fastened him to it. He humbly obeyed every order of the physician, however painful its consequences might be. The wishes of the father-rector were so many laws to him, and he had no will of his own; it was to be found in that of the brother infirmarian. One day the rector told him to go out and get a little air. In order to obey more perfectly, he asked where he was to go. "Go and recreate yourself," said the rector, and he unthinkingly made a gesture which seemed to point out a particular direction. Joachim took it for granted that that was the way he was to go; and although he was so very weak he went onwards towards a steep hill, where he would have continued his walk, if a father had not come to stop him and explain what the father-rector really meant.

As he got worse and worse, he was at length obliged to take to his bed. One morning, however, Father Mazzini found him making great efforts to dress himself. When he asked him what he was doing, he replied, "I am dressing myself in obedience to the doctor, who told me that I must take four steps round the room every morning."

Although his illness was a very painful one, Joachim never lost his usual serenity. Once when he was asked how he passed the day all alone, and stretched on a bed of suffering, he pointed to his crucifix, and said, "I look in my mirror where I see what I ought to become." Indeed, his mere appearance gave us all consolation, and all was admirable in him. His conformity to the will of God, his love of suffering, his humility, and his submission to the will of others were carried to a heroic extent. Once when Father Mazzini asked when he wished to go to heaven, he cheerfully replied, "I wish to go there when my Jesus wills it." He felt the greatest consolation at being the first of the Congregation to die, and repeated in a tone of triumph, "I shall carry the standard." He had such a tender love towards the Blessed Sacrament, that he often seemed quite transformed into a seraphim. His frequent and loving aspirations and his holy affections affected everyone. One day when he was ravished out of himself by love to God, he said to Father Mazzini, "Get a knife and open my breast, that you may take out my heart, and place it in the tabernacle beside my Jesus." In consequence of his fervor, he was permitted to receive Holy Communion in bed every morning, and he never ceased thanking his superior for having granted him such a favor. God however mortified him by casting him into a state of desolation, but he owned to Father Villani that whenever he communicated he felt celestial joy.

When he was most dangerously ill, his love for the Blessed Virgin shone forth with wonderful ardor. He was always kissing a picture of her which he held in his hands, and he recited the rosary several times a day. "The devil never leaves me alone," said he to Father Mazzini, "but he wastes his time, for I can do all, and I hope for all, through my own Mother Mary. Yes, I confidently trust that I shall die under her protection."

He would have rejoiced to die that he might see God; but he also was glad to live that he might be able to suffer more for God. Father Mazzini has often told me that it made him so sad to think that he could not die on the cross, like Jesus, and that the only way to comfort him was to show him that he was beginning to resemble Him, for that his bed was his cross. "But no," he would sorrowfully reply, "this is not a cross to me, on the contrary, it is a haven of rest, for I am aided and strengthened by Jesus crucified, the Man of Sorrows." A little picture of Jesus scourged was placed before him, but as soon as he saw it, he burst into tears, and said with a deep sigh, "O that I could be like Thee, O my Jesus! who wert cruelly scourged for me! Send me sufferings and wounds, O my Jesus! that I may thus resemble Thee!" One day he was seized with such an ardent desire to die, that he might thus go and enjoy the presence of his God, that he seemed to be ravished out of himself; but he soon began to fear that this wish only arose from a desire to flee from the cross. He therefore sent for the father-minister, confessed his scruple to him, and accused himself of his want of love for suffering.

His confidence in the Passion of Christ Jesus was quite moving. "Behold Jesus died for me," he would repeat. "He cannot therefore desert me, He will assuredly conduct me to heaven, and I offer all His merits to His heavenly Father in satisfaction for my sins." He was then asked if he were tempted. "The devil does not leave me alone; but here is my sword of defense," said he, pointing to a large crucifix in his room. As it was afterwards moved into the private chapel, he was asked how he defended himself from the devil when it was gone. "I defeat him with my little sword," he laughingly replied, taking up the small crucifix which hung round his neck.

He wished for sufferings, but he did not wish anyone to feel compassion for him; and he was always unwilling to manifest them to others. Father Mazzini himself had really to cross-question him to get at the truth, and when he, as his superior, required him to tell him all he felt, he obeyed the order with repugnance, for he grieved at not being deprived of all consolation, as Jesus was. He had such a desire to suffer for the love of God, that he never lost any opportunity of doing so. His bed was placed against a window which opened into the chapel, so that the air which came in at the crevices inconvenienced him very much. At first he placed a book on the bed to hinder the wind from blowing in, but on consideration he took it away as a needless luxury. When asked why he had done so, he replied, "The saints strove to procure sufferings, and shall I shun this trifling annoyance which God sends me!" One morning when he had some pills to take, Father Mazzini told him that St. Aloysius Gonzaga not only swallowed them with pleasure, but even chewed them, that he might suffer for Jesus Christ. He had scarcely spoken ere Joachim began to imitate him, and to chew his pills as if they had been the greatest delicacies.

The miserable collation that was sent up to him at dinnertime only gave him pain, for the pleasure of eating was to him a source of torment. When he was at dinner, he offered every mouthful he took to Jesus and holy Mary, and cast his eyes on the crucifix from time to time. He examined to see if he had committed any excess when dinner was over, and grieved that his palate had been capable of receiving pleasure. "My father," he one day said to Father Villani, "is it possible to become pleasing to God by living thus? and can one so dainty as I am ever resemble Jesus Christ?" He was then assured that there was no harm in anything he had done, but he felt such pain at his fancied sensuality that he begged to receive absolution for it. He was obliged to keep on his stockings at night on account of the cold; the last time they were put on, the brother tied them up so tightly with a thick cord, that it was found after his death that it had literally entered the flesh; yet although this must have caused him great suffering for several days, he never said a word about it to anyone. He was so detached from himself, and had so entirely abandoned himself to the care of Providence, that nothing could make him uneasy, and no inconvenience could make him utter a complaint. However ill his bed might be arranged, and however much he had to suffer in consequence, he never asked to have it altered. If the infirmarian lifted him up on the pillow he remained exactly as he placed him, although his weakness often caused him to suffer much in consequence, but this could only be discovered by the expression of his countenance. Father Mazzini however at length ordered him to tell the infirmarian what position was most comfortable to him. When he was asked if he would like to be raised up higher, to have the window open, or to have a fire in his room, or if he would like to eat or to rest, he always replied, "Just as you please." If he at times found it impossible to continue in the same position, he said so through obedience, but he would add, "How weak I am; I cannot bear anything for Jesus Christ!"

His last moments were consecrated to obedience, which

he had practiced so faithfully during his life. For instance, Father Mazzini told him that he must eat a little chicken and a bit of bread before he took the vermicelli soup, after which he was to drink a little wine. Once, however, when he was taking the bread which had been dipped in the soup, he saw that a bit of vermicelli was sticking to it; he immediately tried to take it away, but on seeing that it was still there, he put the bread down and would not touch it. Father Mazzini had also given him an apple to smell. As he was very thirsty, he was tempted to eat it, but as he instantly remembered why he had received it, he at once laid it down again on the bed, "The devil tried to take me by surprise," said he afterwards to Father Mazzini, "but God did not allow me to be overcome."

As he felt that death was at hand, he was most anxious to receive Extreme Unction; and his wish was granted, although the doctors had not yet given him over. "It is the last consolation," said he, "which Jesus Christ has left us." Before he received this sacrament, he made his confession and recited the acts of the theological virtues. He evinced such devotion and joy during its administration, that everyone was affected at it. As he was the first of the Congregation to pass into eternity, he unceasingly repeated, "It is I who carry the standard."

As he believed himself to be guilty of a thousand offenses, and quite unworthy of every kindness, he entreated the father-minister to allow all the fathers and brothers to come to his room. When they were assembled together, Joachim begged their pardon for all the scandal and trouble he had given them, with tears in his eyes, and every mark of deep self-abasement. He then thanked them each and all, for their great charity towards him. This touching scene drew tears from the eyes of all present.

Father Villani has told me that three days before he died, Joachim was suddenly ravished out of himself after

Holy Communion. His face became like that of an angel, and he remained in this supernatural state all day. Towards the evening he was asked how he felt: "I feel Jesus in my heart," said he. It was a day when the discipline is used in common, and Father Mazzini went into his room with his discipline in his hand. Brother Joachim was quite affected at this. "My father," said he, "let me also take the discipline in satisfaction for my sins." To pacify him, Father Mazzini told him to strike his hand, and to unite his sufferings to those of Jesus Christ.

Two days before he died, a disgusting looking fly fell into a little broth which he was going to take. In order not to lose an opportunity of mortification, and also to have at the same time the merit of obedience, he sent for Father Villani. "Father," said he, "I am going to die without having done anything for Jesus Christ. If I cannot now do penance, at least permit me to take this fly." The soup was blessed, and he swallowed it. The evening before he died, the same father came to see him, and found him quite absorbed in God. He asked him what he was doing, when Joachim enthusiastically exclaimed, "Paradise! Paradise!" His death was very different to his illness, for it was peaceful and free from suffering. He preserved the use of reason to the last, and while his body grew weaker and weaker, his mind seemed to become more vigorous. Fathers Villani and Mazzini say that his agony was an uninterrupted act of love, and that he expired in the arms of Jesus and Mary, whose holy names he was unceasingly invoking. He gave up his pure spirit to God on the 18th of April, 1741, at the age of twenty-two, of which four years had been passed in the Congregation.

The next day his body was exposed in the church, and an innumerable concourse of people came around his bier, for his holiness was well known in Ciorani and in the neighborhood. All strove to kiss his feet, and to touch his body with rosaries and scapulars. They also were all anxious to have a portion of his clothes, which they looked upon as so many relics. And God gave proof of His servant's sanctity by many miracles.

Our fathers never wearied in calling to mind his virtues, and they each wished to transmit their memory to posterity, by writing down what they knew regarding the life of this saintly brother. All unite in speaking of his great virtue and constancy in well-doing. I cannot here help citing a beautiful eulogium which our saintly founder, Mgr. D. Alphonsus de Liguori, passed upon him in an inscription: "Frater Joachim Gaudiello, virtutum omnium prædives, ad Christi assimilationem anhelans, in omnibus semetipsum formavit secundum exemplar, patientia in infirmitatibus, mansuetudine in adversis, obedientia insignis. Jesu Christi vitam semper idem omnibus manifestavit: non in ligno crucis, sed cum crucis desiderio, et crucifixi amplexu primus omnium præripuit cælestis gloriæ coronam." And in another inscription it is said, "Frater Joachim, obedientia humiliate, modestia, animique puritate insignis, ac ardenti desiderio se conformandi Christo crucifixo admirabilis; obiit voti compos factus, mense."[10] The following occurrence is still more to his praise.

Our fathers were one day speaking to Mgr. Falcoia of

---

[10] "Brother Joachim Gaudiello, rich in all virtues, pining for the likeness of Christ, formed his very self to the exemplar in all things, patience in infirmities, mildness in adversities, outstanding obedience. He manifested the same life of Jesus Christ in all things: not in the wood of the cross, but with longing for the cross and the embrace of the crucified Christ he was the first of all to seize the crown of glory. ... Brother Joachim was outstanding in obedience, humility, modesty, and purity of mind; as well as admirable in an ardent desire of conforming himself to Christ crucified; he died in possession of his mind to the last."

the admirable virtues of this holy brother, and repeated the above eulogiums to him. His Lordship however at first thought they must be exaggerated. "If the other brothers," said this prelate, "were to read such high-flown praises, they would be scandalized at them, for they would remember the shortcomings they must have observed in him." He was then assured that none of the fathers and brothers had remembered ever having seen him commit the least fault. His Lordship was filled with admiration at this, and exclaimed, "That is indeed marvelous!" As he then began to regret that his portrait had never been taken, owing to a kind of inspiration from on high, he got our fathers to raise the sepulchral stone, and to take his likeness as well as they could. Joachim had been then dead ten days, yet his face looked as fresh and ruddy as if he were in a sweet sleep. Father Rossi was amongst those who saw him in this state, and he got into such an ecstasy of joy at the sight, that he fell upon his neck and embraced him with ardor. It was in this manner that the picture in our house at Ciorani was taken. As there was very little space under the portrait, there was only room for these words: "Frater Joachim Gaudiello Bracilianensis, Congregationis S. S. Redemptoris alumnus, in qua vivens dedit omnium virtutum exemplum; in amplexu crucifixi quem ardente amaverat obiit juranis die XVIII. mensis aprilis anno Dom. MDCCXLI., et ætatis suæ XXII."[11]

---

[11] Brother Joachim Gaudiello of Bracigliano, a sheaf of the Congregation of the Holy Redeemer, in which during his life he gave an example of all virtues; in the embrace fo the crucified Christ whom he loved with a burning fire, he died on 18th April in the year 1742 in his 22nd year of age.

The Life of
VITUS CURZIUS
Lay-Brother of the Congregation of the Most Holy
Redeemer.

The life of
VITUS CURZIUS
Lay-Brother of the Congregation of the
Most Holy Redeemer

By St. Alphonsus de Liguori.

S we often had occasion to speak of Brother Vitus Curzius in the Life of Father Sarnelli, of whom he was the constant companion, we will now give a few details of his own life. He was born at Aquaviva, in the diocese of Bari, of most respectable parents, in the year 1760. One of his brothers was a medical man, and the other was a canon in the college of his native town.

In order to show the extent of God's goodness to this young man, we must mention that he was exceedingly passionate until he was twenty-six years of age. He was so alive to the least injury that he fought several duels in which he nearly lost his life. On one occasion amongst others, he felt so offended at a doctor, that he shot him. Another time he had the boldness to fire at a military officer; but God did not permit him to have the misfortune of hitting his mark. After he left Procida, where he had been the treasurer of the Marquis of Vasto, he went to Naples and worked in the house of D. Cæsar Sportelli, who was the Marquis's agent and his own intimate friend. Don Cæsar had at this time resolved to leave the world, which he soon afterwards did by entering the Congregation of the Most Holy Redeemer, where he died in the odor of sanctity. His tomb was opened four months after his death, when it was found that his body was quite flexible, and blood issued from an incision which was made in his foot. Now one day when he was conversing with Vitus Curzius, he began to speak to him about the new congregation, which had been commenced at Scala under the title of that of the Most Holy Redeemer, through the pious exertions of Mgr. Falcoia, who was Father Cæsar's director. Vitus had scarcely heard the particulars of it, ere he entreated to be admitted into it as a lay-brother, as he felt sure that God called him thither.

He had gained this certainty regarding his vocation to the new institute in the following manner: "In a dream," said he, "I saw a number of priests ascending a high mountain; I tried to follow them, but all my efforts were in vain; I fell backwards after each step, or if I succeeded in getting over a little ground, I soon lost all I had gained. Stupefied and discouraged at these repeated failures, I remained at the foot of the mountain in sorrow, when one of these priests came up to me, and held out his hand to me. By this assistance I was enabled to get to the summit as easily as the others had done." One day when he was out walking with Father Sportelli after this dream had occurred, he met one of the fathers of the Congregation, and although he had never seen him before, he pointed him out to his companion, Father Sportelli, saying, "There is the priest who held out his hand to me."[12] He presented himself for approval and was accepted, but he was told to stay at Naples until the superior at Scala should send for him. He had indeed some time to wait, and this delay as to his definitive reception amongst us pained him greatly,

---

[12] Father Tannoja says this father was Alphonsus himself, and that the saintly author omits to mention this through his characteristic humility.

and he longed and sighed for the hour of deliverance from this evil world. One day however he went to Father Sportelli in a transport of joy, "for," said he, "I have heard a voice which said, 'Get ready to go, for you must soon set out.'" Indeed, the Congregation had only been established eight days, when he was sent for to Scala, in November, 1732. The first day he arrived he was ordered to serve at dinner. As his greatest failing was a horror of humiliation, the devil represented to him that such an office was absurd and ignominious. "What," whispered the evil one, "are you to serve at dinner just as if you were a mere servant?" This temptation beset him so much, that he felt inclined to be revenged on him who had ventured to give him such an office. However, as he saw that a man of rank who aspired to be received amongst us also, had the office of server, his good angel suggested to him, "Can you not do what he can do?" He thus conquered his repugnance and began to serve quite calmly.

From this time he became a special child of grace, and celestial consolations abounded in his heart. He was so enlightened during meditation, especially on the mysteries of the birth and passion of Christ, and his feelings were so sensibly affected, that he could not help bursting into tears, and sobbing to such a degree that it seemed as if the violence of his love for God would really suffocate him. This took place in a special manner when he received Holy Communion, which he did almost every day. I often witnessed this myself, and had to wait some time before he could receive the sacred host. His tears and sighs also lasted for a good while after he had communicated. This plenitude of divine grace lasted for nearly a year.

As he had then made great progress in virtue, God deprived him of this sensible fervor that he might attain a more perfect kind of meditation, and imperceptibly brought him to a state of contemplation. He however himself began to fear that God had abandoned him. "What has come over me?" said he; "I cannot meditate. It is very true that I wish to be united to God, but if I had to give an account of what I have been thinking about I could not do it, and I should not even be able to tell how the time had been spent." Enlightened however by the graces conveyed in this the sublimest kind of prayer, he realized the vanity of laboring for any temporal possession, since all on earth is as smoke, which passeth away. He ceased to think of his home and of the friends of his youth, and only thought of how he might become closely united to his God. He always kept his eyes cast down to the ground, and his very appearance showed the recollectedness of his soul. He became quite a model of humility and mortification, and he who had formerly been so susceptible and proud, and who had such an aversion to every menial office, did not now disdain publicly to carry the manure to the garden, or to draw water for the community. This last office was by no means an easy one, for the well was at a distance from the house, and every time he went there, he had to go up the steep mount of Scala with a heavy pitcher in his hand; yet when he arrived at our house he used to kneel down before the large crucifix at the entrance before he had deposited his burden, that he might offer up the fatigue it cost him to God. He always went thither with his head bare, in winter as well as in summer, through reverence for the presence of God, unless he was expressly forbidden to do so. He never went near a fire in winter. He was also for some time in the habit of taking off his shoes and stockings when he went to dig in the garden, and he used to stand working there with his feet buried in the clay; but when the superiors heard of it they forbade him to do so again. One day the bishop of Scala told him to empty out all the water in a large cistern near his palace. As there was a great quantity of water, his nature revolted at such a laborious undertaking, but he courageously pursued it to the end. He was heard repeating to himself, "You have made a great fuss, and you may be as tired as you please, but you must do it all the same, Brother Vitus." Another time he was ordered to help to saw some boards. As he had never done anything of the kind before, he was quite exhausted with this laborious office. After he had borne the greatest fatigue for two hours, the workman who was sawing with him said in a tone of extreme compassion, "Do rest for a little, Brother Vitus." "No, no," he courageously replied, "we must finish what obedience has put before us." Another time, when he was cleaning out the dirtiest part of the house, a priest said in passing, "Bah! what an offensive smell there is here, Brother Vitus!" "O how much worse it smells in hell!" he replied.

It so happened that once for nearly a whole winter it was forgotten to give him any warm clothing, and he went about in his summer things without saying a word, although our house at Ciorani is so cold. All the time he was at Iliceto, where there is another of our houses, he slept on a board, with nothing but a trunk for a pillow. In order to mortify himself still more, he wanted to suck the sore of an old man, but he was forbidden to do it. He wore a sharp pointed iron girdle about two palms in length. He also took the discipline to blood with such frequency and violence, that he broke a nerve in his leg by it, from which he suffered for the rest of his life. His dinner often consisted in nothing but a little soup and bread, for he divided the different portions, and that was all he set aside for himself. As he was very inexperienced in all culinary matters at first, he one day made some unleavened bread, which soon became as hard as lead, and which it was impossible to set before the community. However, he had the patience to go on eating it day by day until it was all done. He fasted on bread and water on Saturdays, in honor of our Blessed Mother Mary, and he did this even during mission time, although our lay-brothers have then to go through immense fatigue.

He never made excuses when reproved. One day our father-minister told him not to put so much fruit on the table, as he thought it superfluous. As Vitus had acted in obedience to the rector, he went on putting the same quantity. The minister was annoyed at this, and scolded him and gave him several mortifications for his disobedience, but he never said a word in extenuation of what he had done. At length the father-minister heard of the superior's wishes, and while he ceased to reprove him, he admired his patience in bearing reprimands which he had never merited.

Another time when the superior could not find an important manuscript which one of our fathers had accidentally burned, he asked Brother Vitus if he knew what had become of it, and he vaguely replied that it must have been burned. As this answer gave cause to suspect that he was guilty of its destruction, he received a severe reproof, which he bore in patient silence, to shelter the father who really had destroyed it.

His love for his neighbor was truly admirable. As soon as he resolved to join us, he distributed all he had among the poor. His charity also towards the sick was inexpressibly great, and he not only exercised it towards the members of the Congregation, but even towards strangers. The attention which Brother Vitus paid to a secular priest who was taken ill in our house at Ciorani, proves the extent of his charity. This priest was suffering from a most offensive and troublesome malady, and it lasted for twenty days; yet Brother Vitus never left him night or day, and as he was too weak to move, Vitus had to lift him about and do everything he required. Holy Week occurred at this time, yet he cheerfully denied himself the gratification of assisting at the devotions of Holy Thursday, that he might not leave his dear invalid. When he was at Scala he sometimes had to go to Amalfi to buy provisions for the use of the community. When he returned he was at liberty to get the porters to carry them up the mountain, for it is very steep, but if he saw that they were overcome by the weight of their burden and by the difficulty of the ascent, he would say, "Now you must rest, and I will help you." And he would take their loads from them, and carry them up the mountain himself, although they often weighed more than two hundred pounds.

One day when one of the fathers of the Congregation went to Scala, he heard of this extraordinary act of charity from two porters whom he met, who began to inquire of him about Brother Vitus. When he told them that he was no more, they sorrowfully exclaimed, "O what a saint Brother Vitus was! When he gave us goods to carry, he paid us for doing it, and then carried them himself." When he was at Scala, he felt such compassion for the sufferings of Father Sarnelli, who was ill at the time, that he took his own palliasse and added it to his, to try and make him more comfortable, although he was in consequence obliged to lie on the boards himself.

His favorite virtue was that of obedience, and in it consists the essence of religious life. He used to say that a lay-brother should resemble the bell which is fastened round the necks of cows, which never rings unless they move. "So a brother," he would add, "ought never to stir to do anything unless prompted to do so by holy obedience."

Indeed he was, as it were, a martyr to this virtue; for while he was at our house at Iliceto, the superior sent him to a distant village to pass the night. The holy brother asked for admittance in a monastery in this neighborhood, but they refused to receive him. He was therefore obliged to sleep in the open air, and that in a most unhealthy place, and as the weather was also very unfavorable at the time, it brought on the illness of which he died. It came on so suddenly, and with such violence, that he was unable to return to St. Mary's, and had to go to bed at the house of a charitable priest at the very entrance of Iliceto. He bore the sufferings of a tedious illness with admirable patience, and never complained of anything. He never objected to any remedy, and punctually obeyed the doctor's orders.

When he was near death, his confessor asked him whether he would rather live or die. "I only wish what God's wishes," he replied, "but if I might make a choice, I should prefer to die, that I might be free from all danger of offending God, and that I might see Him and be with Him in heaven, if, as I trust, He in His mercy has vouchsafed me the grace of salvation." Before the holy viaticum was administered to him he was asked if he would like to go to confession, but he answered that by God's grace he had nothing more to mention, and he died in a state of heavenly peace on Saturday the 18th of September, 1745. After his death the inhabitants of the place said to one another, "A saint is dead," and they were eager to have relics of him. The crowd which followed his corpse to our church showed the veneration of the Faithful towards him. There are many more wonderful things which might be related of this holy brother, but I have not space to mention them.

Short Life of
FRANCIS TARTAGLIONE
Lay-Brother of the Congregation of the
Most Holy Redeemer

Short life of
Francis Tartaglione
Lay-Brother of the Congregation of the
Most Holy Redeemer

By Father Tannoja.

ROTHER Francis Tartaglione, that model of true humility, was born in the territory of Marcianisi, in the diocese of Capua, on the 7th of August, 1713. He was inclined to piety from his very infancy, and could therefore never take pleasure in the world which lieth at enmity with God. Indeed, when he was but twelve years of age, he determined to enter religion. As he admired the exemplary lives of the lay-brothers of the Society of Jesus, he requested to be admitted amongst them, and this was the more readily acceded to as he was an excellent tailor. His conduct was most edifying whilst he was with them, and the Jesuit Fathers were quite satisfied with him, but as God wished him to enter our Congregation, he became so ill that they sent him away. When he returned to the world, he led quite a monastic life, and as soon as he regained his health he began to frequent the sacraments and carefully shunned idleness.

Our Father Alphonsus and several of his brethren were at this time established in the house of the Villa of the Slaves, and they labored as missionaries in the diocese of Cajazzo as well as in that of Capua. When Brother Francis heard that he was on a mission at Recauata, which is not far from Marcianisi, he went there in company with several other pious young men, for he was prepossessed in his favor by the marvelous things he had heard about him. He went, however, rather through curiosity than with any intention of attending the exercises of the mission; but all he heard there made such a deep impression on him, that after listening to the sermon on hell, he resolved to leave the world and to join us. As soon as the sermon was over, therefore, he left his companions, and followed Father Alphonsus to our house, and he there cast himself at his feet and strove by many entreaties and prayers to prevail on him to receive him into the Congregation. Alphonsus was much moved at the urgency of his appeal, and sent him to Father Mazzini, who said to him, "My good friend, our table is not like that of the Jesuits, and we have not the comforts which they have. Those who are in our Congregation must suffer, for we are in great poverty and distress." Francis was not discouraged by all this however. "I am ready to suffer everything in order to save my soul," he replied. Father Mazzini then urged him at least to return to Marcianisi to think over his resolution more deliberately, and to obtain the consent of his parents. "No, father," replied the fervent Francis. "If I return home I shall not come back here again. I know how artful the devil is. I wish to be saved, and I can do very well without my parents' consent." He then cast himself at the father's feet, and with many tears entreated him to receive him, and assured him that his mind was perfectly made up on the subject. Father Mazzini was at length convinced that he was really called by God. He spoke to Alphonsus about him, and took him with him to our house of the Villa of the Slaves when the mission was over. Francis was not only a very handsome young man, but he possessed the greatest vivacity of manner; but after he entered the house of God he soon became very different, Father Mazzini wrote us word. He was always humble and submissive. He was ready to undertake every kind of labor, and although he was our tailor, he also undertook the most fatiguing offices, and he also helped to carry the materials for the building of our house. This good brother's patience and good humor amidst the poverty and misery we then endured, served as a model to us all, and his example incited us to aim at the highest perfection.

After this, he went to our house at Ciorani, where he was greatly beloved by Father Rossi, the rector. Humility and obedience were his distinctive virtues. He united a great love of meditation to that of labor, so that during the most distracting occupations, he was always recollected and united to God. His aspirations were so frequent that they formed one continued prayer. He crucified his flesh by chains, haircloth, and disciplines, and neglected no opportunity of mortifying his senses. He ate little, and slept still less. Indeed, the life of penance which our Father Alphonsus led, caused everyone either to imitate his austerities as far as their strength would permit, or to quit the Congregation and return to the world.

The most striking virtue in Brother Francis was his courageous determination to overcome himself and to subdue his passions. Once when he felt great repugnance in dressing a large and disgusting-looking wound which one of our asses had on the back bone, he licked away the putrid matter which issued from it, and thus triumphed over his delicacy. Our Father Amarante happened to pass while he was doing it. He was filled with astonishment at seeing such a heroic action, but as he wished to test his virtue, he angrily reproved him, and said in a tone of assumed indignation, "Has your director given you leave to do such things?" "And had this tongue obtained its confessor's permission when it uttered blasphemies?" said Brother Francis, thus humbling himself still more than before. He then went away in great confusion at having been discovered, and left Father Amarante in still greater confusion at his action and at his reply.

One day the lazzaroni met him mounted on an ass when he was on his way back from Castellamare. As the road was narrow and the banks on each side were high, they began to throw stones at him, and as they took him for a priest, they mocked him and cried out, "O! if the poor mother who made her son a priest could see how gallantly he now looks riding on an ass!" As the brother thought that God had permitted this to happen as a punishment for his sins, he got down, and threw himself on his knees before them. "Strike, my friends," said he; "strike a sinner." This unlooked-for action filled them with shame, and they ceased to ill use him, and went away, saying, "Alas! we have struck a saint!" About this time, it became necessary to have a lay-brother at our house at Naples, to receive the fathers when they came there. Alphonsus selected Brother Francis for this purpose, and he manifested the greatest charity in his new employment. He often had so many different commissions to execute he hardly knew where to begin, but he did them all so well that he always pleased everyone, and we never heard a single complaint of anything he did. How often did he not go without his dinner to give it to the fathers who might arrive just as he was going to partake of it himself! He endeavored to follow all the good examples Brother Vitus Curzius had given him at Ciorani, and he never neglected any opportunity of imitating his profound humility and exceeding charity.

During the vexatious proceedings we had to endure concerning our house at Nocera, it was to him that our Father Alphonsus sent all the letters on the subject, and it was his business to convey them to their respective addresses. He had therefore often to take papers to

Counselor Vitale, and to the Marquis Brancone, the secretary of state, with whom he also sometimes had to converse by word of mouth, and the good brother's humility and recollection filled them with affection for himself and esteem for our Congregation. They looked upon him less as a lay-brother than as a saint, and they never failed to commend themselves to his prayers. D. Hercules de Liguori, our Father Alphonsus's brother, always treated him as if he had been his own brother. As we had rooms in his house, he often came to ask his advice and gave him different things to transact for him. He often asked him to his table, and when he went to Marianella, he used to leave his house and his family under his care.

The fathers of the Congregation of Pious Workmen had the greatest respect for him, and so had the fathers of the Oratory and those of the Chinese College. Indeed Father Fatigati, one of the fathers of the latter, had the greatest possible affection for him. In a word, Brother Tartaglione was everywhere regarded as a man of rare virtue, and he enjoyed the highest reputation throughout Naples. He gave many signal proofs of his virtue whilst he was in this city. The one I am now going to relate is worthy of special mention. As his appearance was most attractive, a lady who had often met him was so in love with him for his beauty, that she forgot her God and her station in life, and conceived a criminal attachment towards him. One day when she again met him, she stopped her carriage and called him to her, and asked him to come to her house, saying that she had some important business to communicate to him. As the good brother imagined that it was something which concerned the Congregation, he went there without loss of time. When he arrived, the lady had him shown into her own room, and caused him to be seated; she then dismissed her servant, and she discovered to him the criminal passion which had taken root in her heart. "Madam," replied the brother with horror, "there is a God, and there is a hell. The brothers of our Congregation are not in the habit of committing such crimes." After this he got up and tried to escape, but the lady impudently endeavored to embrace him and to detain him, and continued her immodest solicitations. Upon this the brother rushed to the door, and succeeded in getting free. Then in a loud tone of voice he said as he was going out, "I quite understand you, Madam; you shall be attended to." And more dead than alive, he fled away trembling with fear and terror, but without having fallen into the snares of the tempter.

As I do not mean to write a panegyric, but to give a true history from which others may derive benefit, I will mention the faults of this good brother as well as his virtues. I cannot therefore pass over one temptation to which he yielded, although it was so far from hindering his progress in the paths of perfection, that it only caused him to go onwards with redoubled energy. Once when he was in the refectory in our house at Nocera, he was so angry at some remark which another brother made to him, that he threw a glass at him which was in his hands at the moment. He had no sooner yielded to this burst of passion than he repented of what he had done, and asked that his sin might be visited by some exemplary punishment. The ancient fathers of the Congregation thought that this offense was too serious to be passed over, and that he ought instantly to be dismissed without regard to his merit or longstanding in the Congregation. Our Father Alphonsus, however, fortunately happened to be in the house, and was more lenient towards him. He did not excuse his fault, which he too looked upon as a most serious one; but he thought it was in a great degree to be attributed to surprise, and not to any deliberate malice. For this reason, after he had stripped him of the habit, and dispensed him from the vows, he sent him to Ciorani, where he made him go through a novitiate of six months under my direction, and in the exercise of divers mortifications which he himself appointed. Brother Francis bore all with patience, and if his fall had given us scandal, his submission to all the penances enjoined on him gave us far greater cause for edification. This incident proves that no virtue is so solid that it may not fall into sin, and that our only security consists in the powerful succor of God's grace, for our own strength is weakness.

Alphonsus also wrote Brother Francis a letter to complete his shame, but it only made him embrace the chastisement more thankfully and lovingly than before. In reply he sent him the following letter, which was preserved on account of the remarkable sentiments it contains. "My dear father," said he, "I heartily thank you for not having expelled me from the Congregation. God will reward you for your charity towards me. Methinks He is at a loss what more He can do in order to make me love Him! I feel great sorrow for the fault I committed, but that which appears to be a disgrace in the eyes of men, is really a favor from God. I often repeat, 'O happy fault,' for in all it has caused me to suffer, I have only been made to resemble Jesus Christ. He too was humbled and despised, He too was despoiled of his own garments, and clad in a robe of derision. Why should I shrink from being dressed as a secular? I will frankly tell you that the first time I went out of the house I was so absorbed in contemplating Jesus clad as a fool, that I did not even perceive that I had on a secular dress. My meditation is one unbroken thanksgiving, and I attribute all that has befallen me to the love of God, and the protecting care of Mary our Blessed Mother; for no sooner had I committed this excess—for it really was an excess—than I had recourse to her aid by two Ave Marias. I then went before the Blessed Sacrament, and made a vow to bear any description of penance rather than leave the Congregation. I feel great joy now; I even complain of my punishment being too light; I needed it in order to arouse me from my tepidity and sloth. I cast myself at your feet, and humbly entreat you to forgive me. I also cast myself at the feet of all the fathers and brothers whom I have scandalized, and I trust they do not forget to pray to God for me."

After he had performed his penance, and gone through his six months' probation, to my great satisfaction, and that of Father Rossi, the rector, the habit of our Congregation was restored to him, and he was again admitted to make his profession. He was then sent back to Naples, where he remained until he died. When he passed into a better world, I asked Father Garzilli, who had been his director for some time, to give me some account of him, and I received the following answer: "What I most admired in Brother Francis, and what filled me with confusion, was his patience under every trial, and his unflinching perseverance in overcoming himself. He was always the same, and practiced every virtue with heroic constancy. He was a man of prayer; he frequented the sacraments as our rule prescribes, and communicated still more frequently than that. As soon as he had done his work, he passed the rest of the time at the church. He used to hear as many masses as he could, and never neglected to go where there was the forty hours' exposition. He was very fond of reading saints' Lives and other pious books, and if he had not time to do so during the day, he made up for it at night. What was the most admirable in him is that, during the thirty years he was alone at Naples without being under obedience to anyone, no one ever had the slightest complaint to make of him."

The thought of death was always before his mind. "During the short visits I used to pay him," said Brother

Ilardo, "he never spoke of anything but of death and the shortness of life." "Every Christian," he used to say, "ought to have this before his eyes, because he will thus be always afraid to displease God, and will never lose His grace." Whenever he heard the clock strike, he said, "Another quarter of an hour of our life has passed."

His death took place at Naples, on the night of Monday in Passion Week, which fell that year on the 21st of March, 1774. He was sixty years of age at the time. He had a presentiment of his death a little while before, and prepared for it by increased fervor and devotion. He went to confession and communion on the very morning he died. As he had a room above that which was occupied by a respectable widow, who lived there with her three sons, he used to pass the evening with them when he was alone. When he went upstairs, he took two of the young men with him, and they slept in his room, that they might be witnesses of his conduct. They invited him to supper on the Sunday evening, but he refused, saying that he had already eaten a little dry toast and salad. He went upstairs, accompanied as usual by the widow's two sons.

As they heard him groan after he had got into bed, they asked what was the matter, but he replied that it was nothing. However, he got so much worse that he at length fell on the floor in an apoplectic fit. The two young men hurried to the spot, and found that he was speechless. They instantly called their mother, who got assistance from without, and a priest was sent for, who arrived just in time to give him the last absolution.

D. Hercules de Liguori felt his loss keenly, and all who had known Brother Francis shared in his sorrow. As Hercules had really loved him tenderly, he would not allow his obsequies to take place in Naples. "He has done so much for me," said he, "that I will not be ungrateful to him. I will have him buried amongst his brothers, and he shall share in their prayers." He therefore sent the body in a carriage to Nocera, accompanied by his chaplain. The corpse arrived at seven o'clock in the evening, and he was interred next morning. Blessed are they who die the death of the just! still more blessed are they in whom it has been preceded by a virtuous and holy life.

FINIS

www.ingramcontent.com/pod-product-compliance
Lightning Source LLC
Chambersburg PA
CBHW030914140626
46545CB00016B/1299